CONDUCTING INSANITY EVALUATIONS

Conducting Insanity Evaluations

Richard Rogers, Ph.D.

 VAN NOSTRAND REINHOLD COMPANY

New York

Manufactured in the United States of America.

Published by Van Nostrand Reinhold Company Inc.
115 Fifth Avenue
New York, New York 10003

Van Nostrand Reinhold Company Limited
Molly Millars Lane
Wokingham, Berkshire RG11 2PY, England

Van Nostrand Reinhold
480 La Trobe Street
Melbourne, Victoria 3000, Australia

Macmillan of Canada
Division of Canada Publishing Corporation
164 Commander Boulevard
Agincourt, Ontario MIS 3C7, Canada

15 14 13 12 11 10 9 8 7 6 5 4 3 2

Library of Congress Cataloging-in-Publication Data
Rogers, Richard, 1950–
  Conducting insanity evaluations.
  Bibliography: p.
  Includes index.
  1. Mental illness—Diagnosis. I. Title.
RC469.R58 1986   616.89′075   86–4059
ISBN 0–442–27945–0

Contents

Preface

This book emerged from a continuing need for an integrative source on insanity evaluations that would combine the legal framework and empirical data with the clinical practicalities of forensic work. Too often, clinicians struggle with complicated issues of criminal responsibility and, despite their sincere efforts, do not fully appreciate either the legal standards or clinical methods in evaluating insanity.

Conducting Insanity Evaluations was written both for clinicians with little formal training in forensic psychiatry and psychology and for those with an extensive background in the assessment of criminal responsibility. For non-forensic clinicians, it offers a useful outline for translating insanity standards into psychological constructs and for application of traditional and innovative methods to the evaluation of criminal responsibility. For clinicians well versed in insanity evaluations, it provides a review of relevant case law, recent empirical research, and advances in psycholegal assessment. In addition, the book presents a substantial data base from six established forensic centers in the United States on the clinical characteristics of sane and insane defendants.

This book is also intended as a resource for attorneys whose practice includes insanity and other related defenses. Attorneys share with clinicians the responsibility for ethical, high quality evaluations that address comprehensively the clinical issues of criminal responsibility. Dicussions of clinical methods and relevant issues such as malingering, amnesia, and clinical decision-making provide legal professionals with a basis to evaluate the quality of insanity evaluations and to prepare for expert testimony.

I would like to express my genuine appreciation to R. E. Turner, M.D., Director and Psychiatrist-in-Charge, and Lana Stermac, Ph.D., Staff Psychologist, at Metropolitan Toronto Forensic Service (METFORS), Clarke Institute of Psychiatry, for their thorough review of this book.

I am also indebted to several outstanding individuals for their specialized expertise. These include Ingo Kielitz, Ph.D., Director of the Institute of Mental Disability and the Law, National Center for State Courts, for his thoughtful critique of legal issues; The Honorable G. Arthur Martin, Justice of the Supreme Court of Ontario, for his review of the Canadian standard of criminal responsibility; Ron Langevin, Ph.D., Senior Psychologist, and Stephen Hucker, M.D. Chief of Forensic Service, Clarke Institute of Psychiatry, for their critical review of laboratory approaches; and Lawrence Egel, Ph.D., Professor of Psychology, Governors State University, for his thorough commentary on neuropsychological testing.

I would also like to thank the many secretaries whose competence and good-naturedness greatly helped in maintaining my own sanity. In Chicago, Cloe Reid and Carole Goosby were responsible for major portions of the text. In Toronto, it has been primarily a team effort led by Yvonne Kornelson with valuable contributions by Rosemary Campioni, Margaret James, Kim Thompson and Janice Thomas.

Finally, I would like to publicly acknowledge my wife, Jan, and her fine contributions particularly in completing the library research for the final chapters. The extent of her contributions were aptly summarized this spring by a librarian who politely inquired, "Whose book is this anyway?"

RICHARD ROGERS

CONDUCTING INSANITY EVALUATIONS

Introduction

Conducting Insanity Evaluations was written to provide a clear and concise outline of the diagnostic methods used and the clinical problems frequently experienced in insanity evaluations. While the literature is rich with discussions of legal theory and public policy issues of criminal responsibility, the resources available to the forensic practitioner remain fragmented. This book synthesizes the diverse clinical and forensic literature pertinent to the clinical determination of criminal responsibility.

GOALS OF AN EVALUATION

Forensic psychiatrists or psychologists must examine closely their psychological reasons when they become involved in such complicated and controversial evaluations. In an area so closely connected to their sense of morality, inquiry into the motivation and desire for ongoing involvement may be invaluable.

Forensic clinicians should clarify their areas of expertise and the degree to which such expertise is pertinent to their conducting insanity evaluations. Given the process of forensic consultation, there is a continuing pressure to overstep one's expertise, particularly in highly publicized insanity trials.

Forensic clinicians may clarify the specific standards of criminal responsibility and identify the important clinical issues related to those standards. This step includes the complex and difficult task of translating general legal concepts into specific psychological constructs, each with its array of observable clinical characteristics. This approach is in direct contrast to the simplistic approach that "psychosis equals insanity."

Clinicians are offered a coherent model of integrating diagnostic methods. On a fundamental level, this involves the establishment of specific clinical guidelines for conducting extensive interviews with defendants and witnesses. It further involves careful examination of psychometric approaches and their potential relevance to the issue of criminal responsibility. Finally, forensic clinicians must integrate these sources of clinical data to establish diagnoses and render an expert opinion.

Forensic psychiatrists or psychologists will be more aware of the limitations of self-report information in the context of a retrospective evaluation. These limitations involve a spectrum of dissimulation from deception and malingering to psychogenic and organic amnestic syndromes. Limitations and distortions of memory, conscious or otherwise, greatly complicate the evaluative process.

Forensic clinicians exercise the willingness and courage to render retrospective diagnoses and concomitant opinions only when they believe there is a high probability that those opinions are accurate. The question is not whether clinicians endorse this statement in principle but whether they exercise it in their day-to-day forensic practice. Forensic experts are not asked to testify to what is possible, commonsensical, or more likely to be true than not; they are asked to testify within a reasonable degree of medical or scientific certainty on the basis of established scientific knowledge and accepted, standardized methods. There are sometimes great pressures on forensic clinicians not to render a no opinion.

Forensic clinicians must remain current on research and leading appellate decisions pertaining to insanity evaluations. These include both reports on traditional diagnostic methods and innovations in forensic evaluations.

Those clinicians who choose to conduct insanity evaluations must fully appreciate the importance of such evaluations for the defendant, the criminal justice system, and their profession. This awareness invokes such global attitudes as a commitment to excellence and comprehensiveness. It further suggests a poignant understanding of how important this assessment process is and how it may dramatically alter both the lives of the defendant and victim and their respective families and friends.

EVALUATION FORMAT

This book is divided into two major parts, one that addresses specific content areas of particular relevance to criminal responsibility evaluations and one that examines the process issues of conducting such evaluations. In addition, current empirical data are presented throughout on criminal responsibility assessments regarding symptomatology and diagnostic groupings.

Four chapters address clinical issues, including the clinician's role in insanity evaluations, making the legal standards clinically operational, malingering and deception, and amnesia and memory impairment. Each topic examines from clinical practice and empirical research general considerations for the forensic clinician in the assessment of criminal responsibility. The second part is devoted to clinical methods, examining in detail the evaluative process in conducting insanity evaluations, their goals and structure. In addition, it reviews traditional psychological testing, current advances in psycholegal assessment, and traditional laboratory studies.

The book provides a conceptual and clinical synthesis of content and process issues in insanity evaluations. Chapter 2 addresses the complex translation process from clinical symptoms through retrospective diagnoses and estimates of psychological impairment to conclusory opinions regarding criminal responsibility. Chapter 9 provides a synthesis of clinical findings (i.e., from interviews and psychometric and laboratory procedures) and an integration of such findings into a clinical determination of criminal responsibility. This integration includes the relative weighting of different sources of clinical data as well as the relevance of these data to the final determination.

Empirical data are presented throughout the book. These include previously unpublished data involving several collaborative studies from six forensic centers in the United States. These studies (see Appendix I for a more complete description) examined the psychological impairment of criminal defendants at the time of the crime. Clinical data on the presence and severity of critical symptoms and diagnostic groupings are presented for those clinically evaluated as sane and insane.

STANDARDS OF CRIMINAL RESPONSIBILITY

The exemption of certain individuals from culpability may be traced from ancient times. Both in the Justinian code of the sixth century as well as by ancient Hebrew law, children and insane persons were not held responsible for their acts (Weiner, 1980). In Anglo-Saxon tradition the definition of sanity was held, during the seventeenth and eighteenth centuries, as a commonsensical notion decided by the judge and jury without the assistance or influence of professionals. According to Coke (in Goldstein, 1967) an insane person is one "who completely loses his memory or understanding, a lunatic who sometimes has understanding and sometimes not, and an idiot" (p. 10). Depending on the prevailing religious views, such individuals might be seen either as possessed by the devil or marked by God for misfortune, each of which could result in death or torture. Other early criteria for insanity included the Canon Law of Bracton, archdeacon of Barnstable, who in 1265 set forth the first explicit standard, "an insane person is a person who does not know what he is doing, is lacking mind and reason, and is not far removed from brutes" (in Bromberg, 1979, p. 5). According to Quen (1978), Bracton is credited with a codification of British law and definition of the components of crime to include a physical element or behavior (i.e., actus rea) and a mental element or purpose (i.e., mens rea). Without the requisite mental state or purpose, a crime could not be committed, thus excusing infants because of their innocence and mad persons because of their lack of reason.

An early influential case was that of Arnold in 1724. Described by Bromberg (1979), Arnold, "a known lunatic," shot and wounded Lord Onslow, whom he apparently believed had existed in his belly and had occasioned him much trouble. According to the testimony of twenty-two lay witnesses, Arnold was known to talk to himself and to inhuman creatures and to break out into a passion of cursing or violent laughter. A presiding judge articulated the following standard of criminal responsibility (Bromberg, 1979, p. 6): "It must be a man totally deprived of his understanding and memory and doth not know what he is doing, no more than an infant, than a brute, or a wild beast." This case has been cited (e.g., Robitscher, 1966) as referring to pervasive impairment of reason and is often described as the *wild beast test*. Based on this charge, Edward Arnold (known locally as crazy Ned) was found guilty of the charges. As noted by Quen (1978), the term, *brute,* referred to farm animals, and *wild beasts* at this period in the United Kingdom were primarily restricted to badgers, foxes, deer, and rabbits. Emphasis should therefore be placed on the absence of intellectual ability rather than the image of a violent, unrestrained beast.

The second prominent case establishing the standard of criminal responsibility was that of James Hadfield in 1800. As described by Quen (1978), Hadfield was convinced that only his death would prevent God from destroying the world. Since suicide was a moral crime and a mortal sin, he attempted the regicide of King George III as a circuitous method of causing his death through capital punishment. Hadfield was unsuccessful both in his attempt on George III and in causing his own death. He was acquitted on the basis of insanity by a directed verdict (Bromberg, 1979). A new, somewhat broadened standard was presented to replace the earlier formulations with what is referred to as the *delusion test* in which delusions become a basis of the criminal behavior.

The emergence of the *right-wrong test* was promulgated in the Bellingham case of 1812 (Robitscher, 1966). In this case, the jury was presented with the following standard: "the single question was whether, when he committed the offense, he had sufficient understanding to distinguish good from evil, right from wrong and that the murder was a crime not only against the laws of God but against the laws of his country" (p. 56). Bellingham, who had successfully assassinated the prime minister because of perceived injustices, was found guilty in a trial described by Isaac Ray (see Stearns, 1945, p. 578) as a miscarriage of justice committed with "indecent haste" and carried out with vengeful rapidity. Within the period of a week, John Bellingham was detained, tried, executed, and dissected. This case, despite what Quen (1978) refers to as "judicial murder," set the stage for the classic M'Naghten case.

A fourth prominent case, *Regina v. Oxford,* involved an attempt on the life of Queen Victoria and Prince Albert in 1840. As described by Robitscher (1966), the assailant, Edward Oxford, was found not guilty based on the delusion test set forth in the Hadfield case. Of particular interest in this case is the first known mention of volitional aspects of criminal responsibility. Quen quoted the original opinion by Justice Denman in 1840, "If some controlling disease was, in truth, the acting power within him which he could not resist then he will not be responsible" (1978, p. 239). Such findings of nonresponsibility on the basis of an irresistible impulse were occasionally utilized during this period until their exclusion by the M'Naghten standard.

M'Naghten Standard

The most celebrated case in Anglo-American history is that of Daniel M'Naghten, who was described as having an elaborate system of paranoid delusions that held the prime minister personally responsible for M'Naghten's financial and interpersonal misfortunes. Based on these paranoid beliefs, M'Naghten mistakenly assassinated the prime minister's secretary, Edward Drummond. Quen (1981, pp. 4–5) quoted M'Naghten's statement at arraignment; "The Tories in my native city have compelled me to do this. They followed me and persecuted me where ever I go and have entirely destroyed my peace of mind. . . . They have accused me of crimes which I am not guilty; in fact, they wish to murder me." As noted by Robitscher (1966), M'Naghten believed that the prime minister and the Tory party were after him because he had voted against them in the last election. The lengthy and highly publicized trial resulted in M'Naghten's acquittal as not guilty by reason of insanity (NGRI). This trial was also remarkable for its inclusion of nine prominent medical witnesses, including the well-known American psychiatrist Isaac Ray, all of whom testified that Daniel M'Naghten was insane (Weiner, 1980). Although M'Naghten was committed to the insane asylum of Broadmoor, where he spent the final 20 years of his life, neither the government nor the public was assuaged by this disposition (Simon, 1983). This theme that attempted or successful assassinations of heads of state should only be excusable under the strictest standards has its modern counterpart in the outrage following the Hinckley acquittal and the concomitant demands for a more stringent standard (e.g., American Bar Association, 1983; American Psychiatric Association, 1983).

Queen Victoria was openly angry and disapproving of the M'Naghten verdict. Since this was the fifth attempt (see Simon, 1983) on the life of either royalty or the prime minister since 1800, the queen was alarmed that such an acquittal might encourage other dissidents. Queen Victoria (in Golding, 1983 p. 3) bitterly described the legal system in which defense attorneys could press for an NGRI verdict in trials such as those of Oxford and M'Naghten "whilst everybody is morally convinced that both malefactors were perfectly conscious and aware of what they did." The strong indignation felt by the queen, the House of Lords, and the public resulted in the convening of fifteen judges from the common law courts to respond to a series of questions regarding insanity (Simon, 1967). The judges, including Lord Chief Justice Tindel who had presided at the M'Naghten trial, were evidently influenced in their decisions by public and private pressures as well as other current social and political crises facing the United Kingdom (see Quen,1978). Fourteen of the fifteen judges formulated a stricter standard, subsequently known as the M'Naghten standard.

This standard stated that jurors ought to be told in all cases that every person is to be presumed to be sane and to possess a sufficient degree of reason to be responsible for his crimes, until the contrary be proven to their satisfaction. Also, to establish the defense on the ground of insanity, it must be clearly proved that, at the time of the commission of the act, the party accused was "laboring under such a defect of reason from the disease of the mind as not to know the nature and the quality of the act he was doing; or if he did, that he did not know what he was doing was wrong" [8 Eng. Rep. 718, 720 (1843)]. The judges also addressed the role of delusions in establishing criminal responsibility. They concluded that delusions involving the redressing or revenging of nonexistent wrongs or delusions that such behavior served some public good would be punishable if the perpetrator knew, at the time of committing such an act, that he or she was acting contrary to the criminal law. Further, they held that the defendant would not be responsible if the crime involved homicide in a delusion of self-defense in which the defendant misperceived the victim as attempting to kill the defendant (Simon, 1967).

Queen Victoria and the House of Lords were successful in achieving their immediate goal: that another Daniel M'Naghten would not be acquitted by reason of insanity. Although M'Naghten probably had a chronic paranoid schizophrenic disorder (see Keilitz and Fulton, 1983), it is likely that he would have been found guilty based on the revised standard that bears his name (Stone, 1975).

The M'Naghten decision also addressed the admissability of expert testimony by medical witnesses who were involved in the retrospective evaluation of the defendant and had no prior knowledge of the defendant. The court held (Simon, 1967) that, while the ultimate issue is a legal matter to be decided by the jury, such experts could comment on the mental functioning and sanity of the defendant. This finding established the precedent for expert testimony in the retrospective assessment of criminal responsibility.

Despite the popularity of the M'Naghten standard with the populace and the queen, it raised considerable controversy in other sectors of British society. Lawyers and members of Parliament protested the ambiguity of the words *wrong* and *know* as an overly simplistic interpretation of criminal responsibility (Quen, 1978). The standard was further attacked by British and American psychiatrists as being too narrowly defined and excluding a broader class of severely disturbed individuals who lacked the volitional capacity to avoid criminal behavior. Isaac Ray (in Bromberg, 1979, p. 44) maintained that the M'Naghten standard was the result of "only the most deplorable ignorance of mental operations of the insane." Such attacks did not pass without judicial notice, as observed in an 1845 case in which the jury was instructed to disregard definitions of insanity, "especially such fantastic and shadowy definitions as in Ray" (Bromberg, 1979, p. 46).

The M'Naghten standard, despite these early criticisms, became deeply entrenched in Anglo-American justice (Goldstein, 1967). The M'Naghten standard was a prevailing standard in the United States for more than a century, with significant alterations being made only since the 1950s. Two themes may be extracted from the M'Naghten controversy: the first theme, as alluded to earlier, is that any standard that exculpates regicide or its equivalent is too lenient. This theme is most clearly seen in the parallels between Daniel M'Naghten and John Warnock Hinckley, Jr. (see Golding, 1983; Beis, 1984). Earlier attempts at insanity acquittals for obviously disturbed would-be presidential assassins (Dix, 1984; Freedman, 1983) presaged the outrage experienced by the 1981 assassination attempt against President Reagan.

The second theme involves establishing an acceptable threshold for what type of impairment versus severity of the impairment is necessary to qualify for an acquittal. This second theme established by the M'Naghten standard addresses whether the standard of criminal responsibility should be exclusively cognitive. Such an approach (see Goldstein, 1967) is predicated on the belief that cognition or intellect exerts primary control over individuals' actions. Other observers (Brooks, 1974) argue that volition, impulses, and behavior may not, in all individuals, be subjected to cognitive control and therefore advocate the need for the volitional prong to the insanity defense. This unresolved controversy can be traced from the Arnold case to the most recent case law.

New Hampshire Standard

The New Hampshire Standard was a result of extensive correspondence between Charles Doe, chief justice of the New Hampshire Supreme Court, and Isaac Ray, the renowned Connecticut psychiatrist. Doe, stimulated by the writings of Ray (see Stearns, 1945), formulated the standard that if the criminal behavior was a product of mental illness, then the individual should be exculpated (Quen, 1978).

The New Hampshire Standard was established in the 1869 trial of an ax murderer (i.e., *State v. Pike*). The jury was instructed that if the homicide was the result of insanity, the defendant must be found not guilty (Quen, 1978, p. 243). When Pike's conviction was appealed, Charles Doe wrote the unanimous decision, which is crystallized in the following statement: "an act caused by mental illness is not a crime" (Quen, 1978, p. 243). Doe also ruled that it was within the domain of the jury to establish what constitutes insanity, and not for the judiciary to specify what that standard might be (Bromberg, 1979).

The New Hampshire Standard was viewed as a singular exception to the formerly pervasive M'Naghten standard, allowing expert testimony regarding the defendant's mental illness including both cognitive and volitional elements. The standard attacked what was seen as the undue narrowness of the M'Naghten rule with its arbitrary exclusion of severely disturbed individuals (Robitscher, 1966).

Modifying M'Naghten: Irresistible Impulse

Irresistible impulse represented a broadening of the M'Naghten standard to include severe impairment of volition or self-control in individuals who are cognitively aware of the wrongfulness of their actions. Goldstein (1967) has noted that the concept of irresistible impulse has led to disparate and perhaps competing formulations. These include subtle differences in wording (Goldstein, 1967, p. 69) such as, actions beyond his or her control, incapable of choosing the right and refraining from doing the wrong, unable to resist doing wrong, incapable of resisting and controlling an impulse, and uncontrollable and irresistible impulse. Variations of irresistible impulse were reported contemporaneously with M'Naghten's trial, including *State v. Thompson* in 1834 (in Simon, 1967) and *Commonwealth v.*

Mosler, an 1846 Pennsylvania case (in Keilitz and Fulton, 1983); *Parsons v. State* and *Davis v. United States* are generally regarded as the influential cases in combining the M'Naghten standard with a loss of volitional control.

Parsons v. State was an 1887 Alabama case in which it was asserted that a defendant who knew right from wrong might still be acquitted with the presence of the following two conditions: (1) "if by reason of duress of such mental disease, he had so far lost the power to choose between the right and wrong and to avoid doing the act in question, as that his free agency was at that time destroyed; (2) and if, at the same time, the alleged crime was so connected with mental disease with relation of cause and effect, as to have been the product of it solely" [2 So. 854, 866–867 (Ala. 1887)]. The federal counterpart to *Parsons* was *Davis v. United States* in which it was stated that the accused would be acquitted if "his will, by which I mean the governing power of his mind, has otherwise been voluntarily so completely destroyed that his actions are not subject to, but are beyond his control" [165 U.S. 373, 378 (1897)].

Standards of irresistible impulse have created much debate. It is generally accepted by jurists (see Robitscher, 1966) that this standard does not apply to states of passion—as actions blinded by anger or jealousy—since there is no direct linkage between such states and a mental disorder. It has been argued that the irresistible impulse standard should be applied primarily to psychotic disorders or severe obsessive compulsive disorders that impair self-control or choice of actions (Beis, 1984). A less convincing argument has been made by Davidson (1952) that such a standard should be applied to sexual paraphilias, in which the individual is overpowered by sexual urges. He argued that many sex offenders have uncontrollable sexual urges, which are indiscriminant and without concern for apprehension. This is not consistent with available research on large samples of sex offenders (Groth, 1979). The crux of the issue is how to distinguish between an irresistible impulse and an unresisted impulse (Robitscher, 1966; Shapiro, 1984; Gutheil and Appelbaum, 1982). One option adopted by military courts and other jurisdictions (Goldstein, 1967) is the "police at the elbow" criterion. This criteron argues that if the impulse was so overwhelming and out of control that the individual would have committed the act in the presence of a law enforcement officer, then that person should be exempt from responsibility. This represents a conservative approach to irresistible impulses that would likely exclude all but the most severely impaired individuals. It again places a greater emphasis on cognitive awareness in assuming that awareness of imminent apprehension would deter most rational individuals.

This standard gained some currency during the emergence of dynamic psychology in the 1920s (Bromberg, 1979). It emphasizes determinants beyond the defendant's awareness and therefore control, despite an intellectual apprehension, which is consistent with ego psychology formulations (Goldstein, 1967). A psychodynamic study of 300 murderers by Bromberg (1979) formulated a variety of unconscious motivations.

Mounting criticism of the irresistible impulse, or loss of control, standard has been heard both in psychiatric and lay communities. A survey of psychiatrists (in Goldstein, 1967, p. 74) found that a majority believed that the concept was neither psychiatrically nor legally sound. Recent Supreme Court decisions curtail its application to addictions [*United States v. Lions,* 731 F.2d 243 (1984)] and compulsive gambling [*United States v. Tornero,* 735 F.2d 725 (1984)]. At present, the combined M'Naghten and irresistible impulse standard is found in only four states (Keilitz and Fulton, 1983).

Diminished Responsibility

Diminished responsibility, also referred to as partial responsibility or diminished capacity, was an attempt to establish a middle ground between sanity and insanity. It has as its underlying assumption that those who had less comprehension or criminal intent should receive proportionately less punishment (Bromberg, 1979). Thus, diminished responsibility does not address exculpation but the defendant's degree of guilt.

An early case in establishing the doctrine of diminished responsibility was *People v. Wells,* a 1949 California case (33 Cal. 2d 330, 202 P.2d 53). As reported by Bromberg (1979) Wells, an inmate serving a life sentence, was taken to the warden's office on a charge of misconduct. When Wells apparently became obstreperous, he was asked to leave. Wells sat on the floor outside the warden's office, refusing to move, and eventually assaulted a correctional officer with a cuspidor. He was tried under Section 4500 of the California Penal Code, "every person undergoing a life sentence in a State prison of this State, who, with malice aforethought, commits an assault upon the person of another . . . by any means of force likely to produce great bodily harm, is punishable with death" (Bromberg, 1979, p.73). An evaluation by a prison psychiatrist (Goldstein, 1967) indicated that Wells was emotionally disturbed and had reacted out of severe fear. The trial judge, however, excluded all evidence of his mental state. This finding was overturned by the California Supreme Court since the testimony regarding his emotional state reflected on an element of the charge: malice aforethought. A similar case, *People v. Gorshen,* [51 Cal. 2d 716, 336 P.2d 492 (1959)] established what is referred to as the Wells-Gorshen doctrine; this allows the introduction of testimony regarding specific intent for the purpose of reducing the original charge. This doctrine (see Brooks, 1974) has been applied primarily in California for cases of first degree murder. A similar formulation has been articulated in federal courts. For example, in *U.S. v. Brawner* [471 F.2d 969 (D.C. Cir. 1972)], it was held that "expert testimony as to a defendant's abnormal mental condition may be received and considered, as tending to show, in a responsible way, that defendant did not have the specific mental state required by a particular crime or degree of crime—even though he was aware that his act was wrongful and was able to control it, and hence not entitled to complete exoneration" (p. 998).

An attempt to broaden the Wells-Gorshen doctrine of diminished responsibility proposed that any evidence regarding a mental disease or defect should be admissible if it is relevant in proving that the defendant's mens rea was an element of the offense (American Law Institute, 1962). As noted by Stone (1975) the model penal code allows for any testimony regarding extreme mental or emotional disturbance and how this disturbance affected the defendant's thinking and reasoning at the time of the offense. Moreover, this code requires the adoption of the defendant's perspective in examining the reasonableness of his or her actions.

Diminished responsibility, although allowed into evidence in approximately fifteen states (Weiner, 1980), has come under increasing attack for the ambiguity of its criteria and the unevenness of its application. Appellate decisions have normally denied the use of diminished responsibility in cases of alcoholism, pathological intoxication, side effects of prescribed medication (see Bromberg, 1979), and drug use and withdrawal (Brooks, 1974, 1980; Beis, 1984). Further, courts have attempted to limit this doctrine on the basis of an abnormal mental condition and not simply the result of genetic or environmental influences (*U.S. v. Brawner*, p. 1002). Response from clinicians has been varied from those who emphasize the worthiness and humanitarian intent of this standard (e.g., Dix, 1971) to those who question the feasibility of such evaluations (e.g., MacDonald, 1976). Perhaps the most radical position is that promulgated by Diamond (1961), who advocated that the psychiatrist should testify to the broadest range of mental and emotional abnormalities as they relate to criminal behavior and not be limited to legal questions. Diamond further advocated that the social and cultural issues be allowed into testimony in cases of diminished responsibility and argues that such data be considered part of the legal doctrine (i.e., under what mental state should punishment be mitigated?). He also affirmed the competence of clinicians to establish legal intent. With respect to the doctrine, courts have usually resisted opening the flood gates and have circumscribed the applicability of diminished responsibility, at least in comparison to other countries (see e.g., Zeegers, 1981; Gold, 1981). The complexities of clinically evaluating the concept of legal intent have been well documented (e.g., Meyers, 1965) and certainly require much further empirical investigation (see Keasey and Sales, 1977, for an empirical study of mens rea in children). Without such clear understanding based on clinical research, forensic psychiatrists and psychologists may well be accused of treading legal turf in offering evidence beyond their expertise (Dickey, Remmington, and Schultz, 1980).

The Durham Standard

The Durham standard, established under the aegis of the Bazelon court, afforded the widest range of expert testimony regarding criminal responsibility. This standard, sometimes referred to as the *product rule,* stated [*Durham* v. *United States,* 241 F.2d 862 (D.C. cir. 1954) 874–875], "an accused is not criminally responsible if his unlawful act was a product of a mental disease or mental defect. . . . we use 'defect' in a sense of a condition which is not considered capable of either improvement or deterioration which may be either congenital or the result of an injury, or the residual effect of a physical or mental disease." Writing the majority decision, Judge Bazelon argued that the then current District of Columbia standard (i.e., M'Naghten plus irresistible impulse) was too circumscribed and did not take into account the advances in psychiatric knowledge (Brooks, 1974).

Establishment of the Durham standard was based on an appeal of a conviction for housebreaking. The defendant, Monty Durham, was a 26-year-old with a history of both previous criminal convictions and past psychiatric hospitalizations. He had been diagnosed at different times as having a psychosis with a psychopathic personality and psychopathic personality without other mental disorder. He was civilly committed to St. Elizabeth's hospital for sixteen months before he was adjudged competent to stand trial. Testimony during Durham's trial was equivocal about whether he was mentally disturbed, but the judge concluded that he did not meet the current insanity standard. Parallel to the case of Daniel M'Naghten, it has been suggested (Stone, 1975) that Monty Durham would not qualify under the Durham standard, given the lack of any direct cause or relationship between his mental impairment and criminal actions.

The Durham standard was heralded by several leaders in forensic psychiatry (e.g., Robitscher, 1966) as a great advance toward humanizing archaic laws as well as an improvement for the psychiatric profession. This enthusiasm was shared by all except judges and prosecutors who viewed this change with skepticism and hostility and as an erosion of the current standards of culpability that might lead to mass acquittals (Brooks, 1974). Further, practicing psychiatrists, like those at St. Elizabeth's hospital, were ambivalent about the new standard in defining *disease and defect* and *product.* Problems abounded in the application of the standard. What mental disorder is sufficient to qualify for the standard? Would antisocial personality disorders qualify? Would drug abuse and child molestation [listed in *Diagnostic and Statistical Manual of Mental Disorders* (DSM II)] qualify? Opposition mounted regarding the ambiguity of the standard and the problems in defining its components? This led Goldstein (1967) to conclude that the Durham standard was a nonrule (p.84). Further, its intention in having forensic experts offer understandable and descriptive information regarding the defendant's mental condition in language comprehensible to the jury was, from a judicial perspective, bastardized by experts testifying in arcane and conclusory terms. The chief criticism by Bazelon's court, which eventually led to the repeal of the Durham standard, was this offering of conclusory opinions without adequate and understandable substantiation. Bazelon complained (in Huckabee, 1980, p. 17) that Durham did not do "nearly enough to eliminate the experts' stranglehold on the process."

Further, the Durham standard did not gain wide acceptance from other jurisdictions; although reviewed by thirty states and five federal courts, its formulation was consistently rejected. Only two states, Vermont and Maine, adopted the Durham standard and restricted its use to civil cases (Simon, 1983). This standard differed in emphasis from the 1869 New Hampshire standard. While the New Hampshire standard placed the responsibility on the jury to formulate its standard of criminal responsibility, the Durham standard, because of its construction, was seen as preempting this function (Quen, 1978).

An additional concern was the increasing numbers of individuals acquitted under this liberalized standard. Although there was apparently some rise in the number of insanity acquittals, estimates of acquittals across a 4-year period following the adoption of Durham ranged from thirty-seven (Weiner, 1980) to forty-nine (Brooks, 1974) per year. Thus, what was viewed by many professionals as opening the flood gates might better be conceptualized as increasing the trickle.

Bazelon's court showed growing disenchantment with the administration of the Durham standard. Their growing discontent is noted in their subsequent decisions—for example, *Blocker v. U.S.,* [288 F.2d 853 (D.C. Cir. 1961)]; *Carter v. U.S.,* [252 F.2d 608 (D.C. Cir. 1957)]; and *Rollerson v. U.S.,* [343 F.2d 269 (D.C. Cir. 1964)]. In 1972, the grand experiment was over. Bazelon's court unanimously repealed the Durham standard in favor of the ALI (American Law Institute) standard in *United States v. Brawner* [471 F.2d 969 (D.C. Cir. 1972)].

An important but overlooked lesson of the Durham experiment is the inherently inverse relationship between ambiguity and arbitrariness. While its predecessors (i.e., M'Naghten and irresistible impulse) were roundly criticized for their arbitrariness in excusing only few and finding culpable many other severely impaired individuals, the Durham standard, formulated to avoid such overrefined distinctions, offered a more general (i.e., more ambiguous) formulation. The Durham standard, in turn, became roundly criticized for its ambiguity and lack of clear (i.e., arbitrary) standards. Thus, every formulation of criminal responsibility may be subjected to the opposing criticisms of arbitrariness and ambiguity.

The ALI Standard

The ALI (American Law Institute) standard, unlike other standards that were hastily constructed in response to a particular case, was the result of 10 years of dialogue from 1952 to 1962. This undertaking, underwritten by the Rockefeller Foundation, included judges, law professors, behavioral scientists, and other professionals. This group, as described by one of its participants (see Freedman, 1983), was "occupationally stable" and had "an unshakable middle class foundation" (p. 25). Their meetings were dominated by Judge Learned Hand, who was venerated for his legal erudition combined with personal warmth. This group attempted to reconceptualize and redefine the cognitive and volitional elements associated with criminal responsibility. Toward this end, they offered several changes in language to broaden the M'Naghten standard's cognitive component and to redefine the irresistible impulse or volitional element (see Goldstein, 1967). These changes ran counter the recommendations of the institute's Psychiatric Advisory Board, which advocated acceptance of the Durham standard (Freedman, Guttmacher, and Overholser, 1961).

This new standard, similar to all new standards, was heralded as a solution to the problem of equitable standards of criminal responsibility. As noted in *United States v. Freeman* (cited in Brooks, 1974, pp. 167 and 168) the ALI test is "an infinite improvement over the M'Naghten Rules. It reflects the evolution of modern psychiatry too long circumscribed "by the outrage of a frightened queen." This standard, as articulated in the final draft (American Law Institute, 1962), states:

A person is not responsible for criminal conduct, if at the time of such conduct as the result of a mental disease or defect, he lacks substantial capacity either to appreciate the criminality (wrongfulness) of his conduct or to conform his conduct to the requirements of law. As used in this article, the terms 'mental disease or defect' do not include an abnormality manifested only by repeated criminal or otherwise antisocial conduct.

This standard was gradually adopted in federal jurisdictions—for example, *Wion v. United States,* [325 F.2d 420, 427, (10th Cir. 1963)] and *United*

States v. Freeman, [357 F.2d 606 (2d Cir. 1966)]—as well as state jurisdictions.

Momentum for the adoption of the ALI standard increased when the standard received the endorsement of the major professional organizations including the American Academy of Psychiatry and Law (Pollack, 1976), the American Psychiatric Association, and the American Bar Association (Huckabee, 1980). Contrary to Davidson's prediction in 1952 that the M'Naghten standard was so deeply embedded in U.S. law as to be impervious to change (Davidson, 1952, p. 3), the ALI test had already been adopted in five states and two federal circuit courts by 1967. The standard is currently utilized, with some minor modifications, in twenty-five states (see Keilitz and Fulton, 1983, for a summary of the states and variations within the standard) and until recently in all federal jurisdictions. In addition, case law (see Brooks, 1974) provided reformulations of the ALI standard in various federal circuit jurisdictions. These have included removal of the statement excluding sociopaths (i.e., "an abnormality manifested only by repeated criminal or otherwise antisocial conduct" [American Law Institute, 1962]), and addressing the concept of substantial capacity.

The initial enthusiasm for the ALI standard was predictably tempered by growing criticism. Although one of the intents of ALI was to introduce greater flexibility than found in the so-called straightjacket of M'Naghten, it was criticized for its "vagueness and rubber yard stick quality" (Huckabee, 1980, p. 20), a criticism echoed by others (e.g., Freedman, Guttmacher, and Overholser, 1961; Bromberg, 1979). Quen (1978), commenting on the interminable and unresolvable discussions of terms such as *appreciate* and *substantial capacity,* described such debates as "characterized by a pathological obsessional concern, on the part of the legal and medical professionals, with the magic of words" (p. 26).

A second criticism (again predictable) against the ALI standard was that it allowed too many defendants to be acquitted. Goldstein (1967) observed that it is doubtful that any new standard, given the complex political and social pressures, can be held primarily responsible for increases in the acquittal rate. Although it is generally believed that the ALI standard is more liberal than M'Naghten (i.e., easier to secure an acquittal), little research has investigated this belief. One dramatic increase was seen in Oregon (Keilitz, 1985) where the acquittal rate jumped from 7 to 73 per year. One of the few empirical studies comparing M'Naghten to ALI (Sauer and Mullens, 1976) noted a moderate increase in the number of individuals found not responsible when Maryland shifted from M'Naghten to ALI. This change in percentage (7.9% to 19.21%) was parallel with an overall increase in pretrial examinations. Rogers and Clark (1985) asked experienced forensic clinicians to apply both the M'Naghten and ALI standards to 125 defendants being evaluated for criminal responsibility. The differences between the two standards were very modest, with 2.4% qualifying for ALI but not M'Naghten. While these limited data suggest small increases with the adoption of ALI, such findings are likely to have little effect on those who oppose anything but the most conservative insanity standards.

Guilty But Mentally Ill Standard

The most recent modification of criminal responsibility standards was the adoption in Michigan of the guilty but mentally ill (GBMI) standard in 1975 (Mich. Comp. Ann. 330, 1400a). Following a Michigan Supreme Court decision, *People v. McQuillan* (392 Mich. 511, 221 N.W. 2d 569, 1974), NGRI patients could no longer receive an automatic and indefinite commitment but must meet the general standard of civil commitment. The immediate result of such a decision (see Institute of Mental Disability and the Law, 1984) was the re-evaluation of 270 institutionalized acquittees and the subsequent discharge of approximately 150 of them. Of these discharged NGRI patients, one was subsequently arrested on charges of murder and another on two counts of rape. Responding to the public outcry and indignation, the Michigan legislature passed GBMI legislation with the implicit goal to reduce the incidence of insanity acquittals with the potential for early release into the community.

The GBMI standard drafted by the Michigan legislature stated that defendants would qualify as GBMI if they had a sufficient mental impairment at the time of the offense. Mental illness, for the purposes of this statute, was defined as "a substantial disorder of thought or mood which significantly impairs judgement, behavior, capacity to recognize reality, or ability to cope with the ordinary demands of life" (Robey, 1978, p. 377). It further specifies the exclusion of individuals found NGRI and provides the option of psychiatric treatment in the department of mental health for those convicted under the GBMI statute. This definition of mental illness for the GBMI standard has been adopted with minor modifications by five additional states, and different criteria are used in five other jurisdiction, with the exception being South Dakota, which does not statutorily define mental illness (McGraw and Keilitz, 1984).

The GBMI standard was passed in Michigan and several other states following highly publicized cases in which the NGRI standard was raised. For example, GBMI legislation was passed in Illinois following the rearrest for homicide of two NGRI acquittees (Weiner, 1985). Despite the fact that neither defendant was acquitted for the second offense, these highly publicized murders became a rallying point in demonstrating the abuses of the existing standards of insanity.

The GBMI standard has been opposed on both conceptual and procedural grounds by interested professional associations. According to the Institute of Mental Disability and the Law (1984), opposition to the GBMI verdict has been registered from the American Bar Association, American Psychiatric Association, American Psychological Association, and National Mental Health Association. The American Bar Association (in Beis, 1984, p. 287) characterized the GBMI verdict as "a moral sleight-of-hand which simply will not do." The American Psychiatric Association (1983, p. 9) characterized the GBMI plea as an "abolitionist position in disguise," attempting to whitewash the complex problems in the administration of criminal responsibility standards.

The few proponents of such legislation argue that the GBMI verdict offers an intermediate position for those not meeting the insanity standard. In a similar vein, Watkins (1981) suggested that the GBMI verdict offers a workable middle ground because "fact finders must face the vagaries of conflicting psychiatric opinion" (p. 290); he paradoxically admitted that such a verdict is based on the "same confused psychiatric theory that underlies the insanity defense" (p. 307). Watkins further stated that the GBMI verdict is an acknowledgment of the underlying conflict between medical and ethical models of mental illness with an obvious resolution in favor of the ethical model. No attempt was made to clarify the differences between these two models. DeVito (1980) also advocates the adoption of the GBMI standard and was instrumental as commissioner of mental health in its adoption in Illinois. He suggested that responsibility is an important clinical issue and argued that a GBMI verdict (i.e., making the defendant responsible) might have a positive therapeutic impact. He did not discuss, however, the therapeutic impact of the concomitant incarceration.

A major criticism of the GBMI standard is its considerable overlap with current insanity standards. Several legal commentators (e.g., Mesritz, 1976; Grostic, 1978; Stelzner and Piatt, 1983) have addressed the absence of any clear boundaries between the NGRI and GBMI standards. They suggested that juries may mistakenly utilize the GBMI verdict or see it as a compromise between sanity and insanity. In a thorough review of GBMI practices, the Institute of Mental Disability and the Law (1984) found no evidence that GBMI offenders received any more favorable legal disposition than their guilty counterparts. They found, for example, that GBMI offenders were no more likely to receive treatment than any other convicted offenders. Further, the institute was unable to find empirical data suggesting that the GBMI verdict was a mitigating factor in sentencing. The authors cited an analogous study that found no significant differences in sentencing among those found guilty without raising insanity, those institutionalized following an insanity acquittal, and those incarcerated after unsuccessfully raising an insanity defense. Finally, the GBMI verdict has been seen by some attorneys (Weiner, 1985) as a way to avoid the death penalty; even this circumscribed use has been questioned by an Indiana court that imposed the death sentence in the case of James Harris (see Dickinson, 1984).

A final consideration is whether the GBMI standard satisfied the legislative intent of curtailing the insanity defense. Despite anecdotal data regarding a small number of defendants who would qualify for an NGRI finding that were mistakenly found GBMI (Robey, 1978), the limited data available (i.e., Criss and Racine, 1980; Smith and Hall, 1982; Keilitz, 1984) suggested that the GBMI standard has resulted in no significant reduction in the numbers of defendants acquitted by reason of insanity. These studies are limited in generalizability to Michigan samples and archival examination of variables and their relationship to the GBMI standard.

THE ACQUITTAL OF HINCKLEY

The acquittal of John Wanock Hinckley, Jr., for the attempted assassination of Ronald Reagan in 1981 fueled intense debate over the efficacy and validity of the insanity defense. It resulted in an immediate and unprecedented review of the trial by the legislature, which called before its Senate subcommittee both the members of the jury and expert witnesses (Subcommittee on Criminal Law of the U.S. Senate, 1982). Surveys of the public conducted following Hinckley's acquittal indicated strong dissatisfaction with the disposition (Hans and Slater, 1983) and beliefs that the insanity standard was used too frequently and allowed defendants to escape from the responsibility of their crimes (Jeffrey and Pasewark, 1983). In this latter study, Jeffrey and Pasewark completed a follow-up survey in which they presented the respondents with the statistics on the comparative rarity both of raising the defense and its success. In spite of this information, approximately 40% of the respondents continued to believe in the overuse and abuse of the insanity plea. This may be partially explained by the selective overreporting of Hinckley and other celebrated cases (see Steadman and Cocozza, 1978) and because of the fusion in the public's mind of unrestrained violence and mental illness (Cavanaugh and Rogers, 1982).

Professional organization, perhaps in response to the public condemnation of the Hinckley verdict, began to issue official statements regarding the insanity defense. The two most prominent of these statements (i.e., American Bar Association and American Psychiatric Association) were aimed at solving the problem—that is, in the spirit of M'Naghten, preventing any future Hinckleys from exculpation. In February 1983, the American Bar Association issued its official position on the insanity defense. It argued, predictably, for a curtailment of the ALI standard by substituting the M'Naghten word *unable* for the ALI term *substantial capacity*.

In addition, the American Bar Association (1983) advocated the elimination of the second prong of the ALI test (i.e., "ability to conform one's conduct to the requirements of law"), asserting that "there is still no accurate scientific basis for measuring one's capacity for self control or for callibrating the impairment of such capacity" (pp. 4, 5). The American Bar Association's conclusion that the cognitive form is more objective than the volitional is not substantiated by empirical data. Ironically, the only study that investigated the components of the ALI standard (Rogers, 1984a) found that experienced forensic clinicians were slightly more reliable in their application of the volitional than the cognitive elements (i.e., kappa = .80 and .75 respectively) and differentiate equally well between sane and insane defendants. The American Psychiatric Association (1983) adopted essentially the same position as the American Bar Association (1983) both with respect to the substitution of the term *unable* and the removal of the volitional prong of the ALI standard. Consistent with the American Bar Association, this latter change was suggested because of the weaker scientific evidence regarding volition and because expert testimony on volition is "more likely to produce confusion for jurors than the psychiatric testimony relevant to the defendant's appreciation or understanding" (p. 11). The American Psychiatric Association also defined mental disease or retardation as essentially a psychosis, or a condition that "grossly and demonstrably impairs a person's perception or understanding of reality," relative to the standard of criminal responsibility (p. 12). In contrast, the American Psychological Association exercised considerable restraint in calling for empirical research on current insanity standards and their alternatives before implementing any modifications.

These efforts have culminated in the 1984 passage of a hybrid-cognitive only standard, integrating components of ALI and M'Naghten, for use in federal jurisdictions. This is known as the Insanity Reform Act [Section 402 (a) Chapter 1 of title 18, United States code 5.20]. This standard specified (p. 201), "as a result of a severe mental disease or defect, he was unable to appreciate the nature and quality or wrongfulness of his acts." This criterion combined the ALI concept of appreciate with the M'Naghten concepts of unable and nature and quality. Further, the prestigious National Conference of Commissioners on Uniform State Laws (1984) has recently proposed model legislation similarly limited to cognitive capacity. This latter standard employed as a criterion "substantially unable to appreciate the wrongfulness of the conduct" (p. 2). Ironically, this innovation represents only a slight shift from the original M'Naghten controversy (Keilitz, 1985).

An integral factor in the administration of the insanity defense is the postacquittal disposition of acquittees. As more systematic programs for the detention, treatment, and outpatient follow-up of NGRI defendants are implemented, the greater is the likelihood that the current preoccupation with the wording of these standards may abate. Several innovations in the treatment of insanity acquittees include the adoption in Oregon of a psychiatric security board that oversees the inpatient and outpatient care of NGRI patients (Bloom, Rogers, and Manson, 1982; Rogers and Bloom, 1982; Bloom and Bloom, 1981) and court-mandated specialized outpatient treatment for NGRI patients (e.g., Rogers and Cavanaugh, 1981c; Silver, 1983). The development of a systems approach to the postacquittal phase of NGRI patients (see Golding, 1983) may be instrumental in both increasing the delivery of services and ensuring the continued existence of the insanity plea.

CONCLUSION

The history and development of the insanity defense have been marked by an ongoing struggle in the calibration of criminal responsibility. Anglo-American law is predicated on exculpation of those few defendants who lacked the prerequisite mental state while carrying out their criminal behavior. As observed by Judge David Bazelon (in Keilitz and Fulton, 1983, p. 8), "our collective conscious does not allow punishment where it can not impose blame." The inevitable conflict over the expansion/curtailment of criminal responsibility standards depends on important extralegal factors such as the sociopolitical climate, attitudes toward crime, recent assassination attempts, and the credibility of the medical and mental health professions. It is anticipated that there will be a continued although slight pendulum effect from highly circumscribed to broader definitions of insanity. Three general alternatives are (1) cognitive only, (2) cognitive-volitional, and (3) unspecified deficit (i.e., a matter of the severity, not type, of impairment). At present, the curtailment trend is beginning to lose momentum although it is likely to be at least several decades before any liberalization of the standard is observed.

PART I

Clinical Issues

Chapter I

The Clinician's Role in Insanity Evaluations

The clinician's role in insanity evaluations can be divided into four general areas: (1) agency and professional role, (2) clinician's dynamics, (3) extraneous defendant and victim characteristics, and (4) clinical and ethical issues. This chapter addresses the following issues in criminal responsibility assessments: To whom does the clinician owe his or her loyalties? How does he or she conceptualize his or her role in such evaluations as an advocate, an impartial consultant, or a therapist? What is a clinician's motivation in becoming involved in criminal responsibility evaluations? To what extent do extraneous defendant or victim characteristics influence the clinician? What are the limits of the clinician's expertise? How does the clinician address the adversarial nature of criminal responsibility evaluations through either informed consent or Miranda-type warnings?

AGENCY AND PROFESSIONAL ROLE

The concept of agency refers to an individual person or component of a legal system for whom the clinician is working. Within the context of the criminal justice system, *agency* may refer to the defendant, the defense attorney, the state's attorney, or the judge. Further, the concept of agency is not necessarily determined by who is paying the clinician's professional fees or by who originally contacted the clinician. Financial compensation and initial business transactions do not address the underlying crucial issue: toward what end and for whose purposes should the clinician be involved in insanity evaluations?

It may be argued, from one perspective, that such questions of agency have little impact on the clinician who is attempting to complete an objective and comprehensive assessment of the defendant. In contrast, agency may be seen as exerting a subtle but important influence on the clinician's approach to the defendant as well as his or her interactions with the court. Whether the clinician sees the defendant, one of the attorneys, or the court as the primary agent may well influence that professional's willingness to have pretrial conferences, to discuss courtroom strategy, to admit openly alternative explanations, and to limit/expand the scope of expert testimony. The clinician who feels he or she is working for the court may have a greater aura of objectivity than those who identify with either the attorney or the defendant. It is important for each clinician who has adopted this position to engage in careful self-inquiry to ascertain whether such professional disinterest is genuine.

The forensic clinician may perceive him- or herself as the agent of either attorney or the defendant. This orientation may, in turn, cause potential bias in the insanity evaluation. Those who advocate this position argue that the very basis of the adversarial court system is for each side to make the best case. Such proponents would argue that any loss in the clinician's objectivity might be offset by the clinician's greater understanding of the defendant's psychological state and that any increased likelihood of bias would be neutralized by the adversarial process and testimony by opposing experts.

Treatment Role

Several prominent psychiatrists (e.g., Pollack, 1976; Diamond, 1959) have suggested that most forensic clinicians operate from a clear treatment orientation from which they attempt to meet the best needs of the patient. To what extent forensic clinicians either identify primarily with treatment or are influenced by a treatment orientation is unknown. Such influences are likely to be less true for those individuals with formal training or supervision in forensic evaluations or who work primarily in an evaluative role. Conversely, professionals who provide mostly nonforensic treatment should be aware of the potential influence that such an orientation may have on the forensic evaluations.

Advocate Role

Another role may be that of an advocate who perceives his or her responsibility as maximizing the client's (defendant or attorney) case. Such a formulation sometimes borders on what is referred to, in colloquial and graphic descriptions, as a "hired gun" or a "psychiatric whore." Such pejorative labels are indicative of the strong emotional feelings evoked by individuals who have apparently lost any semblance of impartiality or objectivity. This radical position as an advocate often reflects a lack of experience or training; for example, forensic clinicians, who receive all their referrals from a particular defense or prosecuting attorney, may unintentionally adopt a similar attitudinal set as that of the defense or state attorney. It is always preferable for the forensic clinician to have a broad base of referrals for criminal responsibility evaluations to avoid adopting such attitudes. Toward this end, the forensic clinician may wish to keep track of his or her expert opinions regarding insanity and referral sources to see if any strong correlation exists.

Impartial Role

A third role is that of the impartial expert (see Wasyliw, Cavanaugh, and Rogers, 1985). From this perspective the forensic clinician attempts to "allow the chips to fall where they may" and not have a vested interest in the outcome. This role is easier to achieve when the expert works for the court system as opposed to any particular attorney. It is my opinion that such a role is best suited for the forensic clinician although it does not prevent him or her from being influenced by many of the dynamic issues discussed in the rest of the chapter.

Perhaps, the more important issue is not what particular role forensic clinicians choose but how they articulate this choice to their clients and to the court. Much of the present confusion and distrust of forensic clinicians in insanity evaluations is a result of their lack of clarity regarding how they perceive their roles. This sometimes leads to feelings of betrayal when clinicians, assumed to be objective, present themselves in an advocate or treatment role. The remedy would be for attorneys to ask forensic clinicians, as part of their testimony, to describe how they perceived their role as a forensic expert.

CLINICIAN DYNAMICS

What is a forensic clinician's motivation for being involved in insanity evaluations? Such an involvement normally lacks substantial financial incentives (as compared, e.g., to personal injury evaluations), and it is unlikely to elicit any strong approbation from one's colleagues. Clinicians must ask themselves why they want to be involved in difficult adversarial evaluations that frequently eventuate in stressful and, at times, gruelling courtroom testimony. Do clinicians see themselves as humanitarians, persons who mete out justice, or societal protectors? Since that motivation is a complex and multidetermined process, there is no simple answer. Self-inquiry is perhaps most helpful in sorting out to what extent the clinician may be conducting insanity evaluations for the wrong reasons—for example, if he or she is acting as a frustrated attorney or judge.

The emotional response of the forensic clinician to particular crimes is worthy of self-examination. For example, if the clinician is repulsed by certain types of criminal behavior, then this may well preclude his or her unbiased consultation. Common examples of heinous crimes may include mass murder, torture, or violent sexual assaults on children. Clinicians should not be expected to have no negative emotional responses to particular crimes but should sort out which crimes or particular fact patterns they experience as revolting or abhorrent. By excluding such cases, forensic clinicians acknowledge their human reactions and willingness to exclude themselves deliberately from potentially biased evaluations. Conversely, there may be rare circumstances like the murder of a wife-battering spouse, in which the forensic clinician has strongly positive feelings toward the defendant's action that would again introduce bias into the evaluation.

A third dynamic issue is the clinician's attitudes toward criminal behavior. Implicit within this attitudinal set is how clinicians learn to deal with their antisocial or aggressive impulses. It has been postulated that those who strictly control their deviant impulses may be less tolerant of expression of such impulses by others. Conversely, it could be argued that forensic clinicians who developmentally were allowed greater expression of aggressive or antisocial impulses might be more sympathetic toward criminal behavior by others. These formulations are unproved and merit further inquiry. Without becoming excessively introspective, the clinician's experience as a victim of crimes, particularly violent crimes, should be examined. The dynamic issue does not center on whether or not the clinician was victimized but rather what was his or her adaptation following the crime and how did this effect his or her attitude toward similar perpetrators? Such an appraisal might also include family and close friends of a clinician who have been victims of violent crimes. Although forensic clinicians are rarely asked whether they have been victims of similar crimes, which is routinely done with voir dire of prospective jurors, such a question should be considered in the cross-examination of each forensic expert. Although it is possible for a clinician who was sexually abused to render an objective evaluation of a child molester, such evaluations, depending on the trauma and postadjustment, might well be biased. Certainly an opposing attorney, sophisticated in cross examining psychological experts, would likely neutralize the testimony of an evaluator who has been a victim of a serious crime similar to that perpetrated by the defendant.

A related issue is characterized by Monahan (1980) as who is the victim? The extent to which forensic clinicians in a criminal responsibility evaluation perceive either the perpetrator or the target of criminal behavior as a victim may well influence their final clinical opinion. To varying degrees, forensic clinicians may view the perpetrator as having been victimized through parental and social deprivation, poverty, racial or sexual discrimination, or inadequate coping mechanisms. In contrast, other clinicians may focus primarily on the target, or actual victims, of criminal acts, emphasizing the psychological and physical assaults to the individual's integrity, the acute and chronic stress reactions, and the overall increased sense of vulnerability that these individuals experience. In weighing these alternative approaches, the forensic clinician must consider whether he or she would be unduly influenced by experiences such as seeing gory pictures of the crime scene or interviewing the defendant's mother.

The final dynamic issue that clinicians must consider is their attitude toward the legal issue of sanity. Do they see insane individuals as "getting off"? Further, do the clinicians equate insanity with senselessness? How do they feel about their role in double stigmatization, labeling individuals "insane," implying both madness and badness? Is the clinician unduly influenced by the availability of treatment for insane individuals that was frequently denied guilty individuals? Each clinician must examine his or her attitudes in conducting assessments of criminal responsibility.

EXTRANEOUS DEFENDANT AND VICTIM CHARACTERISTICS

An important area of inquiry is the extent to which the forensic clinician identifies with or relates to either the defendant or victim. Each forensic clinician must be aware of the potential biasing influence of the likability of a particular defendant. One influence may be similarities with respect to education, socioeconomic status, and ethnic or racial background. A second, and perhaps subtler, form of identification is similarities between either the defendant or victim and someone toward whom the clinician has strong emotional feelings (either positive or negative). For example, if the victim of a violent rape reminded a male clinician of his spouse, the clinician may be strongly biased particularly if his wife had ever been a victim of sexual abuse. Under these circumstances, the forensic clinician should exclude him- or herself from that particular insanity evaluation. In most cases, it is important that clinicians be aware of the extent to which they identify with the defendant and victim as well as their general emotional reaction (like or dislike) to both of them. Such an awareness may assist in minimizing such influences. Although no research has examined such biasing influences in general evaluations of criminal responsibility, such data are available regarding specialized procedures. For example, generalizability studies of the Rogers Criminal Responsibility Assessment Scales (R-CRAS) (Rogers,

1984*a;* see also chapter 7) indicate that clinicians employing this procedure render similar opinions irrespective of sociodemographic characteristics such as age, race, sex, education, and prior mental history. For clinicians who do not employ such procedures, it may be helpful both for self-inquiry and subsequent testimony to keep records of general sociodemographic data and diagnoses, cross tabulated by expert opinions. Such data would facilitate the identification of any blatant biases (e.g., never finding a black who meets the criminal responsibility standard).

One approach to limiting possible contamination by extraneous factors is minimizing the flow of irrelevant data. While forensic clinicians want to be comprehensive in their evaluation of all pertinent police and clinical information, they at the same time, may wish to minimize data not directly pertaining to criminal responsibility. The usefulness of detailed photographs of the crime scene, which may assist in understanding the defendant's actions, may well be outweighed by their potential biasing influence on a clinician. Likewise, viewing family pictures of either the defendant or victim may inappropriately influence clinicians without augmenting their relevant knowledge of the individual.

A third area in which clinicians may be unduly influenced is by empathizing with the defendant's emotional responses and current attitudes toward his or her criminal behavior. Certainly the defendant's emotional response is an important component in determining criminal responsibility, but a forensic clinician must also be aware of its potentially biasing influence. For example, a forensic clinician may be alienated by a defendant's expressions of indifference or positively moved by strong and sincere feelings of remorse. Again, such emotional reactions are important components of such determinations but should not be the only determining factor.

Finally, forensic clinicians must be aware of social and professional pressures that have an impact on their perceptions of either the victim or the defendant. For example, an expression of strong negative or positive feelings by a secretary, correctional officer, or colleague regarding the defendant or victim may influence the way the clinician identifies with or relates to the defendant. Thus, clinicians must be aware of the subtle influences caused by extraneous remarks. Common examples are correctional officers commenting on either the niceness or viciousness of a particular defendant, nonprofessional staff expressing dismay or disgust after having reviewed the records, and comments regarding lack of personal hygiene of a defendant. Social pressures become more blatant in celebrated cases of criminal responsibility where everyone (professional; and non professional alike) is willing and at times insistent on expressing personal views. For example, in Chicago, following the arrest of a highly publicized mass murderer, John Wayne Gacey, there emerged so-called gallows humor in the form of Gacey jokes. Such moral condemnation and public indignation of heinous crimes must be examined by the forensic clinician in a self-critical manner to minimize the effect of such subtle yet pervasive social influences.

CLINICAL AND ETHICAL ISSUES

Forensic clinicians have the responsibility of giving a Miranda-type warning at the onset of the evaluation. This warning includes an open discussion of the purpose of the evaluation, its nonconfidentiality, the possible legal consequences of cooperating or not cooperating with such an evaluation, and the defendant's right to remain silent or not respond to any component of the evaluation. It is not what clinicians state about these issues at the onset of the insanity evaluation but the degree of understanding that the defendant demonstrates with respect to such warnings that is important. Research on informed consent (Lidz, Meisel, Zerubavel, Carter, Sestak, and Roth, 1984) has demonstrated that the simple verbalization, "I understand," is often not a true indication of the patient's understanding. This issue can be largely obviated if the clinician asks the defendant to restate the warnings in his or her own words and, perhaps, to give examples of how such warnings may apply to him or her. The question of seriousness must be addressed: how much importance does the defendant attach to these warnings? For example, if the defendant perceives this process as purposeless or irrelevant to him- or herself, it may be difficult for the defendant to weigh carefully the alternatives. Three options are available to forensic clinicians who believe their defendant lacks sufficient understanding of the Miranda-type warning: (1) to carefully explain and educate the defendant, (2) to refer the defendant to his or her attorney for further consultation, and/or (3) to consider whether or not the defendant is competent to stand trial. These issues are presented in ascending order; for the majority of defendants, the first option is sufficient.

Forensic clinicians have an ethical responsibility to clarify their role in insanity evaluations. This clarification frequently involves a concerted effort to correct potential stereotypes about mental health professionals—for example, the assumption that clinicians serve the best interest of the client in insanity evaluations. As is discussed in later chapters, forensic clinicians are not benign or (from the defendant's perspective) well intentioned. Many defendants, particularly those of less than average intelligence, persist in believing that doctors and other mental health professionals are on their side and will make things better. The following sections address the specific components of Miranda-type warnings in criminal responsibility evaluations.

Purpose

The purpose of criminal responsibility evaluations must be clearly explained to the defendant. This includes an explanation of the clinician's goals of establishing diagnoses of the defendant at the time of the crime and rendering an opinion (or making other conclusory statements) on the legal standard of insanity. It is important that the defendant has a reasonable understanding of what it means to be considered sane or insane and what are the potential consequences of either disposition. In some jurisdictions it may also be necessary to distinguish the standard of guilty but mentally ill (GBMI) from sanity/insanity.

Nonconfidential Relationship

The defendant must have a clear understanding that typical insanity evaluations lack the confidentiality found in most mental health professional–patient relationships. This may be especially true for clinicians retained by the defense attorney who may reach conclusions that are upsetting to the defendant. For example, the defense-retained clinician may make statements about how sick the defendant is or be forced on cross-examination to make other adverse remarks concerning the defendant. The defendant should know that a summary of his or her statements will be included in a report to one or more attorneys; that this report may, as a matter of law, become available to both attorneys and the judge; that the forensic clinician may testify regarding this evaluation in the presence of the defendant in open court, and that all the testimony will be a matter of public record. Regarding this final issue, it is important that the forensic clinician not dramatize the publicity element of an individual case since most not guilty by reason of insanity (NGRI) trials receive little public attention.

Right Not to Cooperate

Defendants must be informed of their right to cooperate or not cooperate with criminal responsibility evaluations. How defendants exercise their choice is exclusively the responsibility of the defendant and his or her attorney. The clinician must be wary of wearing two hats in attempting to assist or persuade the defendant in making such a decision. It may be helpful to ask the defense attorney, on a routine basis, to discuss with defendants their decision to cooperate prior to the beginning of the evaluation. This is not necessarily a dichotomous decision; defendants may choose to avoid or limit their report in certain circumscribed areas. If this occurs, forensic clinicians must be aware of their own emotional response to such refusals or objections. If clinicians become either highly persistent or respond with negative emotions (e.g., anger or disappointment), they may be giving the defendant a double message. Such mixed communications may persuade defendants to give up their resolve to limit self-disclosures. This would certainly undermine the purpose and intent of Miranda-type warnings.

The clinician may wish to inform the defendant of potential consequences of cooperating or not cooperating with the insanity evaluation. This may include a brief statement concerning the potential negative impact of noncooperation on the trier of fact, if the clinician is knowledgeable about such consequences. A common assumption in the legal arena is that a noncooperative individual has something to hide; to what extent this assumption is true or influences legal dispositions has not been empirically examined. In addition, the clinician may wish to state briefly the potential consequences, both positive and negative, of cooperating with an insanity evaluation. It should be emphasized that it would be unethical for the clinician to attempt to persuade the defendant to making either decision since this might undermine the defendant's decision and misrepresent his or her options.

While similar in design, the Miranda-type warnings have several differences with the broader doctrine of informed consent. The informed consent doctrine, which has been applied to both evaluation and treatment, involves a thorough understanding of the procedures, the specific risks and benefits of such procedures, as well as alternative procedures. An area of discussion is whether the informed consent doctrine should be applied to psycholegal evaluations like criminal responsibility. One difference in the utilization of informed consent versus the Miranda-type warnings is the emphasis on the description of potential risks, including the likelihood and severity of adverse effects. Does the clinician have the responsibility to inform each defendant in an insanity evaluation that "I find 3 out of 4 defendants I evaluate as sane" or "If you agree to take the MMPI and have been lying, there is a strong likelihood I will be able to detect it"?

A second difference between informed consent and the Miranda-type warnings is a consideration of alternatives. In evaluations of criminal responsibility, informed consent may include a discussion of other available experts both from the same, as well as other related professions. Other alternatives, which might be presented would include selection of assessment methods and use of corroborative data sources.

Whether insanity evaluations should be included within the informed consent doctrine has not been sufficiently explored. In current practice, forensic clinicians infrequently address either of these two additional issues raised by the informed consent doctrine in conducting insanity evaluations.

LIMITS OF EXPERTISE

The qualification of a forensic clinician as an expert is primarily an individual decision and responsibility. The courts are typically unsophisticated at winnowing out real from pseudo-experts. They have a tendency to allow most psychiatrists and psychologists to testify, assuming that the trier of fact (judge or jury) will be able to determine and give greater weight to the true expert. This is a highly questionable assumption. It is therefore necessary for each forensic clinician to evaluate his or her relevant training, experience, and research in evaluating criminal responsibility. Solid clinical training, while forming the essential basis of forensic evaluations, is not a substitute for specialized forensic experience. Research on psychologists applying for their diplomate in forensic psychology has documented the difference between general clinical and specialized forensic training and experience (see Rosenhan, 1983).

What are reasonable qualifications for an expert in criminal responsibility evaluations? Certainly most psychiatrists and psychologists who have passed their respective specialty boards (i.e., board certified by the American Board of Forensic Psychiatry and diplomate status through the American Board of Forensic Psychology) are qualified. The more difficult question is what are minimal qualifications, particularly in nonurban areas where training and professional experience may be severely circumscribed. Even under such conditions, the clinician should make every effort to obtain close hands-on supervision from an established forensic expert on at least a dozen cases before functioning as an independent expert. Particularly for the sole practitioner, continued expert supervision for the first several years of forensic practice is invaluable in improving the quality and comprehensiveness of such evaluation. It is the author's firm position that to initiate insanity evaluations without substantial training and/or supervision is unethical (see American Psychological Association, 1981) because this area of specialization requires more than a general clinical background. In addition, it is the responsibility of each forensic clinician to decide whether particular insanity evaluations are beyond the scope of his or her expertise. Thus, in complex evaluations or those involving specific issues such as substance abuse or neurological factors, the expert may choose to have a consultation or to decline further involvement in that particular case.

An area of debate in criminal responsibility evaluations is whether or not the expert should render an opinion or conclusory statements regarding specific legal standards. The three basic options are to present testimony on (1) diagnosis only, (2) diagnosis and elements of the criminal responsibility standard, and (3) diagnosis, elements of the insanity standard, and expert opinion regarding sanity. This issue must be addressed both on empirical as well as ethical issues. From an empirical perspective, is there any difference in the impact of testimony across the three conditions? No research has been done on the differential impact of such expert testimony on the triers of fact.

Much of the controversy on the ethics of expert testimony is based on the unproven assumption that such differences do exist. I would like to suggest an alternative conceptualization—namely, that the fundamental process is one of *translation;* that is, the triers of fact attempt to translate what the expert is saying into terms meaningful to themselves on the question of the sanity/insanity of this particular defendant. The clarity of presentation (i.e., how clearly the expert communicates regarding the psychological functioning of the defendant at the time of the crime) may well have a greater impact than the style of presentation (i.e., diagnosis; diagnosis and components of standard; or diagnosis, components of standard, and final opinion). Most specifically, it is not the simple articulation of any of the three options but a coherent explanation of the defendant and his or her impairment that influences triers of fact. It is the responsibility of both attorneys to ensure that the triers of fact understand not only the expert's conclusion but also his or her logic, reasoning, and a coherent description of symptomatology that supported the conclusion.

The author's position on conclusory statements is to allow (but not to insist) experts to make conclusory statements. This is based on the underlying premise that the forensic experts' role in a criminal responsibility evaluation is to translate their clinical findings into an understandable conceptual framework for the triers of fact. From this paradigm, it is the ethical responsibility of each forensic expert to ascertain on an individual case-by-case basis whether rendering a concluding opinion will clarify or obscure what the expert intends to communicate.

Proponents (e.g., Morse, 1982) for limiting expert testimony raise several valid issues. First, are forensic clinicians overstepping their level of expertise? Second, are they invading the province of the judge or jury in attempting to decide the merits of the case? Third, are clinicians overstating their degree of certainty in rendering an expert opinion on sanity? The first issue is an important ethical responsibility for each forensic clinician. It is improbable that any conclusive statement could be made regarding the general role of forensic psychologists and psychiatrists (if one disregards the minority of evaluative nihilists, who in the name of Thomas Szasz deny any useful role for psychological assessment) and their overall expertise in criminal responsibility evaluations. The second issue may be conceptualized on both empirical and systems levels. Empirically, no data exist on the use of information from experts and its impact on both judge and jury decisions. On a systems level, the forensic professional serves as a consultant to the legal system; it is therefore for the responsibility of the legal system to determine what role, if any, forensic psychologists and psychiatrists play in insanity determinations. The third issue is the one most open to differing views. Clinicians have an ethical obligation to render a no opinion under any circumstances in which they do not have an high degree of certainty, whatever the clinical or legal issue. It is the responsibility both of the clinician and the attorneys to explore thoroughly the expert's certainty as well as the presence of alternative explanations/opinions.

Professional organizations have differing views on what should be allowed during testimony. In a task force in the mid-1970s on psychologists' involvement in the criminal justice system, Monahan (1978) cautioned against rendering conclusory opinions in criminal forensic evaluations. The basis of this opinion was apparently the low degree of accuracy in predictions of dangerousness, a factor unrelated to criminal responsibility assessments. When the American Psychological Association subsequently considered an official opinion regarding the insanity defense (1984), it did not address the issue of conclusory statements. Similarly, the American Psychiatric Association (1983) did not prohibit its members from rendering opinions regarding criminal responsibility although it did express concern about the potential for abuse in this area. This lack of definiteness is appropriate considering the need for more extensive and well-designed research with respect to the differential impact of such testimony and the expertise of forensic evaluators. In the aftermath of the Hinckley trial, Senator Spector (Subcommittee on Criminal Law in the U.S. Senate, 1982, p. 196) proposed a curtailment of psychiatric testimony in insanity trials "to prevent them from dominating and confusing the juries with multisyllabic scientific theories answering to the ultimate question of criminal responsibility." An alternative position is for forensic clinicians to avoid, on an ethical basis, any testimony that obfuscates rather than elucidates the mental state of the defendant at the time of the crime.

WHOLE TRUTH VERSUS PARTIAL TRUTH

Expert witnesses are typically required to swear an oath regarding the honesty and completeness of their statements. While this oath has slight variations from jurisdiction to jurisdiction, it typically includes a phrase regarding the whole truth. Is the purpose of such a stipulation to avoid mental reservations (or other forms of psychological finger crossing), or is it a mandate for the expert to present every relevant facet of the defendant? The point of view utilized by forensic clinicians will be instrumental in assessing their ethical responsibility both in presenting conflicting clinical data and alternative explanations for the defendant's criminal conduct. There is no question that this responsibility exists; the question is how active or passive the forensic expert should be in carrying out this responsibility. Arguments from a passive role are that the parameters of consultation are determined by the legal system, that attempts to offer conflicting data or alternative explanations would be disruptive to the courtroom process, and that a more active stance would discourage future business.

Certainly, forensic experts serve neither the defendant nor their professional career by alienating members of the court. Several issues must be considered in how experts may take a more active role in ensuring that their testimony addresses the whole truth. First, being on the witness stand is not the place to make gratuitous remarks like "By the way, he told me he had lied to the other psychiatrist." The clinician's responsibility is to make the attorney for whom he or she is testifying aware of both the strengths and weaknesses of the evaluation and alternative formulations. Further, in essential areas, the clinician should discuss with the attorney how these weaknesses can be presented to the court to provide honest and balanced testimony. Such admissions on direct examination may frequently increase rather than diminish the credibility and persuadability of a particular expert. Neither the judge nor the jury expect the expert to be infallible; admissions on direct regarding weaknesses of the evaluation may render the expert more believable. Further, if such admissions are only brought out by cross examination the expert may be seen as partisan and less objective, or possibly as having something to hide.

More problematical is the situation in which the attorney, who calls forensic experts to testify, refuses to bring out weaknesses or conflicting clinical data. Experts have two alternatives in such a situation. The first is to expand on their responses during direct and cross-examination in order to clarify these issues (it is difficult for the attorney calling the expert to object or ask his or her expert to limit responses without damaging the case). Second, the expert may wish to discuss these weaknesses with the opposing attorney to ensure that they are thoroughly explored either during the expert's testimony or the testimony of opposing experts. Most attorneys will recognize and accept the expert's genuine need to be as accurate and comprehensive as possible. Many of the issues surrounding the ethical responsibilities of telling the whole truth in insanity evaluations can be avoided if weaknesses and alternative explanations are clearly discussed in the written evaluation. This report, which is typically made available to both attorneys prior to testimony, shifts much of the responsibility back to the legal system concerning which areas each attorney may wish to explore.

CERTAINTY OF CLINICAL OPINIONS

Clinicians are asked, when rendering expert opinion, to testify to a reasonable degree of medical or scientific certainty. At what point is this threshold reached? Certainly a mere preponderance of evidence (i.e., more likely than not) is insufficient to meet the standard. Further, arbitrarily assigning percentage (e.g., 90% sure) may be viewed as arbitrary and capricious if there is no clearly delineated decision model. In addressing this issue, three components of clinical decision making must be addressed: (1) the strength of the clinical methods, (2) the clarity of the symptoms presented, and (3) relative absence of competing explanations. Forensic clinicians may wish to address each of these components in establishing for themselves the threshold of certainty between an opinion and no opinion.

The following decision model outlines one systematic approach to establishing the certainty of clinical opinion in criminal responsibility:

$$\begin{array}{c} \text{Certainty} \\ \text{of opinion} \end{array} = \begin{array}{c} \text{Accuracy of} \\ \text{diagnostic} \\ \text{methods} \end{array} + \begin{array}{c} \text{Consistency} \\ \text{of clinical} \\ \text{presentation} \end{array} + \frac{\text{Relative strength of the opinion}}{\text{Strength of alternative explanations}}$$

First, the accuracy of diagnostic methods refers to the effectiveness of the specific clinical approaches in differentiating the diagnostic patterns associated with responsibility and nonresponsibility. Second, the consistency of symptom presentation is a judgment of how clearly and coherently the reported psychological impairment fits known diagnostic entities and what impact this symptom constellation and its concomitant impairment may have on the defendant's criminal behavior. Third, the relative strength of the opinion must be considered in light of competing explanations and whether or not this clinical presentation could have alternative explanations either diagnostically or with respect to responsibility. An additional issue not included in the model is consequential bias, or how clinicians weight their decision toward responsibility or nonresponsibility. Given the ambiguities of criminal responsibility evaluations, is it better to err in the direction of sanity or insanity? The clinician may adopt a variety of weightings (e.g., better to evaluate a responsible individual as insane than to assess as guilty a nonresponsible individual or a defendant is healthy until proven sick). Such weightings of the decision process must be made explicit in the expert's mind as well as the presentation to the court. This decision model assists only in clarifying the complexities of ascertaining the degree of certainty of an expert opinion; it does not simplify that process.

There is great pressure, frequently from both attorneys, on forensic experts to be definite and to state (if the opinion is favorable) their opinion with great vigor and resolve. The forensic clinician's ethical responsibility is to resist such overstatements regarding the certainty of his or her opinion and, where necessary, to render a no opinion.

ATTORNEYS AND THE EVALUATIVE PROCESS

Forensic professionals' accessibility to attorneys during insanity evaluations must be carefully considered. The clinicians must weigh their needs for communication with the attorneys and the possible responsibility to keep them abreast of evaluations against the potential biasing effect of discussing the evaluation prior to its completion. The potential for bias in openly discussing an incomplete evaluation with attorneys from either side is frequently underestimated. Zusman and Simon (1983), who studied extensively the discrepancies between defense and plaintiff experts in civil forensic evaluations, concluded that initially neutral experts became increasingly biased through frequent contact with attorneys. Such biasing is frequently subtle because the forensic expert begins to adopt a particular attorney's fact pattern or conceptualization. After the insanity evaluation has been initiated, there is no justification for discussing its details with either attorney. If additional information is needed, such requests may be handled by secretaries and staff as long as attorneys have been informed of this procedure prior to the evaluation. Although both attorneys may argue for the right to know or that the expert is partisan (this may be justified if the expert discusses the case with only one side), the power of such arguments may be minimized if written policy/procedures are distributed to the attorneys prior to the acceptance of the referral.

Forensic clinicians may also wish to limit their initial contacts with both attorneys prior to the evaluation. If forensic clinicians have access to clinical and legal records regarding a particular defendant, they may draw their own conclusions regarding the sequence of criminal behavior and the defendant's psychological state. Although it is intellectually stimulating to have an attorney conceptualize his or her fact pattern, logic, and tentative conclusions about the defendant, the potential biasing effect of such a presentation outweighs its informational usefulness. Such limitations are a matter of degree rather than kind; it is entirely proper for either attorney to make a 10-to-15-minute presentation highlighting the type of insanity evaluation and discussing the expert's approach and responsibilities if retained on this particular case.

Another issue is how a forensic expert handles aggressive attorneys. Research reported by Bartol (1983) identified a subcategory of attorneys labeled "ineffective aggressives." The forensic clinician must differentiate between his or her evaluation of the defendant and the aggressiveness or alienating impact of either attorney.

Forensic clinicians must address their role in preparation for testifying. Do clinicians make themselves available to both sides in preparation for expert testimony? If they do not, to what extent are they being partisan? Conversely, if the clinician's written report and test data are available to the opposing attorney, are there sufficient reasons for a pretrial conference? Many clinicians are wary of pretrial conferences with opposing counsel since the primary purpose of such meetings may be to trip up the expert. If, however, the experts have been straightforward about the strengths and limitations of their evaluation in the written report and pointed out alternative explanations to their opinion, there are unlikely to be any surprises. Further, such conferences may also assist the expert in understanding the attorney's way of thinking and potential avenues for cross-examination. An additional question may involve compensation of the expert for his or her time in conference with the opposing counsel. This is certainly not the responsibility of the counsel retaining the expert and it should not be gratis (in some jurisdictions the mechanism for compensation of an expert not retained by that side is cumbersome at best). As a general guideline, it is best for forensic experts to make themselves available to both sides prior to testifying, although the amount of time and intensity of contact may vary widely from case to case.

Chapter 2

Addressing the Legal Standards

The primary goal of this chapter provides a step-by-step translation of legal standards into psychologically meaningful concepts. This involves operationalizing the standards of criminal responsibility into their integral parts and assessing each component. This process of translation is carried out for the three most prevalent insanity standards [i.e., the M'Naghten standard, the M'Naghten–irresistible impulse standard, and the American Law Institute (ALI) standard] and the guilty but mentally ill (GBMI) standard. This is intended to provide practical guidelines of legal criteria for the forensic clinician to implement in his or her evaluations of criminal responsibility.

The forensic clinician is engaged in two interrelated processes that establish what the standard means in psychological terms and how the standard applies to a particular defendant. The first process is one of concretization, moving from a highly abstract legal standard and related psychological concepts to specific observable patterns of behavior and symptoms of a mental disorder. In contrast, the second process is one of synthesis and abstraction; it includes the incorporation of clinical data from the defendant (i.e., self-report, behavioral observations, corroborative information) into a current and retrospective diagnosis that is integrated with the severity and degree of impairment at the time of the offense into a conclusory opinion of how the defendant fits or does not fit the standard of criminal responsibility. This chapter addresses, the first of these two processes, and chapter 9 addresses the second.

This translation process from legal standards to forensic practice is characterized by evolution and refinement (see Roesch and Golding, 1980). Changes both in mental health and criminal justice will have concomitant effects on this multistep process. Such changes are most clearly observed in the evolving diagnostic standards noted in the adoption of the *Diagnostic and Statistical Manual of Mental Disorders,* Third Edition (DSM III) and progress toward *DSM III-R.* In a parallel manner, there are continuing modifications of the legal standards established both through legislation and case law. It is therefore the responsibility of the forensic clinician to be aware of any additional modifications of the legal standards within each jurisdiction that he or she conducts insanity evaluations.

M'NAGHTEN STANDARD

As of 1983 the M'Naghten standard is applied in sixteen states (see Keilitz and Fulton, 1983). It has been adopted by statute in three states (i.e., Louisiana, Minnesota, and South Dakota) and by case law in thirteen (i.e., Arizona, Florida, Iowa, Kansas, Mississippi, Nebraska, Nevada, New Jersey, North Carolina, Oklahoma, Pennsylvania, South Carolina, and Washington). For an individual to be found insane under the M'Naghten standard, he or she must be "laboring under such a defect of reason, from disease of the mind, as not to know the nature and quality of the act he was doing; or if he knew it, that he did not know he was doing what was wrong." [10 cl. & F. 200, 8 Eng. Rep. 718 (1843)]. This standard may be examined as five interrelated concepts (Figure 2.1).

Disease of the Mind

Interpretations of this first concept have varied from a broad conceptualization including any diagnosable mental disorder (Davidson, 1965) to a more restricted position that requires severe impairment, usually in the

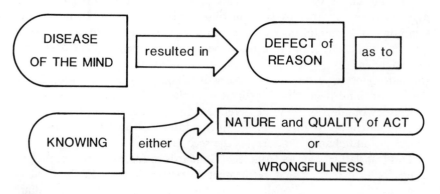

Figure 2.1
M'Naghten standard.

form of a psychosis (Brooks, 1974). This stricter interpretation was based on the earlier diagnostic standards of *DSM II* in which any severe impairment was typically characterized as a psychosis. This rule of thumb (i.e., psychosis as one precondition of insanity) is less relevant under the current diagnostic nomenclature. In *DSM III,* the term *psychosis* is limited to a specific cluster of symptoms and does not necessarily reflect the severity of the disorder. Thus, an individual with a major depressive disorder or a dissociative disorder could experience pervasive impairment without warranting a specific diagnosis of psychosis. It would therefore be more appropriate to take into account both the severity and type of disorder in establishing the existence of a disease of the mind. Therefore, the concept of disease of the mind establishes the basis of the sanity standard, with the four additional concepts limiting its usage to only the most severely impaired (see Goldstein, 1967).

Goldstein (1967) noted that the concept of disease of the mind excludes voluntary intoxication (either by alcohol or drugs) and strong emotional states. Further, the concept of disease is construed to refer to a disorder of fixed or prolonged nature in contrast to any transitory emotional state.

Defect of Reason

Defect of reason specifies the type of impairment necessary for exculpability as a result of a mental disease. For an individual to be found nonresponsible, he or she must show marked loss in the ability to think logically and rationally. In applying a decision-making model, such an individual must show a substantial decrement in the ability to weigh alternatives, consider logical outcomes, and make a reasoned decision. This concept involves the defendant's capacity for rational deductive thinking, which is predicated on the accuracy of his or her perceptions. Thus, a deluded individual, while thinking logically (e.g., "You are a monster about to injure me and others. I will kill you and thus save my life."), would still evidence a defect of reason since this thinking cannot possibly be rational, given marked distortions of the defendant's delusional beliefs (see Brooks, 1974). A second component of rational thinking is the defendant's capacity to organize and synthesize his or her thoughts. Therefore, marked deficits in the structure of thinking may well indicate a defect of reason. This is likely to be manifested (see Spitzer and Endicott, 1978) in disorganized thinking with clinical symptoms such as loose associations (i.e., derailment), perseveration, and markedly illogical thinking.

A clinical evaluation of defect of reason requires a complex judgment in evaluating an individual's ability to perceive alternatives and to make a rational decision in analyzing and synthesizing such alternatives. There are no explicit criteria for establishing the threshold for effective reason (see e.g., Whitlock, 1963), although each element of this concept may be reviewed systematically (e.g., Rogers, 1984*a*).

Knowing

The knowing component of the M'Naghten standard has been the subject of much controversy regarding whether the word *know* refers only to a cognitive or intellectual apprehension or to a more encompassing affective understanding as well (Brooks, 1974). In *People v. Wolff* [61 Cal. 2d 795, 800, P.2d, 40 Cal. Rptr. 271, 274 (1964)] the California Supreme Court defined knowing as "knowledge fused with affect." Such distinctions between intellectual and emotional understanding are imprecise since it is difficult to imagine how one could lose emotional awareness without concomitant loss of intellectual awareness. The term *emotional understanding* is apparently linked to the defendant's ability to recognize and respond on an emotional level to the importance of his or her actions. Thus, if homicide, while intellectually understood by the defendant, evoked from the defendant as little emotional acknowledgment as threading a needle, then that person might qualify under this concept. The concept of emotional understanding includes an evaluation of the defendant's affective arousal, inappropriate affect, and conflicted or ambivalent emotions. The forensic clinician must be careful in establishing the extent to which impairment in emotional awareness and/or expression is evidence of an incapacity to know.

The large majority of cases using the M'Naghten standard's component of knowing are evaluated on the individual's general understanding and comprehension of his or her actions. As noted by Goldstein (1967), the concept of knowing refers in particular to the defendant's criminal action in contradistinction to knowing in a broader or more abstract sense. Finally, the importance of cognitive understanding is underscored by the earlier concept in which the impairment must be based on a defect of reason.

Nature and Quality of the Act

This fourth component of the M'Naghten standard addresses the defendant's comprehension of his or her criminal conduct. It is divided into nature, which is generally defined (e.g., Davidson, 1965; Goldstein, 1967; Brooks, 1974) as the physical characteristics of what the defendant did and under what circumstances. Thus, if the defendant truly believed the alleged victim was a beast of burden, he or she might potentially be excused for the ensuing assaultive behavior (i.e., in attempting to mount the victim) on the basis of not comprehending the nature and circumstances of that behavior. However, it is extremely rare that an individual will not understand the nature of his or her behavior (Davidson, 1964).

The quality of the act has been recognized to have a broader interpretation than the mere physical actions that transpired. Quality has been defined as an acknowledgment of the harmfulness of one's conduct (Davidson, 1965) and its potential or actual consequences for the victim. The threshold question is whether the defendant was able to recognize what was the likely outcome of his or her conduct. An example would be a delusional woman who, while attempting to baptize the devil out of her baby, accidentally drowned the child without a clear awareness of the potential harmfulness of her particular behavior. The Wisconsin Supreme Court addressed the concept of quality in a 1962 case, *State v. Esser* [16 Wis. 2d 567, 115 N.W. 2d (1962)], in which it was stated that the defendant must have a clear realization of his or her behavior and that a vague awareness without real insight was insufficient with respect to the quality of the act.

Wrongfulness

As delineated by Brooks (1974, p. 145), the concept of wrongfulness may be defined as "(1) that which is illegal or contrary to law; (2) that which is contrary to public morality; (3) that which is contrary to the actor's private morality." Courts typically define wrongfulness in terms of incapacity to recognize illegal behavior or behavior that is contrary to law or private morals and delusionally based (i.e., definitions 1 and 3). Thus, while the original M'Naghten decision defined wrongfulness as "acting contrary to law" (cited in Goldstein, 1967, p. 51), this has been broadened in most jurisdictions to include moral wrongfulness.

Davidson (1965), in establishing wrongfulness under the M'Naghten standard, suggested a careful investigation of the defendant's behavior prior to and following the criminal actions. He suggested that behaviors such as turning oneself in, statements of remorse, and attempts to avoid prosecution may be evidence of wrongfulness. Similarly, he indicated that preparatory behavior for the criminal act and behavior that was intended to avoid subsequent arrest should be considered. Examination of these factors may be helpful in the majority of cases. A major exception involves the defendant whose delusional beliefs include the government and law enforcement personnel. For example, if the defendant believes that police are really masquerading terrorists, then attempts to evade them would not address the wrongfulness of his or her actions.

Several potential problems emerge in the implementation of the wrongfulness component. Wrongfulness can be examined on two parameters: (1)

the clarity and unequivocalness of the defendant's intentions and behavior and (2) the perceived seriousness of a wrongful behavior. For example, a manic investor may be fully aware of the wrongfulness of his or her business transactions but convinced of their inconsequentiality (e.g., "just a technicality"). In addition, the defendant may have strong conflicting beliefs regarding the wrongfulness of his or her actions. For instance, a defendant may hold rigidly to a code of honor that justifies vengeance against anyone who disgraces his or her family. The primary determinant in this case is the basis of this code of honor and whether it and subsequent actions are derived from mental illness. Psychotic symptoms might include a gross misapprehension of who the defendant is (e.g., a chivalrous knight), a gross misperception of another's conduct (e.g., a friendly wink as irrefutable proof of a romantic liaison), or a gross misconstruction of the significance of a situation (e.g., a harmless joke misread as malicious and devastating humiliation). Such determinations are greatly complicated by defendants' subsequent needs, intentional and unintentional, to provide psychological justification for their criminal actions.

A related issue, defendants who deliberately carry out criminal behavior so that they will be punished, was raised by the Group for the Advancement of Psychiatry (1983). Does the defendant who showed remorse and deliberately committed a criminal act in order to be punished comprehend the wrongfulness of this conduct? In this example, the defendant obviously understands the illegality of the behavior and may also find it morally repugnant. Would this person meet the M'Naghten criteria for wrongfulness? Probably yes, if the actions were based on delusional beliefs in which he or she was serving a grossly distorted moral imperative (i.e., through his or her punishment) in knowingly committing these wrongs. In most cases, however, the self-destructive behavior is neither as clear cut nor directly related to delusional thinking; in such cases, defendants would not likely qualify with respect to the wrongfulness component of the M'Naghten standard.

IRRESISTIBLE IMPULSE

The combined M'Naghten–irresistible impulse standard has fallen into disfavor and is recognized (i.e., as of 1983) in only four jurisdictions: Colorado, Georgia, New Mexico, and Virginia (Keilitz and Fulton, 1983). The addition of irresistible impulse was intended to broaden the standard so that individuals who met the M'Naghten rule (i.e., knew the nature and quality of their act and knew that it was wrong), but who, on the basis of a mental disorder, lost the capacity to control their behavior were rendered nonresponsible. One of the most influential cases establishing the combined

M'Naghten–irresistible rule was *Parsons v. State* (cited in Goldstein, 1967), which articulated in addition to the M'Naghten rule the acquittal of a defendant when "(1) if, by reason of the duress of such mental disease, he had so far lost the power to choose between the right and wrong, and to avoid doing the act in question, as that his free agency was at the time destroyed; (2) and if at the time, the alleged crime was so connected with such mental disease, in the relation of cause and effect, as to have caused the product of it solely" (p. 68). This standard includes three important components based on a mental disease: (1) loss of power to choose (2) between right and wrong and (3) inability to avoid doing the act. While there is considerable variation in the language of existing standards, these three components are addressed. The most elaborate of the combined M'Naghten–irresistible impulse standards is statutorily defined in Colorado (cited in McDonald):

[A] person who is so diseased or defective in mind at the time of the commission of the act as to be incapable of distinguishing right from wrong with respect to that act, or being able to distinguish, has suffered such an impairment of mind by disease or defect as to destroy the will power and to render him incapable of choosing the right and refraining from doing the wrong is not accountable; and this is so howsoever such insanity may be manifested, by irresistible impulse or otherwise. But care should be taken not to confuse such mental disease or defect with moral obliquity, mental depravity, or passion growing out of anger, revenge, hatred, or other motives, and kindred evil conditions, for when the act is induced by any of these causes the person is accountable to the law. [1976, p. 67]

The following sections examine the implementation of the three primary criteria for the irresistible impulse standard. The combined M'Naghten–irresistible impulse standard is schematized in Figure 2.2.

Loss of Power to Choose

The loss of volitional-behavioral capacity is the pivotal issue in establishing irresistible impulse. This loss of power to choose must be the result of a mental disease or defect and is described variously as the absence/incapacity of free agency, will, will power, and mental power (in Goldstein, 1967; Keilitz and Fulton, 1983). Further, this loss of power to choose must not be the result solely of any strong emotional reaction. Thus, emotional states flowing from moments of rage would not by itself excuse the defendant (Goldstein, 1967).

The fundamental issue underlying the determination of loss of power to choose is establishing what various authors have referred to as distinction between irresistible and unresisted impulse (e.g., Shapiro, 1984; American

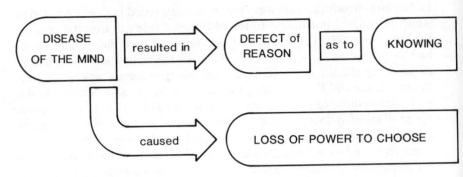

Psychiatric Association, 1983). As most forensic practitioners would attest, the majority of defendants experiences at least some ambivalence and conflict about engaging in a criminal activity. The issue is twofold: Does the individual want to resist the criminal act? If so, does the defendant have the capacity to resist? Thus, even the severest compulsions do not preclude the intention/desire of an individual to engage in criminal behavior.

The loss of power to choose must reflect some internal imperative to carry out behavior that is forbidden both on a societal as well as a personal basis. This internal imperative may be experienced symptomatically as an over-riding compulsion (i.e., a pattern of repetitive behaviors that the defendant is incapable of resisting), although this is a fairly rare occurrence. One such example, is a defendant with a compulsion to explore other's personal possessions; in this particular case he was apprehended by a homeowner who awoke to find the defendant in his bedroom looking through his family photos. More commonly the loss of volitional capacity is experienced as an internal and nonnegotiable demand. This internal demand must meet the following criteria:

Must be unable to be satisfied by other available alternatives. In the preceding example the defendant must have an internal need to enter this home and then to see these particular family portraits or other possessions that would not be satisfied by browsing in a book store.

Must be incapable of any extended delay. Although observers hold that the loss of volitional capacity does not have to be sudden (see Goldstein, 1967), a strong internal demand such as that required by the standard should certainly not be delayed indefinitely (if it were, then it would clearly be resistible). The individual's capacity to resist an impulse and his or her coping methods for resisting may indicate adequate behavioral control. This may not hold true where there has been a sudden loss of a coping method (as in the death of a spouse).

Must experience this loss of volitional capacity with a sustained negative

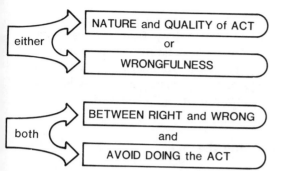

either {
NATURE and QUALITY of ACT
or
WRONGFULNESS
}

both {
BETWEEN RIGHT and WRONG
and
AVOID DOING the ACT
}

Figure 2.2
Combined M'Naghten–irresistible impulse standard.

effect on the individual's day-to-day functioning. If this loss is based on a mental illness (see Davidson, 1965) it should have a disinhibiting and/or disorganizing effect on the individual's overall functioning. Thus, a pattern of mental illness and problems of behavioral control should be identifiable. In assessing the defendant's mental disorder, the forensic clinician should ascertain the defendant's overall psychological impairment, capacity to be choiceful and purposeful in major areas of life, and capability of resisting impulses forbidden both personally and legally.

Right and Wrong

This component of the irresistible impulse standard refers to the capacity of defendants to choose between right and wrong and refrain from criminal behavior. Wrongfulness has been previously defined as a component of the M'Naghten standard; rightfulness, by extrapolation, is behavior that is either legally or morally correct. The forensic clinician must establish the basis on which the defendant perceived his or her behavior as right or wrong since the clarity of this distinction is closely related to the individual's capacity to resist. If, for example, a mentally retarded defendant does not resist his or her angry impulses, based only on the belief that he or she may receive parental punishment, then this defendant has less volitional control than if he or she realized the gravity of societal/criminal sanctions. The forensic clinician must address how, on this occasion, the knowledge of right and wrong does not allow the individual to resist criminal behavior. One formulation considered in several jurisdictions (see Goldstein, 1967) was the policeman at-the-elbow rule. This formulation asked whether the immediate presence of a law enforcement officer would inhibit or substantially modify the criminal behavior. While this may be useful as a general guideline, an important consideration is that for those individuals struggling for behavioral control, the presence of any authority figure might result in a temporary avoidance of criminal activity. Realizing this limitation, the forensic clinician may wish to use the policeman-at-the-elbow formulation as part of the clinical inquiry. Other hypotheticals, including the presence of a member of the clergy or family, may assist the clinician in establishing the defendant's ability to avoid wrongful behavior.

Avoid Doing the Act

This component strongly emphasizes the inevitability of the behavior and its uncontrollability as observed in the language of irresistible impulse standard (Goldstein, 1967): "acts beyond his control," being "overwhelmed" and "unable to control his actions or impulses." The forensic clinician must address how, at the time of the offense, the criminal behavior became an inevitable and psychologically necessary expression of the mental illness. The following clinical issues must be addressed:

1. The clinician must establish what are the determinants of the uncontrollable behavior and whether or not it is based on a mental disorder. This involves a complex judgment of the role of situational variables, temporary emotional states, and substance abuse in this loss of behavioral control.
2. The clinician must establish the extent to which the defendant was able to foresee his or her vulnerability in a particular situation and thereby avoid it. For example, if a pedophile were to babysit for a particularly attractive child, he may knowingly be placing himself in a situation where his behavior will become uncontrollable. In other words, how preventable was this behavior?
3. The forensic clinician must assess how the defendant attempted to resist or avoid the criminal actions. The clinician must carefully assess the defendant's various motivations in establishing the defendant's intentions and the uncontrollability of his or her behavior.

An area of controversy in forensic psychology and psychiatry is the role of the unconscious in criminal behavior. One classic explanation for criminal behavior is that it represents the unconscious expression of repressed aggressive and sexual impulses. According to this formulation (see e.g., Tanay, 1978; Bromberg, 1979) since the determinants of behavior are unconscious, the crime is uncontrollable. Deviant behavior would therefore be construed as superego lacunae or impulses beyond the individual's ability to control or sublimate. Further, such loss of control is construed as evidence of a mental disorder. Such reasoning may become tautological (i.e., "you act out because you are mentally ill; you are mentally ill because you act out"). This is not to argue that the unconscious plays no role in the production of criminal behavior; rather, it suggests that the forensic clinician begin first with the defendant's mental functioning, carefully evaluating severity and degree of impairment and its impact on the criminal behavior. To begin with the criminal behavior and to attempt to formulate psychological explanations for such behavior is untenable, given the criteria of criminal responsibility standards.

ALI STANDARD

This standard is utilized as of 1984 in twenty-four states (Alabama, Alaska, Arkansas, California, Connecticut, Delaware, Hawaii, Illinois, Indiana, Kentucky, Maine, Maryland, Massachusetts, Michigan, Missouri, Ohio, Oregon, Tennessee, Texas, Utah, Vermont, West Virginia, Wisconsin, and Wyoming). The ALI standard (American Law Institute, 1962) states that a defendant is not culpable if "as a result of a mental disease or defect, he lacks substantial capacity either to appreciate the criminality (wrongfulness) of his conduct or to conform his conduct to the requirements of law." This standard specifically excludes "any abnormality manifested by repeated criminal or otherwise antisocial conduct." This standard includes five operative concepts (Brooks, 1974): (1) mental disease or defect, (2) lack of substantial capacity, (3) appreciation, (4) criminality or wrongfulness, and (5) conformity of conduct to the requirements of law (Fig. 2.3).

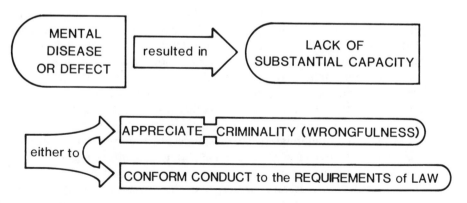

Figure 2.3
ALI standard.

Mental Disease or Defect

This criterion, while paralleling mental disease in the M'Naghten standard, specifies both functional and organic disorders. In defining this concept, most jurisdictions adopted *McDonald v. United States* [312 F.2d 847 (D.C. Cir. 1962)], adopted "any abnormal condition of the mind which substantially affects mental or emotional processes and substantially impairs behavior controls." This definition continues to be used in most states (Weiner, 1985). Considerable discussion has focused on what diagnoses constitute a disease or defect. It has been argued that any disorder (with the possible exclusion of antisocial personality disorders) would be sufficient to qualify if that diagnosis is found in a current diagnostic nomenclature, *DSM III*. Others have discouraged the utilization of personality disorders, arguing that they are insufficient to meet the criminal responsibility standard (e.g., Rachlin, Halpern, and Portnow, 1984). Rogers (1984*a*) suggested that no class of disorders should be summarily excluded while acknowledging the improbability of some disorders, meeting the insanity standard. These disorders include psychosexual dysfunctions, simple phobias, most somatoform disorders, and the majority of personality disorders. As with the M'Naghten standard, it is the responsibility of the forensic clinician to examine any severe disorder and utilize the subsequent criteria for establishing the defendant's criminal responsibility. The American Psychiatric Association (Insanity Defense Work Group, 1983, p. 685) suggested that disorders leading to exculpation typically be of "the severity (if not always the quality) of conditions that psychiatrists diagnose as psychoses." It should be observed that this statement applies more to proposed revisions of criminal responsibility standards than the simplistic exclusion of all nonpsychotic disorders.

Additional debate has centered on the inclusion/exclusion of antisocial personality disorders. The original ALI standard excluded any disorder manifested only by repeated criminal or otherwise antisocial conduct. The rough translation of this concept as a definition of a sociopath has been questioned both on legal (e.g., *United States v. Currens*, [290 F.2d 751 (3d Cir. 1961)]) and psychiatric (Overholser, 1962) grounds. To meet the current diagnostic criteria for antisocial personality disorder, the individual must manifest a developmental pattern of maladjustment with impairment at home, at school, and in interpersonal spheres. In addition, as an adult, the individual must evidence impairment not only in conforming to societal expectations but also in meeting social expectations and having a satisfactory work history. It is very unlikely that an individual meeting these diagnostic criteria would have symptoms limited to antisocial or criminal behavior; such behavior would be more consistent with a nonpsychiatric or V diagnosis of adult antisocial behavior.

An alternate approach to examining the dimensions of mental disease or defect is to examine clinical studies of criminal responsibility to see under what conditions the courts have found defendants nonresponsible. These studies have two important limitations: First, the sample size in both studies is rather small, thus limiting generalizability, and second, the findings demonstrate trends and not strict inclusion-exclusion criteria. A study reported by Howard and Clark (1983) examined the clinical records of eighty defendants evaluated for insanity. They found individuals with psychotic disorders and no history of substance abuse were more likely to be found insane than their counterparts. Similarly, Rogers and his colleagues (Rogers, Seman, and Stampley, 1984; Rogers, Cavanaugh, Seman, and Harris, 1984) found individuals with schizophrenic disorders, previous history of psychiatric hospitalization, prior treatment with psychoactive medication, and an absence of drug or alcohol abuse were more likely to be acquitted on grounds of insanity. While these trends are interesting, it should be observed that defendants must be evaluated on a case-by-case basis because nonpsychotic individuals may also be found nonresponsible for their criminal behavior.

Lack of Substantial Capacity

The concept of lack of substantial capacity was adopted by the framers of the ALI standard as a measure of severe but not complete impairment of the defendant's cognitive and volitional abilities at the time of the offense. To quote the drafters of the ALI test (in Huckabee, 1980, p. 20) the term *substantial* is utilized to "support the weight of the judgment; if capacity is greatly impaired, that presumably should be sufficient." The purpose of the concept of substantial capacity is to avoid the use of absolutes (see Brooks, 1974) in making a judgment about major interference or impairment with respect to either of the twin prongs of the ALI standard. Given the imprecision of terms, the forensic clinician must address the threshold question: were the defendant's cognitive-volitional abilities disrupted in a major way during the commission of the offense? Would the offense have occurred without such impairment?

The loss of substantial capacity may result from an interruption, disorganization, or gross distortion of the individual's psychological functioning because of a mental disorder:

Interruption: Most problematical is the determination of a loss of substantial capacity in individuals whose functioning appears to be well integrated except for discrete episodes. Such interruptions are difficult to assess because of their variable nature and the typical absence of such episodes during subsequent assessments in institutional settings. Thus, an individual experiencing a severe bipolar disorder may have a discrete manic episode that severely disrupts his or her cognitive and volitional abilities for relatively brief periods.

Disorganization: Blatantly psychotic individuals may not be able to process their situation adequately, grossly misperceiving environmental stimuli, and may lack the capacity to integrate such stimuli in a meaningful and rational manner. Such individuals, because of their disorganization (e.g., schizophrenic or organic impairment) cannot cognitively appreciate their immediate situation and sufficiently control their subsequent conduct.

Distortion: Individuals may respond to their environment in a coherent and internally logical manner yet severely misconstrue the meaning of others' verbalizations and/or actions. Such misapprehension of meaning based on psychopathology constitutes more of a distorted than disorganized process. Thus, an individual with a paranoid disorder may have intact intellectual functions, with the notable exception of circumscribed persecutory delusions.

Appreciate

The term *appreciate* was adopted into the ALI standard to broaden the earlier concept of knowing beyond intellectual apprehension (see Introduction). The intent of the change was also to assess the defendant's emotional understanding—that is, ability to understand and recognize the significance of his or her conduct. The term *appreciate,* therefore, covers not only a rudimentary awareness of the inappropriateness of actions but also the magnitude of this inappropriateness. As noted in *Wion v. United States* (cited in Rogers, 1984a, p. 5) the term *appreciate* is defined as "mentally capable of knowing what he was doing and mentally capable of knowing that it was wrong."

The forensic clinician must assess the defendant's cognitive abilities in understanding his or her physical actions, the likely or expected outcome of such actions, and the significance of such actions. This includes an awareness of what happened and was expected to happen both to the defendant as the perpetrator of criminal activity (e.g., arrest and possible conviction) as well as to the victims of their activities (e.g., the potentially devastating effects of being raped). Certainly, a mentally retarded individual who did not understand the irreversibility of death would be grossly impaired in his or her comprehension of the results of excessively dunking a younger sibling in the tub and the legal consequences of such behavior. The individual's activities either in preparation for the criminal activity or in an attempt to avoid prosecution (i.e., avoidance of identification, concealment of evidence, and/or evasion of police) often provide clear-cut evidence of the individual's ability to appreciate.

The assessment of emotional understanding, or the significance, of the defendant's criminal activity is frequently more difficult. The defendant's ability to recall his or her perceptions of the importance of the behavior and his or her affective arousal its typically more difficult than remembering the actual events and his of her overt actions. The forensic clinician may wish to address how bad the defendant perceived the criminal behavior. This should be probed thoroughly based on both what happened and relevant hypothetical situations. Examples of hypothetical situations include:

1. How would the defendant respond if he or she were the recipient or victim rather than the perpetrator of the crime?
2. What would have been the defendant's emotional response and actions if such criminal behavior were carried out against a loved one?
3. What was the victim's emotional response to the criminal behavior? Was it understandable—that is, did the defendant know why the victim cried or was angry or upset?
4. What was the defendant's reaction to the victim's expressed emotions?

In summary, the forensic clinician must assess the individual's recognition of his or her behavior, understanding of the likely consequences of such behavior, and awareness of its significance. This evaluation (see Rogers, 1984a) addresses primarily the individual's cognitive abilities but also includes an assessment of the emotional understanding of the importance of that person's criminal conduct to him- or herself and the victims.

Criminality or Wrongfulness

States have adopted either the original term, *criminality* or its alternative, *wrongfulness* (Keilitz and Fulton, 1983). Criminality refers to any conduct for which societal sanctions are imposed to prohibit such conduct for the protection of the community. Criminal behavior is statutorily defined by federal and state law. Defendants are not expected to know the precise wording of the criminal statutes in question or of the specific penalties that may be imposed; rather, defendants should understand that the behavior is criminal and have some awareness of the magnitude of the offense. To meet this component of the ALI standard, the lack of comprehension of criminal behavior must be the result of a mental disease or defect. Nonpsychopathological reasons (e.g., cultural isolation) are not sufficient to qualify for this criterion.

The alternative term, *wrongfulness,* has been adopted in many jurisdictions as being slightly more inclusive than criminality. Wrongfulness augments the concept of criminality by including those defendants who recognized that their conduct was criminal but, on the basis of a delusion, believed it was morally justified (Rogers, 1984*a*). This reasoning is articulated in *U.S. v. Freeman* [357 F.2d 606 (2d Cir. 1966)] and parallels the M'Naghten standard in its definition of wrongfulness.

Conformity of Conduct to the Requirements of the Law

This represents the volitional-behavioral prong of the ALI standard. The term *conformity of conduct* supplanted the earlier irresistible impulse and refers to any marked loss in self-determined purposive behavior at the time of the offense. Conformity of conduct defines the defendant's ability to choose and to withhold important behavior preceding and including the crime in question. A loss of cognitive control is frequently paralleled by a concomitant loss of volitional-behavioral control.

Several dimensions must be considered in examining the conformity of conduct criterion:

1. The standard refers to the capacity to conform, whether or not the defendant exercised this capacity. Reckless or impulsive behavior may not necessarily reflect on the individual's capabilities but on his or her choice.
2. The ability to conform refers only to criminal behavior (i.e., the requirements of law). Deficits in volitional-behavioral control unrelated to criminal behavior do not qualify under this criterion.
3. Assessment of the choicefulness of the criminal behavior involves a careful examination of the individual's perceived options and decision-making abilities. Similar to the M'Naghten–irresistible impulse standard, the forensic clinician must evaluate the deliberateness of the defendant's actions, choices available to the defendant, and the point, if it does exist, when criminal actions became inevitable.

The clinical determination of conformity of conduct is frequently challenging given the retrospectiveness of insanity evaluations. For a variety of reasons, the defendant may wish to portray his or her behavior as uncontrollable and therefore exonerable. For this reason (see Rogers, 1984*a*), the forensic clinician may wish to separate the defendant's reported volitional control from clinically assessed control. Such division allows the clinician to focus on all corroborative sources of clinical information in reaching a decision about the lack of volition. Further, the forensic clinician is cautioned not to confuse ineptness with uncontrollability; bungling of criminal behavior with a high probability of arrest is not necessarily related to either mental illness or criminal responsibility. Similarly, ritualistic behavior may or may not be symptomatic of mental illness and should be carefully evaluated for its relevance to volitional abilities. For example, some defendants with sexual paraphilias may intentionally use ritualistic behavior to heighten their sexual pleasure; such behaviors (dependent, of course, on the impairment) are unlikely to represent uncontrollable behavior. A final dimension of volitional control is the defendant's capacity to foresee and thus avoid potentially explosive situations. If the defendant deliberately places him- or herself in a situation where violence is likely to occur, then this factor of avoidability must also be assessed within the spectrum of volitional-behavioral control.

GUILTY BUT MENTALLY ILL STANDARD

This section focuses on the implementation of the Michigan-based GBMI standard. This standard (see Robey, 1978) requires three decision points: first, that the defendant was guilty of the offense; second, that the defendant experienced a legally defined mental illness at the time of the offense; and third, that the defendant did not meet the insanity standard. For the purposes of this decision model, the guilt of the defendant is strictly under the purview of the fact finder. This exclusion leaves the forensic clinician with two tasks: (1) to assess whether the defendant meets the insanity standard and (2), if not, whether the defendant meets the criteria of mental illness as defined under the GBMI standard. Thus, in any assessment of GBMI criteria, the forensic clinician must first complete a thorough evaluation of insanity prior to addressing the GBMI definition of mental illness.

The Michigan standard defines mental illness as "a substantial disorder of thought or mood which significantly impairs judgment, behavior, capacity to recognize reality, or ability to cope with the ordinary demands of life" (Mich Comp Ann 330.1400a). This standard has been adopted with minor modifications (i.e., as of 1984) by six additional states: Delaware, Georgia, Illinois, Indiana, Kentucky, and New Mexico (Institute of Mental Disability and the Law, 1984). Two other states, Alaska and Pennsylvania, have radically departed from the GBMI standard. Both states (see Institute on Mental Disability and the Law, 1984) have retained the original M'Naghten standard of insanity and have adopted the ALI rule as their GBMI standard. Thus, forensic clinicians in these jurisdictions must examine the criteria included in the ALI formulation in conducting their GBMI evaluations. In two additional states, South Dakota does not specify a GBMI standard nor does it have a legally defined mental illness, and Maryland has recognized the guilty but insane verdict, which appears identical (except for minor changes on wording) to the traditional not guilty by reason of insanity (NGRI) finding. In this latter case, the disposition guilty but insane exculpates the defendant under the same criteria as the ALI standard (i.e., with treatment, not punishment, as the disposition).

The GBMI standard consists of three operative concepts: (1) that the defendant does not qualify for an NGRI finding, (2) that the defendant has a substantial disorder, and (3) that the defendant has significant impairment in one or more areas as a result of that disorder (Fig. 2.4).

Does Not Qualify for the NGRI Standard

This component of the GBMI standard requires, in many jurisdictions, an evaluation of the defendant on the issue of sanity prior to any determinations of GBMI. Thus, a forensic clinician never conducts a GBMI evaluation in these jurisdictions without a prior insanity evaluation. An additional problem is posed when the forensic clinician is unable to reach an opinion regarding sanity with a reasonable degree of medical or scientific certainty. Under these circumstances, it would appear (see Rogers, 1984*a*) appropriate for the forensic clinician to make clear his or her uncertainty regarding the issues of sanity and then proceed to address the GBMI standard. Such an approach would not deprive the triers of fact of valuable

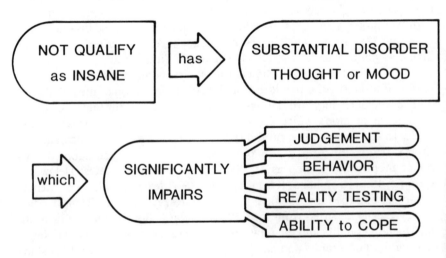

Figure 2.4
GBMI standard.

information in the broader context of criminal responsibility since the GBMI and NGRI standards are addressed concurrently.

Substantial Disorder of Thought or Mood

This component includes two important criteria: explication of the term *substantial* and delineation of disorders of thought and mood. The articulation of the disorder as substantial is an attempt to limit the disorders considered under this standard. The need of clarification is whether the word *substantial* refers to the severity of the disorder (e.g., moderate versus mild depression), the type of disorder (e.g., dysthymic disorder versus adjustment disorder with a depressed mood), or both. From a clinical perspective, it would be most logical to apply the term *substantial* to the severity of disorder since the type of disorder has little relationship to its potential overall impairment of the individual. For example, a severe obsessive compulsive disorder may be as disabling as any schizophrenic disorder.

The clinical determination of substantialness involves a careful investigation both of the severity and extensiveness of the symptoms and their potential impact on the individual's day-to-day functioning. The severity of symptoms may be assessed on several indices including the frequency and duration of the symptoms during the period of the alleged offense, avoidability of the symptoms (i.e., can the defendant ignore or alleviate the symptoms?), and the psychological discomfort and disruption experienced by the individual as a result of the symptoms. The impact of the disorder on day-to-day functioning is considered under the third component, significant impairment. The severity of the disorder may be assessed with respect to individual symptoms and overall severity. Toward this goal the SADS (see chapter 7) offers a model for reliably quantifying psychological symptoms and for determining through the Global Assessment Scale the overall severity of the disorder.

The types of mental disorders considered under the GBMI standard are indistinguishable from those required in an insanity evaluation (Association of Mental Disability and the Law, 1984). Although it has been suggested (Center for Forensic Psychiatry, 1974) as a guideline that disorders of thought refer to schizophrenic and other psychotic disorders and those of mood to major affective disorders, such a formulation is unnecessarily narrow. For example, severe anxiety disorders may clearly show a major mood disturbance, and certain dissociative disorders may manifest disturbances of thought. Other disorders (e.g., borderline personality disorder and paranoid personality disorder) must be carefully reviewed on a selective basis regarding disturbances of mood and/or thought. Thus, the clinician is cautioned against summarily dismissing a disorder on the basis of type without careful consideration of its substantialness and its impairment of thought or mood.

Significant Impairment

Significant impairment, while suffering from definitional ambiguity, applies to a mental disorder that disrupts or disorganizes the individual's day-to-day functioning. These deficits must be a result of the mental disorder and involve an ongoing impairment. This impairment must be within the context of day-to-day functioning and not limited to the criminal behavior (e.g., although many criminals show extraordinarily poor judgment, this is not conclusive evidence of either a mental illness or impairment of judgment as a result of that mental illness). In addition, this criterion specifies that the significant impairment must be in one or more of the following areas: judgment, behavior, capacity to recognize reality, and/or ability to cope with the ordinary demands of life.

Judgment refers to the defendant's ability to perceive and accurately weigh alternatives, assess benefits and risks, and make reasoned decisions (Rogers, 1984a). Such a determination must be made on whether or not he or she exercised that ability. Finally, the impaired judgement must be the result of a mental disorder and must significantly impair his or her decision-making capacity.

Impairment of behavior refers to ongoing disturbances in the defendant's actions. Such behavioral disturbances must be symptomatic of mental disorder. For example, any individual may engage in what appears to be ritualistic behavior; such behavior becomes symptomatic of mental disorder when it is a result of a diagnosable disorder as manifested through some loss of voluntary control. For example, what distinguishes an obsessive compulsive disorder from normal behavior is the individual's inability to resist such behavior. Other disturbances of behavior might include phobic responses, perseveration, and actions as a result of a manic syndrome.

Capacity to recognize reality refers to the intactness of the individual's perception of external stimuli and integration of these perceptions in a consentually validated manner. Impaired reality testing may be the result of either distortion and/or disorganization of the individual's perceptual process. Such impairment may range from being transient and peripheral (i.e., momentary feelings of depersonalization), which would not qualify as GBMI, to blatantly psychotic. A severe impairment of reality testing would likely produce impaired judgment as well and should alert the forensic clinician to re-evaluate the defendant's sanity.

Ability to cope with the ordinary demands of life refers to the defendant's ability to secure and maintain the basic physical and emotional needs.

An inability to meet basic self-care needs must be the result of mental disorder, not the adoption of an alternate life-style (e.g., hobo-type existence) or economic misfortune (e.g., failure of social welfare agencies to provide adequate support). This capacity for self-care is typically measured in the individual's psychological ability to maintain personal hygiene, food and shelter, and minimally adequate social skills. Further, it is likely that an individual who, because of a mental disorder, does not engage in purposeful or goal-oriented activities (e.g., work, hobbies, day treatment program) would also qualify as one who lacks the capacity for self-care.

Marked deficits in judgment are the most commonly found criterion within this component of the GBMI standard. Table 2.1 summarizes the percentage of GBMI defendants meeting the four criteria of significant impairment.

OTHER STANDARDS

Six states utilize standards of insanity not addressed in the preceding formulations. New Hampshire has continued to use the New Hampshire standard that with minor modifications has been its standard since 1870. This rule places the responsibility on the jury to establish the parameters of sanity and insanity. The forensic clinician, under such a system, offers information regarding diagnosis and subsequent impairment but is not asked to address explicitly either legal criteria or psychological constructs regarding criminal responsibility (Emery and Emery, 1984). Similarly, Rhode Island has adopted the justly responsible test (Keilitz and Fulton, 1983), which requires the jury to establish the prevailing community standards of legal and moral responsibility.

New York, by curtailing the ALI standard, and North Dakota, by altering the M'Naghten standard, have devised similar standards employing the first prong of the ALI test, "appreciating the criminality of his con-

Table 2.1
Level of Impairment on the GBMI Criteria

Criteria	Insane (%)	GBMI (%)	Sane (%)
Judgment	100	75	3.3
Behavior	86.4	25	1.1
Capacity to cope with ordinary demands of life	72.7	33.3	3.3
Reality testing	95.5	41.7	0

duct.'' For such formulations the reader is referred to the discussion of the ALI standard. In addition, a hybrid M'Naghten/ALI standard has been adopted by federal jurisdictions under the Insanity Reform Act of 1984. This standard requires the integration of the ALI concept of appreciate with M'Naghten's nature and quality and the combined M'Naghten/ALI wrongfulness. In the application of this hybrid standard, the forensic clinician is referred to the appropriate components of the respective standards. In addition, this new federal rule specifies a severe mental disease or defect, raising another threshold question in distinguishing severe from nonsevere disorders (refer to the analogous discussion of substantial disorder within the GBMI standard).

Montana and Idaho, through legislative action, eliminated their specific standards for insanity. They have opted for the mens rea approach that requires that the defendant have the requisite mental knowledge or intent to commit the offense. As a defense (see Keilitz and Fulton, 1983), there are no explicit criteria available for its implementation.

CONCLUSION

In summary, this chapter has reviewed the relevant legal and psychological literature with respect to specific standards of insanity. Progress has been made over the last several decades in an attempt to articulate more systematically criminal responsibility standards. Legal criteria for criminal responsibility have always been and are likely to continue to be vague definitions relating culpability to psychological impairment. As empirical research continues on standards of criminal responsibility, it will be the responsibility of forensic psychology and psychiatry to offer more explicit models for the courts to consider in their refinement of criminal responsibility standards.

Chapter 3

Malingering and Deception

A cornerstone issue of criminal responsibility evaluations is the clinical assessment of the defendant's completeness and veracity of self-report. In each insanity evaluation, the clinician must address the general issue of deception and rule-in or rule-out malingering. As discussed in chapter 1, insanity evaluations are, by their very nature, adversarial, and this fact thereby increases the likelihood of conscious or unconscious distortion in the defendant's self-report. The far-reaching consequences of such evaluations must have some impact on the defendant's self-report, even though he or she may perceive the forensic evaluator as friendly and empathic. Thus, the clinician is left with a complex task of sorting out the degree of distortion in a patient's self-report and the degree of intentionality inherent in that distortion.

The adversarial nature of insanity evaluations deserves further comment. In most jurisdictions, the clinician is required to inform the defendant of the purpose of the evaluation, its nonconfidentiality (including who will have access to this information), the potential negative consequences for the defendant if he or she chooses to participate in the evaluation, and the defendant's right to limit his or her participation in the evaluation. A clinician who minimizes the importance of such warnings through rapport-building techniques (e.g., high degree of empathy and supportive statements) may unethically avoid or unduly minimize the adversarial nature of the criminal responsibility evaluations. Thus, as noted by Rogers and Cavanaugh (1983a), a clinician may ironically be modeling deception to his or her evaluatees.

It may be valuable for the clinician to discuss early in the evaluation the defendant's perception of what is happening and of the clinician's attitude toward the defendant. For example, a defendant who perceives the clinician is attempting to trick him or her may be accurately perceiving the clinician's intentions, responding to other demand characteristics, or reflecting perceptual distortions like those with a paranoid personality structure. Asking periodically for feedback may assist the clinician in assessing important interactional variables that may dramatically influence the defendant's honesty and the completeness of his or her self-report.

The specific effects of sociodemographic variables such as age, race, and sex on the honesty of a defendant in a criminal responsibility evaluation are not known. Differences in responses have been noted in projective testing and psychotherapy based on the race and gender of the clinician and patient. Anecdotally, it has been observed that male defendants, in their discussion of rape and other sexual assaults, appear to relate differently to a female than a male professional. In one case, a defendant who had been almost boasting about the details of several dozen rapes he had committed became reticent when a female clinician was included in the evaluation and refused any further discussion of sexual matters until she had left. He then spontaneously resumed his discussion of his deviant sexual behavior. It is likely that this defendant's honesty as well as openness were affected by the presence of a woman. In addition, the clinician must be alert to the defendant's attitude toward racial issues and ethnic backgrounds since both may have an impact on the issue of malingering.

Epidemiological data on the prevalence of malingering and deception in criminal responsibility evaluations are presented in Table 3.1. Of individuals clinically evaluated as sane, nearly 20% showed moderate deception with suspected malingering, and 4.5% evidenced definite malingering. These figures are in contrast to those clinically evaluated as insane where only 7.5% manifested a moderate degree of deception and none was seen as definitely malingering, underscoring the substantial prevalence of deception and malingering, particularly with the same defendants.

Several styles of deception have been observed in insanity evaluations. The most common is malingering in which individuals attempt to fabricate deliberately or exaggerate grossly their symptomatology. Malingering, as with other deceptive styles, forms a continuum of responses from a minor shading of self-report to dramatic and preposterous accounts of mental ill-

Table 3.1
Malingering and Deception

	Sane (%)	Insane (%)
Minor distortion or deception	32	15.1
Moderate deception or suspected malingering	19.7	7.5
Definite malingering	4.5	0

ness. Variations of malingering may also involve deliberate distortions of when symptoms occur (e.g., a patient who is genuinely depressed following incarceration may ascribe the same symptoms to the period of criminal behavior). In addition, defendants may not be truthful about the severity of their psychological impairment. For example, an individual who was hallucinating during the time of the criminal behavior may subsequently exaggerate the effects of these hallucinations and attribute control to hallucinated voices that did not exist at the time of the offense. Further, malingering may also take the form of a grossly disturbed self-report that is both highly improbable and suggestive of gross psychotic impairment and includes a denial of any involvement in the criminal behavior. The strategy underlying such an approach is for the defendant to avoid the issue of culpability in an attempt to convince the clinician that, although the defendant may have committed the criminal behavior, he or she was obviously in another world or out of it. This latter approach is sometimes more difficult to identify since the clinician is typically placing greater emphasis on more obvious forms of malingering.

An issue that emerges from the definition of malingering given here is deciding at what point the threshold is reached and the defendant labeled a malingerer? Since defendants cover a wide spectrum from those who openly disclose potentially self-damaging information to those who offer absurd accounts of psychopathology, when does embellishment stop and malingering begin? One position (Ziskin, 1984) is to employ a lower threshold for establishing malingering based on the greater likelihood that malingering does exist in forensic evaluations; whether such an approach would appreciably improve the detection rate is unknown. An opposing view is that a higher threshold be employed for establishing malingering in insanity evaluations based not on likelihood but on the far-reaching consequences of such a determination.

THRESHOLDS OF MALINGERING
Position 1
A lower threshold may improve the detection rate as the likelihood of malingering increases
Position 2
A higher threshold should be employed as the consequences of a misclassification increases

---

As noted by Bonnie (1977), testimony on malingering by one expert is likely to play a determinative role in the final legal outcome, in spite of contrary testimony. This author would therefore suggest a conservative (i.e., higher) standard for the determination of malingering. Again, in the diagnosis of malingering, clinicians must be convinced that the defendant is deliberately fabricating or grossly exaggerating his or her psychopathology.

Malingering is not a dichotomous variable (i.e., present or absent) but a continuum consisting of multiple dimensions. The clinician may want to address individually the components of malingering: degree of intentionality (is he or she attempting deliberately to deceive the clinician?), degree of exaggeration (how bad is the defendant attempting to look?), actual degree of impairment (despite conscious deceptions, to what extent was the defendant psychologically impaired at the time of the crime?). By addressing each of these issues in cases of gross deception, the clinician will offer the clinical data and articulate the reasoning that substantiate his or her conclusion (Table 3.2). It is suggested that the clinician describe a defendant as unreliable when there are either serious questions regarding the defendant's intentionality and/or when the purported distortions are only slight. Second, it is suggested that the clinician describe a defendant as having suspected malingering when there is definitely some intentionality yet the distortions are only moderate in severity and/or may have some psychological basis (i.e., more exaggerated than fabricated). Finally, it is suggested that the clinician label as definite malingering individuals with whom there are unequivocal intentionality and numerous examples of moderate to severe distortion. It is particularly helpful in these latter two categories for the clinician to articulate representative examples of the defendant's behavior as well as outline the clinician's reasoning with respect to both intentionality and distortion.

An often overlooked area is the impact of interactional effects on a defendant's honesty and self-disclosure. The way the clinician represents him- or herself—whether he or she is friendly, inquisitorial, or coolly objective— may influence the defendant's level of trust and willingness to disclose information about the alleged criminal behavior (Jourard and Landsman,

Table 3.2
Typology for Degrees of Malingering

Descriptive Term	Degree of Intentionality	Degree of Distortion	Elaboration versus Fabrication
Unreliable	Questionable	Mild	Either
Suspected malingering	Definite	Mild to moderate	Primarily elaboration
Definite	Unequivocal	Moderate to severe	Both

1960). It would be unfortunate if the clinician's overfriendliness were perceived and responded to as a con, or confrontation as aggression to be defended against. To minimize some of these interactional effects, the clinician should encourage the defendant to make his or her account as spontaneous and uncensored as possible.

CLINICAL INDICATORS OF MALINGERING AND DECEPTION

The prototypical malingerer may be differentiated from the honest or reliable defendant on several parameters. Symptomatically, a malingerer is likely to report symptoms of unusual severity, rare symptoms infrequently observed in psychiatric populations, and an improbably high number of symptoms. The malingerer is likely to endorse symptoms inconsistent with a specific diagnosis, with the course of that disorder, and with the clinical observation. Clinical research (Rogers, 1984b; Resnick, 1984) suggests that the malingerer will endorse more obvious and dramatic symptoms of a particular disorder, report a sudden onset to that disorder, and manifest a greater willingness to discuss his or her psychological symptoms than individuals who are not malingering. In extreme cases of malingering, many of these indices are clearly apparent throughout the evaluative process. More problematic are the evaluations of individuals who are only selectively exaggerating their symptomatology, primarily focusing on the time of the crime.

The remainder of the chapter examines specific indices of malingering in the clinical literature and empirical research. The role of psychological testing in the detection of dissimulation is addressed extensively in chapter 6.

Rarity of Symptoms

Individuals attempting to malinger a severe mental disorder are typically unsophisticated about what symptoms often occur in psychiatric populations and those that are rarely seen. Resnick (1984) provided an excellent discussion concerning defendants' attempts to feign auditory hallucinations. He pointed our that schizophrenic patients are often able to ignore hallucinatory commands, experience hallucinations on an intermittent rather then continuous basis, and have hallucinations that are typically associated with delusions. Resnick also summarized the research of Goodwin, Alderson, and Rosenthal (1971), which reported visual hallucinations of normal-sized people that were color and auditory hallucinations that contained both familiar and unfamiliar voices, of both male and female gender, and that gave clear messages (93% of the time). Resnick further noted that most individuals with true auditory hallucinations have developed effective coping strategies involving changes in activities and interpersonal contact, which diminish the effects of these hallucinations.

Unreported data in a study by Rogers, Thatcher, and Harris (1983) of sixty-four sanity evaluations found that evaluatees rarely reported any evidence of the following symptoms: agitation in the form of hand wringing or pulling or rubbing on hair, skin, clothing; psychomotor retardation in the form of slowed speech, mute or markedly decreased amount of speech, and/or slowed body movements; thought withdrawal (i.e., thoughts being taken away by some external force); somatic delusions (i.e., concerning changes in appearance or body structure); auditory hallucinations in which two or more voices converse with each other; olfactory hallucinations among non-drug abusers; or any symptoms indicative of catatonic behavior. Finally, there was no clinical evidence or self-report that any of the defendants created neologisms either at the time of the crime or during the evaluative process. These clinical data were collected employing the SADS diagnostic interview (see chapter 7) and included symptoms rarely endorsed by either sane or insane defendants.

Symptom Subtlety

A useful dimension in the examination of malingering and deception is the subtlety of individual symptoms. Early research with the Minnesota Multiphasic Personality Inventory (MMPI) discovered that individual items could be divided into those that are obvious (i.e., clearly signify psychological impairment) and subtle (i.e., symptoms that are not readily apparent to the patient). On the basis of this dichotomy, it was observed that individuals attempting to malinger would report a much higher proportion of obvious items than subtle items when compared to nondeceiving subjects. Conversely, patients attempting to minimize their psychological impairment showed a suppression of obvious items in relationship to subtle items. As an expansion of this paradigm, Buckhart, Christian, and Gynther (1978) were successful at discriminating between malingering and nonmalingering individuals on the MMPI by employing a continuum (very obvious, obvious, neutral, subtle, very subtle) with malingerers overendorsing obvious items. Later research has supported these findings with respect to item subtlety on the MMPI and similar measures (Greene, 1980).

Item subtlety may also be utilized in diagnostic interviews. It is usually easier for a malingering defendant to simulate positive symptoms (i.e., those whose presence signifies a mental disorder) than negative symptoms (i.e., those whose absence is characteristic of a mental disorder). Thus, a defendant may find it simpler to fabricate hallucinations or delusions as symptoms of being crazy yet be unaware that constricted or blunted affect, lack of motivation, social withdrawal, and decreased concentration may also be diagnostically important in the simulation of a mental disorder. For example, a clinician should be alerted to the likelihood of malingering when presented with gross psychotic symptoms in an individual who appears motivated for interpersonal contact and has no apparent deficit in attention or concentration. Particularly with inpatient evaluations of suspected malingering, it may be useful to observe the range and depth of the defendant's involvement with others, interest and enthusiasm in general activities, and ability to attend to and concentrate on intellectually related matters in comparison with positive symptoms.

Symptom Consistency

To what extent can the defendant keep his or her story straight? Although some inconsistencies are found in all defendants' self-reports, the more these inconsistencies are blatant and exculpatory, the greater the index of suspicion that this individual is malingering. It is difficult for malingering defendants to reconstruct the period of the offense and present clinical material over several separate interviews in a convincing and consistent manner. Defendants who have well rehearsed their account may often have a rehearsed or rote quality to their report. It is often helpful to ask such defendants to recount the time of the crime using different words and/or comment directly on the rehearsed quality of the presentation. Rehearsed self-reports are not always attempts at deliberate distortion but may also be practice effects from numerous previous self-reports, attempts to control anxiety, or a defense against the emotional trauma associated with the criminal behavior. Therefore, the defendant's motivation for rehearsed self-reports requires further clinical evaluation.

Malingering is frequently identified by highly inconsistent self-reports simply because the defendant becomes confused and does not remember previous fabrications. There is also a tendency among some malingerers to "up the ante" by providing increasingly severe fabrications during later interviews. This is most clearly observed in cases of substance abuse in which the defendant may, between the initial and final interview, double or even triple the reported amounts of his or her intake at the time of the offense. Defendants should be given an opportunity toward the end of the forensic evaluation to respond to apparent inconsistencies in their stories. For inconsistencies that are directly relevant to the defendant's criminal responsibility, it is important that the clinician explore thoroughly each side of the inconsistencies to ascertain the defendant's understanding and intentions in making these discrepant or contradictory statements.

A second approach to symptom consistency is to compare the defendant's current account with either the defendant's statement at the time of the crime or with the observations made by witnesses and arresting officers. For example, a defendant who reported that he had fatally stabbed a robbery victim after untying the victim's hands was confronted with several witnesses' statements that the victim was still tied after the perpetrator had fled. A second example is a defendant who reports in her statement to the police that she had killed a friend as a result of an altercation and later dramatically alters her story to include auditory hallucinations demanding the victim's death. In both these instances, it is helpful to ask the defendant to explain the inconsistencies and to comment on how such disparities might have occurred.

A third approach to symptom inconsistency is to compare the defendant's current report of psychological functioning with clinical observation. If at the time of the evaluation the defendant presents him- or herself as severely psychologically disabled when there is considerable evidence to the contrary, the clinician may make inferences about the veracity of the defendant's report of the alleged offense.

Course of the Disorder

Clinicians have observed (e.g., Ossipov, 1944; Resnick, 1984) that malingering patients frequently report a rapid onset of symptoms just prior to the criminal behavior. In addition, these symptoms are often reported as emerging with considerable severity, which is contrary to the usual development of most major mental disorders (except when precipitated by a psychological trauma or substance abuse) in which symptoms gradually appear and worsen in severity. Similarly, some malingerers report a sudden disappearance of psychological symptoms following the criminal behavior, thus presenting themselves as being temporarily insane to explain their current absence of significant psychopathology. Although brief psychotic states do occur, it is unlikely that such circumscribed episodes would have a pervasive control over the defendant's volition and behavior and would then disappear without residual symptoms.

The sequence of symptoms reported by the defendant may either support or cast doubt on the self-report. For example, with schizophrenic disorders it is likely that there will be a prodromal phase as well as a residual phase, both including social withdrawal, eccentric or bizarre behavior, and oddities in thinking and perception. Thus, the sequencing of symptoms may be so improbable that the veracity of the defendant's self-report must be questioned.

The presence of previous mental disorders may be very helpful in establishing the plausibility of psychological impairment at the time of the crime. In a study of insanity evaluations, 44% of the defendants had prior episodes of a major mental disorder, 21% had antisocial personality disorders, and 26% evidenced other personality disorders. What is more relevant is the degree of connectedness between preexisting mental disorders, reported symptomatology at the time of the crime, and more recently diagnosed mental disorders.

Retrospective Diagnosis

In examining the defendant's self-report for the time of the offense, the clinician must consider the extent to which the defendant's account fits any known diagnostic entity. This is a complex judgment since many defendants may have multiple diagnoses and/or an atypical mental disorder. Although reported and corroborated symptoms that clearly meet both symptoms and associated features of a specific diagnosis may assist in confirming the genuineness of reported symptoms, the absence of such clarity is not pathognomonic of malingering or deception. The clinician must evaluate the plausibility of reported symptoms and the likelihood of an individual's experiencing such disparate symptoms during one discrete period.

Two indicators of potential malingering with respect to retrospective diagnoses are contradictory symptoms and overendorsement of symptoms. Clearly, when a defendant repeatedly endorses symptoms that contradict each other, there is a high index of suspicion of deception. For example, a defendant who indicates severe social withdrawal at the time of the crime but endorses increased involvement with others or an individual who endorses symptoms of inadequacy and worthlessness and yet maintains a grandiose posture may well be attempting to deceive the clinician. More commonly, defendants who are attempting to malinger may simply overendorse a wide range of symptoms and report an improbable number of symptoms in the clinical range for the time of the alleged offense. To establish such an overendorsement, the clinician is advised to follow the diagnostic procedures in chapter 6 regarding clinical interviews and to consider the employment of structured diagnostic interviews (e.g., the SADS). Such individuals are usually fairly consistent in their reported symptoms since they endorse such a wide range of psychopathology but may be identified by the improbable number of psychological symptoms.

A related issue is the extremeness of the reported symptoms. The clinician should consider carefully any defendant's self-report in which there are numerous examples of extreme symptoms since most nonhospitalized patients have relatively few severe symptoms and if the defendant was this grossly impaired how would he or she have been able to carry out the crime or function from day-to-day as well as he or she apparently did? Although there is considerable variability between the severity of symptoms and the level of an individual's functioning (i.e., some are disabled with relatively mild symptoms while others continue to function with moderate to severe symptoms), the extreme symptomatology reported by some defendants would render them incapable of committing the offense.

Paralinguistic Cues

Most research on paralinguistic cues has been conducted from a social psychology paradigm with normal samples in empirical attempts to detect deception. These studies, therefore, have limited generalizability to clinical populations where malingering is suspected. For example, research on facial expressions (see Rogers, 1984b, for a review) has been unsuccessful at distinguishing honest from dishonest responses. Ekman and Friesen (1974) originally postulated the concept of leakage in which the true emotions would subtly emerge and be observable in individuals attempting to dissimulate. Later work by the same authors (1975) suggested that many individuals expressing blended emotions (i.e., mixed or ambivalent feelings) were indistinguishable from those attempting to dissimulate their emotional state. Perhaps more useful is research focusing on individuals' body movements and postural shifts. It has been noted (Ekman and Friesen, 1969) that individuals attempting to deceive have increased movements of their limbs and increased physical tension. These findings have been confirmed by more recent studies (e.g., Feldman, 1976; DePaulo and Rosenthal, 1979).

The role of speech and language patterns in the detection of deception has received considerable attention. For example, researchers (Harrison, Hwalek, Raney, and Fritz, 1978; Baskett and Freedle, 1974) have found increased latency periods between questions and responses and more frequent hesitations in deceitful individuals. While these group differences exist, other factors such as anxiety and ambivalence may also lead to increased latencies. Knapp, Hart, and Dennis (1974) conducted a detailed content analysis with respect to the structure of communication. They found that deceivers had significantly more silent periods, made more sweeping nonspecific statements, made fewer factual statements about themselves, and had a greater frequency of self-disparaging remarks when compared to honest respondents. Their study found no significant differences in facial, gestural, and leg movements between honest and dishonest respondents.

Malingering: Other Considerations

An important issue for the forensic clinician is deciding what factors are most important in determining the honesty of a criminal defendant. More specifically, should the forensic clinician pay primary attention to facial and physical cues, paralinguistic cues, or the content of what is said in making a determination of malingering? This issue has been addressed by several studies employing a social psychology paradigm; these studies have, however, two important limitations: (1) the observers were not active in questioning the subjects but merely observed, and (2) subjects were not considered mentally ill. Maier and Thurber (1968) examined observers' abilities to detect deception under three experimental conditions: (1) watching an actual interview, (2) listening to an audiotape of the same interview, and (3) reading a transcript. The authors found increased accuracy in detecting deception with both audiotapes and transcripts as opposed to observation. Littlepage and Pineault (1978) utilized two video segments of the television program "To Tell the Truth." This research found that verbal content appeared to be the most important factor in detecting dishonesty and that facial and physical cues did not improve this discrimination. Others, like Miller and his associates (Miller, Bauchner, Hocking, Fontes, Kaminsky, and Brendt, 1981), completed a series of experiments utilizing observation, videotapes without sound, audiotapes, and transcripts of interviews. These studies confirmed that auditory information (i.e., content and paralinguistic cues) was more important than nonverbal behavioral cues in determining the honesty of subjects. While noting these two important limitations, this type of research suggests that greater emphasis be placed on verbal and paralinguistic cues than on facial, gestural, or postural cues. These latter cues (see Rogers, 1984b) may actually serve as detractors that confound the clinical assessment of deception.

A related issue in the detection of malingering is whether certain criminal defendants look honest. Zukerman and co-workers conducted a series of studies of interpersonal communication and found that the overall demeanor of the subject was associated by observers with a perception of honesty or deceptiveness regardless of whether the message communicated by subjects was honest or deceptive (Zukerman, Larrance, Hall, DeFrank, and Rosenthal, 1979; Zukerman, Lipets, Koivunaki, and Rosenthal, 1975). They found that characteristics such as facial pleasantness, assertiveness, and dominance in speech were all associated with increased ratings of honesty. In addition, pleasantness in facial cues apparently played a determining role. While these studies have limited generalizability, they suggest that facial pleasantness, assertiveness, and dominance of speech may confound clinicians' ability to determine an individual's degree of honesty.

Little is known about which diagnostic groups if any, are more likely to malinger than others. Sierles (1984) found that those with histories of drug dependencies were most likely to report previous attempts at malingering than other psychiatric or medical patients. Other important variables found by Sierles were alcohol abuse and a self-reported pattern of sociopathic behavior. Finally, the youthfulness of the patient and whether the patient was black yielded small but significant correlations with malingering. Although this study is of academic interest, extensive replications would be necessary before its utilization in criminal responsibility evaluations.

Defensiveness

In evaluations of criminal responsibility, the clinician is much less likely to encounter defendants who are minimizing their psychological impairment at the time of the crime than other forms of deception. Most problematical are those instances in which the defendant apparently experienced an acute episode and is no longer able to accept or remember his or her psychiatric illness. This situation is sometimes accompanied by a complete denial of the criminal behavior or an assertion of self-defense under improbable circumstances. Such denials may serve the individual in a psychologically adaptive manner, assisting him or her in coping with this unacceptable behavior. The clinician must balance his or her psycholegal needs for detailed clinically relevant material with these psychological needs of the defendant in attempting to conduct a comprehensive evaluation.

An additional complication occurs when a defendant denies his or her criminal behavior and the clinician believes there is a reasonable doubt that the individual committed the offense. Since criminal responsibility evaluations are predicated on the defendant's admission of the criminal behavior, what alternatives are available to the clinician under these circumstances? One viable alternative is for the clinician to stop the evaluation if he or she believes that no diagnostic conclusion can be reached. A second alternative, when sufficient corroborative data are available, is to render an opinion on the basis of those data. A third alternative is to evaluate the defendant's competence to stand trial and to determine whether or not the defendant can assist counsel in his or her defense. In such circumstances, if the clinician proceeds with the insanity evaluation, he or she should make explicit the defendant's denial of the criminal behavior and the severity of the individual's psychological impairment. In addition, it may be necessary to make conclusory statements that indicate that *although the defendant denies any involvement in the criminal behavior, the clinician's opinion is that he or she did not suffer at the time of the alleged crime from a mental disorder sufficient to meet the standard of insanity* or *the defendant was experiencing a major mental disorder that had a significant impact on day-to-day behavior. Although the defendant denies any involvement in the offense, he or she was so grossly disturbed at the time of the crime that it is unlikely that he or she was not insane.* The clinician is urged in this latter case to be conservative in the evaluation and to render opinions only on strong corroborative evidence and clinical data that overwhelmingly indicate a relative absence of psychological impairment. In a large number of cases where the defendant denies the criminal charges, it will not be possible for the clinician to render a definite opinion.

Many individuals attempting to minimize their psychological problems will be easily identified by the absence of any reported psychological difficulties. Clinical research has noted that the absence of any admission of common foibles is perhaps the most consistent discriminator of such persons. This finding has been substantiated with extensive research on an MMPI (refer to chapter 6). Concomitant with the denial of common foibles has been the presentation of idealistic self-attributes. Defendants attempting to minimize their psychological impairment will frequently endorse laudable and overly positive statements about their character and their adjustment. Finally, in the examination of obvious and subtle symptoms, such individuals are likely to suppress the obvious symptoms in relationship to the subtle symptoms. This may be observed in both interviews and testing by the endorsement of disproportionally fewer obvious than subtle symptoms. As previously noted, the clinician should be alert for the reluctant teller who only after considerable inquiry admits to blatant psychotic symptoms since this may reflect a pattern of malingering in which the reluctance is employed to lower the clinician's index of suspicion regarding the defendant's presentation.

The final clinical issue in establishing the defendant's degree of honesty is the identification of overly compliant and/or dependent individuals. Such defendants, particularly those who are mildly retarded, may be attempting to please or ingratiate themselves to the clinician. The defendant's level of agreeability is frequently the benchmark of overly compliant individuals. The motivation for such a response style is varied, including deference to authority (i.e., the doctor knows best), feelings of intimidation (i.e., tell them what they want to hear), or characterological adaptation (i.e., based on feelings of passivity and inadequacy). Overly compliant individuals may be clinically differentiated from others by answers to clinical inquiry that clinicians present offering more and more improbable explanations for their behavior that are unrelated to the legal issue. Frequently, such individuals will diminish in their compliance when they are confronted with the unrealistic way they are responding to specific issues. In addition, overly compliant behavior may be minimized by making general nondirected inquiries or by offering multiple alternatives.

CONCLUSION

It is unrealistic for the clinician to expect in any forensic evaluation, including criminal responsibility, that the defendant will respond with complete honesty. Given the adversarial nature of insanity evaluations and the number of conscious and unconscious determinants of the defendant's presentation, it is very likely that some distortions will be found with the vast majority of defendants. The issue is therefore not whether the defendant has distorted the self-report but the severity and extensiveness of such distortions. As noted by Bonnie (1977), any clinician conclusion that a defendant was malingering may play a presumptive role with respect to the legal outcome. Thus, the clinician is cautioned to invoke the diagnosis of malingering only when presented with numerous and convincing examples reflecting either fabrication or gross exaggeration of symptoms. In establishing malingering, the clinician should keep a copy of his or her notes that chronologically demonstrate inconsistencies, rarity of symptoms, or extremeness of symptoms as well as any written observations with respect to visual or paralinguistic cues. Such comprehensiveness minimizes the likelihood of vague impressionistic conclusions on such a crucial issue. Finally, it should be observed that suspected malingering is only a secondary issue in many insanity evaluations since the questionable symptoms, regardless of their authenticity, are insufficient to meet the insanity standard.

Malingering, more than any other clinical issue, must be addressed with respect to each component of the insanity evaluation. Because of this, discussions of malingering are found in chapters on clinical interviews, psychological testing, and laboratory and other specialized approaches. It is essential that any comprehensive examination of malingering include the conceptual issues found in this chapter and their integration with specific clinical methods in Part II. As a distillation of this complex issue, Table 3.3 shows a summary of empirically based indicators of malingering and deception. This table is based on a comprehensive review of recent research on dissimulation in case study, psychometric, and social psychology literature (Rogers, 1984b).

The chapter on psychological testing summarizes for each commonly used test its vulnerability for malingering and what indicators, if any, have been established for the detection of the dissimulation. It should be noted that many clinicians do not use many of the available methods for detecting deception; it is therefore the responsibility of the forensic psychologist or psychiatrist to review carefully test reports of other psychologists with respect to these indicators.

Several specialized methods for the evaluation of deception are presented in chapter 8. These include two methods for uncovering the truth (i.e., hyp-

Table 3.3
Empirical Model of Dissimulation

Indicators	Reliable	Malingering	Defensive	Irrelevant	Unspecified Deception
(Response Styles)					
Severity of symptoms		Extreme severity (cs)			
Consistency of self-report	Consistent (pt)	Consistent (pt)	Consistent (pt)	Inconsistent (pt)	Inconsistent (pt)
Rare symptoms	Unlikely (pt)	Likely (pt)		Likely (pt)	
Sequence of symptoms	Consistent with diagnoses (cs)	Inconsistent with diagnoses (cs)			
Obvious versus subtle symptoms	Balance of obvious and subtle symptoms (pt)	More obvious than subtle symptoms (pt)	Fewer obvious than subtle symptoms (pt)	Obvious symptoms may increase (pt)	
Appearance of symptoms	Gradual onset (cs)	Sudden onset (cs)			
Admission of common foibles	Likely (pt)	Likely (pt)	Unlikely (pt)		
Endorsement of idealistic self-attributes	Unlikely (pt)	Unlikely (pt)	Likely (pt)		
Random pattern of responses	No (pt)	No (pt)	No (pt)	Very likely (pt)	
Symptoms inconsistent with clinical observation	Unlikely (cs)	Likely (cs)			Likely (sp)
Improbable failure rate	No (pt)	Possible (pt)			
Latency of response					Increases (sp)
Responses that are nearly correct	Unlikely (pt)	Possible (pt)			
Vagueness of responses					Great frequency (sp)
Fidgetiness					Likely (sp)
Willingness to discuss symptoms		Often very willing (cs)			
Endorsement of stereotypes of neurosis	Unlikely (pt)	Small percentage (pt)	Unlikely (pt)		

cs-Case studies
pt-Psychological testing
sp-Social psychology research
From Rogers (1984*b*).

nosis and drug-assisted interviews) and one for detecting physiological correlates of deception (i.e., polygraph techniques). Each of these techniques is reviewed with a particular emphasis on the limitations or contraindications of these methods. Of the three approaches, only drug-assisted interviews may have limited clinical applicability to criminal responsibility evaluations.

Chapter 4

Amnesia and Memory Impairment

The assessment of amnesia and other forms of memory impairment is an important component of criminal responsibility evaluations where an accurate representation of the individual's internal psychological state and overt behavior at the time of the offense is essential. Insanity evaluations are particularly vulnerable to amnesia and memory impairment because of their retrospective nature, memory distortions following an emotion-evoking event, substance abuse, conscious or unconscious desire to forget, diminished recall caused by a mental disorder, and occasionally, diminished intellectual ability (e.g., mental retardation or dementia). Further, the assessment of amnesia may be complicated by the presence of several of these factors and/or the desire to distort one's self-report deliberately (i.e., malingering). In addition, the chapter discusses the extensive empirical research on memory distortion, particularly eyewitness research, as it relates to criminal responsibility assessments. Finally, the role of memory loss in the clinical determination of insanity is examined and specific diagnostic strategies recommended.

Amnesia represents one of the most complex syndromes in diagnostic literature. Not only are amnesias diverse in their etiology (i.e., feigned amnesia, organic amnesia, psychogenic amnesia, and mixed etiology), but also each classification has multiple subtypes. Likewise, the clinical characteristics of amnestic syndromes are highly variable, with individuals showing transient, circumscribed, pervasive, and global amnesias. Further, amnestic disorders manifest considerable variation in onset (gradual versus sudden), direction (retrograde versus anterograde), and course (deterioration, no change, gradual recovery, and sudden recovery). Thus, the forensic clinician must become well versed in the forms of amnesias and in evaluating the relevance of memory impairment to the standard of criminal responsibility.

Table 4.1
Degree of Amnesia for Time of Crime

	Sane (%)	Insane (%)
Moderate	10.3	7.7
Severe	5.4	6.6
Pervasive	4.9	4.4

Available empirical data (see Table 4.1) on the presence of amnesia in defendants evaluated for sanity suggest 10% of the sane and 11% of the insane defendants manifested severe or pervasive amnesias. An additional 18% of the entire sample manifested moderate memory loss, with recall of varying degrees of internal and external events for the time of the crime. Additional data (Table 4.2) examined whether there was interference in the accuracy and completeness of the defendant's self-report—e.g., psychotic disorder, organic mental disorder, or substance abuse. Employing this broader standard, 10% of the sane and 50% of the insane individuals experienced either peripheral or substantial interference with their recall at the time of the alleged offense. Thus, both the specific issue of amnesia as well as the general area of memory impairment must be of paramount concern in conducting insanity evaluations.

PSYCHOGENIC VERSUS ORGANIC AMNESIA

This section addresses the phenomenology of psychogenic and organic amnesias with the goal of making a differential diagnosis. The forensic clinician is urged to review primary sources regarding the etiology and course of specific amnestic disorders. The following discussion focuses on psychogenic versus organic amnesia and is followed by a brief description of specific amnestic syndromes.

Psychogenic amnesia is characterized in the *Diagnostic and Statistical*

Table 4.2
Degree of Involuntary Interference with Patient's Self-report

	Sane (%)	Insane (%)
Peripheral	7.8	34.7
Substantial	2.2	15.2
Pervasive	0	2.2

Manual of Mental Disorders (*DSM III,* American Psychiatric Association, 1980) as a memory impairment involving the sudden inability to recall important personal information without any known organic etiology. This disorder is characterized by sudden onset, unawareness of the memory loss, and either severe psychosocial stress or unacceptable impulses and behavior. In addition, psychogenic amnesias are most typically localized—that is, involving a circumscribed period of time including the traumatic event and a short period of time following that event. In contrast, these disorders are least likely to be generalized or continuous amnesias involving global impairment of nonpersonal information. Weiner (1983) cited the following additional diagnostic characteristics of psychogenic amnesia: abrupt termination of amnesia, anterograde amnesia, generally complete recovery if it occurs (i.e., no islands of memory loss like those found with organic disorders), use of hypnosis or amytal interview to recover memory, primary or secondary gains that may prolong psychogenic amnesia.

A hallmark of psychogenic amnesia is its focus on personal memory, primarily those aspects of an individual's life that were directly involved or affected by the traumatic event. Thus, individuals experiencing psychogenic amnesia have no memory impairment with respect to nonpersonal memory (Fisher and Adams, 1964). In addition, Kelly (1980), in reviewing the literature, found no deficits in the learning ability of individuals experiencing psychogenic amnesias. Thus, psychogenic amnesia can usually be distinguished from organic amnesia and feigned amnesia by its onset and course (i.e., sudden onset and termination), direction (anterograde), recoverability (under hypnosis or sodium amytal), focus on personal information, and normal ability to learn new information. In attempting to assess psychogenic amnesia, the clinician may also wish to focus on the disagreeability of the repressed memories (Pratt, 1977) and on whether any recovery may be made on the basis of direct suggestion (Fisher and Adams, 1964).

Organic amnestic syndromes are characterized by deficits in both short- and long-term memory that are attributed to a specific organic factor. This includes an ongoing inability to assimilate new information (i.e., anterograde amnesia) as well as an inability to recall previously learned remote information (retrograde amnesia). In comparison, very remote memory (e.g., childhood events) is frequently less impaired; immediate memory (e.g., the ability to repeat numbers and words) is not impaired. *DSM III* (American Psychiatric Association, 1980) also noted the following clinical features: no loss of general intellectual ability, display of some degree of disorientation, confabulation, either a lack of awareness of the memory deficit or lack of concern over it, and emotional blandness and loss of initiative.

Organic amnesias frequently follow a chronic course with little improvement. In cases where recovery occurs, it is typically slow and includes islands of amnesia (i.e., permanent loss of memory in circumscribed areas). During the course of an organic amnestic disorder, confabulation is typically present in the early stages and subsequently disappears (Weiner, 1983).

SPECIFIC ORGANIC SYNDROMES

The most common organic amnestic syndrome is the alcohol amnestic disorder. This disorder follows extensive alcohol dependence and is typically a result of thiamine deficiency or Korsakoff's disease (American Psychiatric Association, 1980). Korsakoff's disease (Kral, 1959; Kral and Durost, 1953) involves a marked deficit in both recent and remote memory, severe impairment of immediate recall, and disorientation in all three spheres. In addition, Lishman (1971) has observed the clinical features of loss of time sense and the ordering of events in memory; contextual isolation (see also Talland, 1965), in which experiences apparently lose their relationship to other experiences; perseverative thinking; and confabulation during the early stages.

Berlyne (1972) studied confabulation in patients with Korsakoff's disease. He was able to distinguish momentary confabulation, involving the presentation of fictitious material to cover lapses of memory and avoid embarrassment, from fantastic confabulation, in which the patient presents preposterous accounts of his or her experiences. Berlyne found that the great majority of these patients present only momentary confabulation in the early stages of this disorder and relatively few examples of fantastic confabulation.

The diagnosis of alcohol amnestic disorder is infrequently made with defendants in criminal responsibility evaluations. Although a moderate percentage of those defendants evaluated for insanity had histories of alcohol abuse or dependence, the occurrence of an alcohol amnestic disorder is rare. Rogers and Zinbarg (1985) found 35% of the sane and 37% of the insane defendants had prior histories of alcoholism, but none warranted the diagnosis of an alcohol amnestic disorder.

DSM III (American Psychiatric Association, 1980) also provides diagnostic criteria of a barbiturate or similarily acting sedative or hypnotic amnestic disorder. This disorder meets the organic amnestic syndrome described earlier, with an earlier onset (often in the twenties) and a variable course with full recovery possible.

Posttraumatic amnesia resulting from a head injury is highly variable with the degree of severity based on the site and extent of the injury. Kelly (1980) described posttraumatic amnesiacs as having an initial period of confusion in which both perceptions and memory registration are impaired. This period is accompanied by anterograde amnesia in which the patient has a diminished capacity for durable memories that lags behind the resumption of full alertness and consciousness. Further, Kelly reported that retrograde amnesia usually precedes the injury by only a few seconds and commonly shrinks over time.

Memory functions following a concussion typically include brief retrograde amnesia and relatively brief anterograde amnesia prior to recovery (Weiner, 1983). Russell and Nathan (1946) reported that amnesias following head injuries affect recent more than remote memory. He further reported that the duration of the retrograde amnesia increases in relation to the severity of the head injury.

Transient global amnesia is a rare amnestic syndrome most frequently caused by cerebrovascular disease and rarely by temporal lobe tumors, migraine headaches, or sedative-hypnotic drug overdose (Weiner, 1983). This disorder typically occurs in elderly males with a sudden onset that includes confusion and inability to retain information. Lishman (1971) described the following clinical characteristics for transient global amnesia: profound amnesia that usually lasts several hours to a day; affects personal knowledge and current experience; causes retrograde amnesia, extending days to weeks prior to the episode but shrinking rapidly over time; leaves a permanent gap of only several hours for the transient global amnesia episode; and occurs rarely in middle-aged or elderly individuals. Fisher and Adams (1964), in reviewing the symptomatology for transient global amnesia, found that individuals experienced no awareness of memory impairment and a pervasive loss of retention for a circumscribed period (i.e., remembering nothing of what they experienced or were told), had accurate perceptions of knowing people and objectives, and were able to engage in customary habitual acts (e.g., driving). Suarez and Pittluck (1975) found only fifty reported case studies of transient global amnesia in the psychiatric literature, and these were characterized by abrupt onset, spontaneous recovery, and no history of reoccurrence. Given the rarity of this disorder, it is unlikely that bona fide cases will be found in forensic assessments.

Organic amnestic syndromes vary widely with respect to their etiologies. These include space-occupying lesions and infectious diseases (e.g., encephalitis, meningitis, epilepsy, toxic and metabolic disturbances). In addition, amnestic syndromes may result from biologically based psychiatric treatment including temporal lobectomies, which are rarely performed, and electroconvulsive therapy (Squire, 1977). These latter amnestic syndromes are easily diagnosed on the basis of psychiatric treatment history.

Specific amnestic disorders are distinguished from dementia, which involves a general loss of intellectual ability, particularly in the area of abstract functions. Specific deficits include short- and long-term memory, decreased ability to process new or complex information, impaired judgment and impulse control, and personality changes. Early onset dementias may be the result of Alzheimer's disease, Pick's disease, Huntington's chorea, and Jakob-Creutzfeldt diseases (Weiner, 1983). Psychological and neuropsychological testing and neurological evaluations may be helpful in establishing the parameters of the dementia and its impact on remote memory loss at the time of the crime. The impairment of judgment and impulse control frequently observed with demented individuals is often chronic, allowing a thorough assessment based on the defendant's inpatient behavior or corroborative data from significant others.

MALINGERED AMNESIA

An important issue in criminal forensic evaluations is determining the authenticity of the amnesia. The few available studies demonstrate that, among those patients claiming symptoms of an amnestic disorder, malingered amnesia may represent a prominent number. Kiersch (1962) examined ninety-eight reported cases of amnesia that were admitted to two army hospitals (ninety-two male and six female military personnel). This study found that forty-one of the ninety-eight cases were feigned, of which twenty-five consciously admitted the feigning and sixteen admitted it only under hypnosis or amytal interviews. Further, Kiersch found an additional thirteen cases that involved either organic or psychogenic amnesia plus conscious exaggeration. It is interesting to note that thirty-two of the ninety-eight cases were hospitalized pending court martial; of this subgroup, twenty-one admitted to malingered amnesia, with an additional nine exaggerating the extent of their amnesia. Thus, nearly all those with pending legal difficulties employed some deliberate distortion of their memory functioning. In a much earlier study, Hopwood and Snell (1933) examined one hundred patients who claimed amnesia and were facing criminal charges. In this British study, seventy-eight cases were determined to be genuine amnesia, fourteen were malingering, and eight were inconclusive. Parwatikar, Holcomb, and Menninger (1985) found that approximately 30% of pretrial homicide defendants simulated amnesia and could be differentiated from true amnesiacs by lower scores on MMPI scales 1, 2, 3. Certainly, additional research is needed on differential diagnosis and frequency of malingered versus genuine amnesia in court-referred cases.

The clinical approaches in the detection of malingered amnesia parallel the clinical methods utilized with other forms of malingering and deception. The reader is therefore referred to chapter 3 on malingering as well as the discussion of specific diagnostic methods in chapters on clinical interviews, psychological testing, and laboratory methods.

Malingered amnesia is frequently detected through inconsistencies in the individual's self-report. By carefully reviewing the contours of the amnestic period (i.e., the boundary between what is remembered and what is forgotten), it is often possible to detect marked inconsistencies that cannot be explained by the putative amnestic disorder. A subtler approach to the detection of feigned amnesia is an examination of the reported symptoms and the degree to which these symptoms fit a specific diagnostic pattern. This must be done for both organic and psychogenic amnestic syndromes.

The clinician's examination of a reported organic amnesia involves a careful investigation into possible organic etiology. This includes inquires about substance abuse, head injury, intracranial lesions, infectious diseases, toxic and metabolic disturbances, and dementias. The clinician may wish to review the clinical symptoms associated with the reported disorder as a first approach. In many cases, the use of medical, neurological, and neuropsychological consultations will be necessary as will specialized laboratory procedures and establishing the veracity of specific organic amnestic syndromes. From a practical point of view, the clinician will need to assess the relative importance of the questioned amnestic syndrome to the issue of criminal responsibility (e.g., the reported amnesia may be sufficiently circumscribed or so clearly the result of a psychotic process that it obviates the need for extensive consultations) in deciding the extent to which consultations and laboratory procedures are needed to differentiate actual from feigned amnesia.

Feigned psychogenic amnesias may be explored by carefully examining the reported characteristics and addressing the extent to which they fit psychogenic amnesia. Such clinical approaches parallel those employed in differentiating honest from deceptive defendants. In addition, hypnosis and sodium amytal interviews have been employed, with some success, in eliciting changes in psychogenic amnesias and making clinical determinations regarding their authenticity (American Academy of Psychiatry and Law, 1979). These approaches are discussed in greater detail in chapter 8 on laboratory procedures.

A novel approach to the detection of feigned psychogenic amnesia involves the sequential administration of standardized memory questionnaires. Such an approach would allow the forensic clinician to examine across discrete periods of time the consistency of the defendant's reported memory deficits and whether there were gross inconsistencies between reported memory and clinical observation. Herrmann (1982), in reviewing the wide array of memory questionnaires, found that subjects' responses were usually reliable but only moderately corresponded to their actual memory performance. Therefore, moderate inconsistencies between questionnaires and other diagnostic data may reflect inaccurate beliefs regarding memory as opposed to deliberate distortion.

The forensic clinician may wish to select memory questionnaires that are related to the type of reported memory loss. For example, the Everyday

Memory Questionnaire (EMQ) was designed by Sunderland (1980) to address memory loss that is the result of head injuries. This protocol consists of a 28-item questionnaire that examines various aspects of memory deficits with respect to the frequency of their occurrence. Reliability data are not reported and there are no significant validity data. From a different perspective, the Inventory of Memory Experience (Herrmann and Neisser, 1978) examined 72 items on a 7-point scale covering childhood, remote, and recent memory. Research on an abbreviated version of the inventory indicated moderate reliability (reliability coefficients of .46 to .68) with modest evidence that responses were related to actual performance. A third scale, the Memory Scale (see Sehulster, 1981a, 1981b), examined in three sections of 20 items each the patient's degree of forgetting, remembering, and the overall quality of his or her memory. Subjects were moderately consistent ($r = .64$) with test-retest reliability and had low but significant correlations between reported memory and performance on laboratory tests.

Herrmann (1982) reports an additional ten protocols to examine self-reported deficits in memory and learning. Although the clinical use of such protocols in the detection of feigned amnesia has not been empirically addressed, the forensic clinician is encouraged to utilize such protocols as clinical tools while being fully aware of their psychometric limitations. It is expected that, in at least some cases of questionable amnesia, the magnitude of the inconsistencies on sequential administrations of memory questionnaires may augment the clinician's opinion with supportive evidence. Given the lack of empirical data, the forensic clinician should never utilize such inconsistencies, however blatant, as the sole or primary evidence of feigned amnesia.

An innovative approach to questionable amnesia was developed by Schacter (1986c) in a series of studies. Schacter, employing an experimental design with university students, found consistent group differences for actual and simulated amnesia in feeling-of-knowing ratings. These ratings were the degree of confidence that subjects had that they could remember if given more time, cues, or the task of recognizing the forgotten material when presented with two choices. Those simulating amnesia gave lower ratings for both cues and recognition than their amnesiac counterparts. The forensic clinician may wish to ask defendants claiming amnesia whether they believe they could remember the time of the offense if given cues and whether they could recognize a report of their criminal behavior. Responses cannot be used as the sole discriminator between actual and simulated amnesia because of the considerable overlap of group scores (see Schacter, 1986b) and the limited generalizability of this study to mentally disordered individuals in pretrial evaluations.

An additional conclusion from the Schacter studies (1986a) is that clinicians, after reviewing transcripts of subjects' attempts to recall the forgotten material, tended to credit those who tried hard with genuine amnesia. This strategy was unsuccessful since many of those simulating amnesia appeared to be very active while many of those who were actually amnestic put forth little effort. The defendant's attempts to remember is thus an unreliable indicator of the genuineness of the amnesia.

A final caution in assessing the authenticity of amnestic disorders is the possibility of an amnesia with a mixed etiology. Perhaps the most common combination would be psychogenic amnesia and malingering. Weiner (1983) reported that either primary or secondary gains may prolong psychogenic amnesia, but the discrimination between such prolongation and intentional exaggeration may be difficult to establish. Further, it is possible, although rare, that an individual may have a psychogenic amnesia superimposed on an organic amnesia (e.g., an alcoholic amnesiac or demented individual who experiences an emotional trauma) or by having both disorders coexisting (e.g., a brutally raped woman is both traumatized emotionally and receives a serious concussion). Thus, the forensic clinician should be alert that the defendant in a criminal responsibility evaluation may be experiencing a mixed organic-psychogenic amnestic syndrome. More common, as reported earlier by Kiersch (1962), is the likelihood of deliberate exaggeration with either organic or psychogenic amnesia.

In summary, amnesia is a psychiatric syndrome that varies widely in severity and etiology and that is frequently reported in criminal forensic evaluations. Establishment of improbable symptoms through clinical interviews represents the initial approach in uncovering feigned amnesia. For example, psychogenic amnesias should not have a gradual onset, greater loss of general than personal information, or an inability to learn new information. Likewise, organic amnesias do not often show heightened concern or awareness of the memory deficit, substantial impairment of immediate memory, total absence of confusion or disorientation, or complete resolution of their amnesia. Finally, in more complicated cases, it may be necessary to have several specialized consultations to establish and differentiate the specific etiology and its relationship to criminal responsibility.

MEMORY PROCESS AND AMNESIA

The process of remembering (Bradford and Smith, 1979) involves the following stages:

Reception: Reception involves the processing of stimuli through the sensory apparatus, which includes perception and attention. Koson and Robey (1973) reported that deficits in reception may be caused by psychosis, depression, sleep deprivation, hallucinogens, and intoxication.

Registration: Registration is the attentional process of making external stimuli available for memory. Koson and Robey (1973) report that intoxication, brain damage, electroconvulsive therapy, epilepsy, and protein synthesis inhibitors may interfere with registration. Gibbens and Williams (1977) reported in addition to those listed by Koson and Robey that psychotic states may also impair registration.

Retention: Retention refers to the formation of long-term memory through development of permanent memory traces. Deficits in retention have been noted by Koson and Robey (1973) with Korsakoff's disease, cerebrovascular diseases, senile dementia, and intracranial tumors.

Recall: Recall is the ability to retrieve memories of past experiences. Deficits in recall may occur (Koson and Robey, 1973) because of encephalitis, trauma, intoxication, dissociative disorders, and psychosis.

Identification of deficits in the examination of the memory process may facilitate the diagnosis of amnesia. This is less true in the examination of psychogenic amnesias where the impact of mental disorders and severe stress may interfere at several stages in the memory process (Bradford and Smith, 1979).

STATE-DEPENDENT LEARNING

Considerable research has examined the issue of state-dependent learning in which information registered in a drug-altered state shows better recall in a similar drug-altered state. This research (e.g., Goodwin, 1969) has studied state-dependent learning primarily with simple learning and recall tests. Although no research has focused on the utilization of alcohol- or drug-assisted interviews with amnestic criminal defendants, research has shown (i.e., Goodwin, Crane, and Guze, 1969) that alcoholics may spontaneously recall events that occurred during drinking episodes in subsequent periods of intoxication. Utilizing the state-dependent learning paradigm, it may be helpful to employ alcohol-assisted interviews as an adjunctive approach with alcohol amnesiacs.

AMNESTIC DISORDERS AND CRIMINAL RESPONSIBILITY

The presence of any amnesia, feigned or authentic, complicates the determination of the defendant's criminal responsibility (Rubinsky and Brandt, 1986; Hermann, 1986). Rarely does amnesia represent a decisive factor in formulating an expert opinion regarding insanity; the only possible exceptions are automatisms and dissociative disorders, which are discussed briefly later. Amnesia as a syndrome is more important, however, in establishing the defendant's diagnosis and in addressing the honesty and completeness of his or her self-report. Therefore, any reported amnesia must be evaluated carefully to address its authenticity, clinical characteristics (i.e., onset, course, duration), and potential role in the insanity standard. Certainly, the thorough determination of malingering and distortion with respect to amnesia is equally significant for the forensic clinician in his or her examination of other reported psychological symptoms. In addition, the presence of an amnestic syndrome must be clarified in formulating any accurate diagnostic presentation of the defendant. Finally, the role of amnesia in the criminal conduct must be assessed. If marked deficits in memory can be established at the time of the alleged criminal behavior, then the potential impact of such a memory dysfunction on the individual's cognitive and volitional capacity must be examined.

Aligned with criminal responsibility is the capacity to form the requisite mental state, or mens rea, to commit the criminal behavior. Thus, if the defendant did not have the conscious intent to commit a crime, then he or she must be exculpated. For example, a severely demented individual who is unable to distinguish his or her property from that of others may lack the requisite intent to commit home invasion or burglary. In clinical practice, such cases are rarely referred since most are diverted from the criminal justice system.

The defendant's denial or nonacceptance of his or her criminal charges on the basis of amnesia at least may be conceptualized on three distinct levels. The first is total denial; that is, on the basis of amnesia the defendant may deny even the occurrence (e.g., claiming the decedent is still living) of the criminal act. This is extremely rare in criminal responsibility evaluations. The second level is denial of personal involvement; that is, the defendant may claim amnesia and deny any personal involvement in the criminal act although not dispute it was committed. Third is denial of intent; that is, the defendant, on the basis of amnesia, may deny any criminal intent while not disputing involvement: "I might have done it but I would have to have been out of my mind." In each of these three conditions, the forensic clinician must determine whether the amnesia interferes with the defendant's ability to stand trial (see Koson and Robey, 1973) or to understand and appreciate the Miranda-type warning given at the onset of the insanity evaluation. More specifically, a defendant who totally denies, on the basis of an amnesia, the existence of a criminal act may lack the capacity to cooperate with his or her attorney. Further, the defendant who denies any personal involvement because of memory loss may not take seriously the pre-evaluation warning regarding the purpose and possible negative consequences of the insanity evaluation.

There is inevitably some memory loss in every criminal responsibility evaluation. All defendants are simply unable to recall totally their thoughts, emotions, perceptions, and actions preceding, during, and following the criminal behavior. Therefore, the question is one of degree: to what extent does the memory loss interfere with a coherent account of the time of the crime? The great majority of defendants experiences only a peripheral loss of detail regarding their behavior and emotions and a mild to moderate memory loss of their perceptions and thinking. Most individuals presenting amnestic symptoms for the time of the crime have only partial amnesia and remember the majority of their actions. It is important with such defendants, as with all defendants, to distinguish carefully what is speculative or inferential from actual memories.

The most important impact of amnestic disorders on insanity evaluations is on the clinician's degree of certainty. In cases where corroborative data are inadequate, the forensic clinician may not have sufficient clinical data, particularly concerning the defendant's internal psychological state, to render an opinion within the degrees of medical or scientific certainty (see chapter 1). In cases where there is substantial amnesia for the period of the criminal behavior, the clinician is obligated to utilize comprehensively all other available clinical sources. In the absence of such resources, the clinician will have the responsibility for considering whether or not the defendant is fit to stand trial and whether any conclusory statements can be made.

AUTOMATISM AND CRIMINAL RESPONSIBILITY

Automatism has gained greater currency in the United Kingdom and Canada than the United States as a clinical concept to describe behavior for which there is amnesia and an absence of conscious control (see Appendix II for discussion of insane automatism in Canada). McCaldon (1964) has described a spectrum of automatisms. For example, he described hypnotic and posthypnotic states and somnabulism as *normal automatism* since such states may involve automatic behavior without conscious control. He further described organic automatisms as including these caused by epilepsy, cerebral trauma, and alcohol intoxication. He described symptoms associated with epileptic automatism as derealization; depersonalization; olfactory, gustatory, and visual hallucinations; lip smacking and chewing movements; mood changes; clouded consciousness; and psychomotor retardation. He states that such automatisms may have a certain aura of purposiveness in spite of which the defendant may have lacked the requisite intent. This clearly represented a minority position in the examination of epilepsy and directed violence. Exhaustive research into both the ictal and interictal behavior of thousands of epileptics found only highly infrequent expressions of aggression, typically in the form of undirected rage (see chapter 8).

McCaldon (1964, p. 917) described alcohol automatism as based on amnesia and disinhibition of "already shaky controls and acting out of conflicts." Further, Blair (1977) argued that for alcohol intoxication to produce amnesia it would also be likely to impair criminal intent. The writings of both McCaldon and Blair probably reflect differences between Canadian and American conceptualizations of intoxication and criminal behavior although Martin's (1981) more recent work suggests a narrowing of automatism within the Canadian context. Such cases are likely to be viewed by American psychiatrists and psychologists as a foreseeable consequence of voluntary intoxication and that defendants who experience a disinhibitory effect from the alcohol have a greater likelihood of having alcoholic blackouts (Cunnien, 1986). Further, most defendants raising the insanity defense report that their precrime level of alcohol consumption was no different from their characteristic consumption. The argument that the alcohol created the automatism that exculpates the defendant becomes tenuous when the defendant experienced similar and even worse states of intoxication without any evidence of automatism or criminal behavior.

McCaldon (1964) described psychogenic automatism as trancelike dissociative states that defendants may enter as "an escape from reality or an escape from their own repressed and unacceptable impulses" (p. 918). Clearly multiple personality disorders, fugue states, and atypical dissociative disorders may reflect degrees of fragmented personal memory. The relationship of such fragmentation to specific standards of criminal responsibility is difficult to examine on an empirical basis given the rarity of such disorders among criminal defendants. In examining the diagnoses of all defendants evaluated at the Isaac Ray Center over a 6-year period, only one multiple personality disorder and no fugue disorders were found. Further, such losses of personal memory are not ipso facto evidence of nonresponsibility. The clinician must carefully assess the extent to which the defendant's operating personality meets or does not meet the respective legal standards. For example, a defendant in a severe dissociative state may have assumed a different identity but was aware of and chose to engage in his or her criminal behavior. In contrast, one subpersonality of a multiple personality disorder may grossly misperceive his or her current circumstances to delusional proportions and commit homicide under beliefs of self-defense. Howe (1984) provided an excellent summary of dissociative disorders and the complicated issues in their forensic assessment.

MEMORY LOSS AND DISTORTION

Considerable literature examines in detail memory loss and memory distortion. Much of this research (Loftus, 1979; Loftus and Loftus, 1980) examined memory deficits in light of the extensive work on eyewitness research. Such research has shown (e.g., Buckhout, 1974) that individuals experience greater memory loss over time while paradoxically becoming more certain in the accuracy of their memory. In applying these findings to criminal responsibility evaluations, it is quite possible that a defendant may became more adamant about his or her perceptions, thinking, and behavior as a result of this memory process—decrease in accuracy/increase in certainty—beyond or in addition to any conscious intentions to manipulate the situation.

An important determinant in memory recall is the interrelationship of memory and meaning. The individual attempting to recall any important event will attempt to make sense of it. This may lead to either a supplementing or altering of the original memory so that it is plausible and consistent with other apparently known facts (see Loftus, 1975). This is particularly true for incomplete or blurry memories of details surrounding an event. Memory in these instances becomes reorganized toward developing an overall coherent picture, with understandability preempting accuracy. Thus, memory details become permeable and vulnerable to external influences like police interrogation.

The criminal defendant who struggles with a question, How could I have done it?, will attempt to make meaning out of his or her criminal behavior. Since most defendants do not view their behavior as vile or repugnant, certain defendants may experience a cognitive shift with concomitant changes in their actual recall. This change is more likely to be in emphasis than in actual sequence of events. For example, the defendant may emphasize the extenuating circumstances that justify his or her actions in an attempt to make sense out of what happened. The forensic clinician is therefore hampered by the permeability of memory details and the flexibility in emphasis/importance placed on internal psychological events.

The boundary between memory and nonmemory is frequently indistinct. It is difficult for most individuals to separate their actual memories of a past event from what they have been told directly or indirectly about that event. Thus, an individual's actual memory may become attenuated by the presentation of additional information, whether or not that additional information is accurate. Studies (see Loftus, 1979) have demonstrated that observers of a traumatic incident may dramatically alter their memories when given information inconsistent with their original memory. Thus, defendants who observed a film clip of an actual automobile accident may alter their memory both of the physical description as well as of the events based on the subtle insertion of ideas and change in emphasis. In this example, subjects who are asked how fast a red car was traveling may give estimates even though none of the cars was red and will automatically alter their memories and sequence of events on the basis of these subtle cues from interviewers. The forensic clinician must be aware of how he or she may lead and distort the defendant's memory with directed questions (Loftus, 1975; Cole and Lotus, 1979).

Given the vulnerability of the defendant's memory, the forensic clinician must be sensitive to avoiding or minimizing further memory distortions. Toward this end, the following guidelines are offered for clinical inquiry in insanity evaluations.

1. The clinician should use general nondirectional questions, particularly in the initial evaluative phase. This allows the defendant to recall to the best of his or her ability what occurred and what the defendant remembers of his or her internal processes. After the defendant gives a complete and unstructured account, the clinician may wish to ask more specific questions regarding the self-report. There is no need, however, for these questions to be leading (e.g., "What were you actually feeling when X happened?" is preferable to "were you really enraged when X happened?").

2. The sequencing of the defendant's self-report should be logical and, during the initial phases, chronological since the order of recall may influence the extent of recall. Thus, a chronological self-report allows for less structuring and potential contamination of the defendant's memory.

3. The clinician should avoid the loaded premise. This involves the placing of conditional phrases with which the defendant may or may not agree within the clinical inquiry. For example, "After X ridiculed you, what did you do?" may be loaded both factually and emotionally, thereby distorting the defendant's recall. Particularly in the case of emotionally loaded questions, the clinician may antagonize the defendant into disregarding his or her memory and responding with defensiveness or defiance.

4. The clinician should minimize explanatory-type questions interspersed with the defendant's self-report. Such questions interposed with recall may unnecessarily distort the defendant's memory of his or her thinking and motivation. Inquiries focused on what the defendant was thinking about are more acceptable than asking for justifications or explanations.

5. The forensic clinician should minimize the use of speculative questions. This includes questions such as What do you imagine . . . ? What was the victim thinking? and What was likely to have happened if . . . ? Given the indistinct boundary between memory and nonmemory, such speculations may unwittingly be added to the defendant's memory, thereby contaminating further recall.

CONCLUSION

Memory and memory impairment represent fundamental issues in the determination of criminal responsibility. Amnesia constitutes a clinical syndrome with a broad range of possible etiologies: organic, psychogenic, feigned, and mixed. Such memory losses and distortions are important both in establishing a retrospective diagnosis and in the application of the appropriate legal standard.

The assessment of amnesia requires the careful investigation of the apparent memory loss and its characteristics. The forensic clinician assesses the parameters of the amnestic episode, its onset, direction (retrograde or outergrade), and course (e.g., improved, deteriorated, or stable). Following a detailed description of the amnesia, the clinician must evaluate three related issues: (1) whether or not the amnesia is feigned, (2) what is its etiology and diagnosis, and (3) what is its relevance to establishing criminal responsibility.

The clinician should be alert to memory distortions that typically occur after any emotion-evoking event, including participation in a crime. Research from an eyewitness paradigm suggests that memories become increasingly distorted over time while the conviction in the accuracy of these memories paradoxically increases. Criminal defendants are also susceptible to distortions introduced through repeated questioning and attempts at memory recall. The forensic clinician must distinguish unintentional memory distortion from deliberate attempts at malingering and deception.

PART II

Clinical Methods

Chapter 5

Clinical Interviews

Clinical interviews represent the cornerstone of the forensic evaluation process. It is during this component of the assessment process that the clinician has the greatest flexibility in his or her retrospective assessment of the defendant. This flexibility places demands on the clinician to collect precise, detailed, clinically relevant information both for the time of the alleged offense as well as the time of the evaluation. This chapter addresses the goals and diagnostic and legal issues relevant to clinical interviews.

GOALS

The goals of an insanity evaluation interview differ both qualitatively and quantitatively from those of nonforensic evaluations. The assessment of criminal responsibility requires a careful and thoughtful examination of discrete periods of the defendant's life as well as a careful evaluation of the veracity of his or her self-report.

Establishing the Defendant's Credibility

A primary goal of the forensic clinician is to establish the believability of an individual's self-report since this is often the sine qua non of forensic evaluations. The defendant's credibility during the criminal responsibility evaluation puts substantial demands on the clinician throughout the forensic evaluation process. First, defendants are presented with a situation that has far-reaching and potentially devastating consequences for them. The effects of such consequences may consciously influence defendant's self-reports. A second factor connected with the concept of credibility is that of plausibility. Despite attempts to remain objective, the clinician evaluates the veracity of the defendant's self-report against his or her experiences. The reasonableness of the criminal act may influence the evaluator's perceptions of the defendant's honesty. Defendants may be caught in a conflict between being liked by the evaluator (i.e., reasonable) and a desire for self-preservation (i.e., attempt to appear less reasonable or irrational) during the forensic evaluation. It has also been observed that certain individuals have a tendency to become more reasonable in a forensic evaluation, perhaps to their detriment. A third and crucial factor is to establish the defendant's honesty and accuracy of self-report. Given the literature on memory distortion in chapter 4, cases occur in which the defendant may honestly state an inaccurate memory. Thus, the clinician must attempt to corroborate in detail the defendant's account, both for its accuracy and honesty.

A fourth factor in establishing the credibility of a defendant is whether or not he or she admits to the criminal behavior in question. Defendants frequently present themselves at a criminal responsibility evaluation by either denying the criminal behavior or admitting only a rather innocuous portion of that behavior (e.g., breaking and entering but not murder). Such a presentation might reflect the defendant's beliefs (based on a functional or organic amnestic syndrome) or an attempt to deceive. It may be difficult for the clinician to reconcile marked differences between a well-documented police report and a defendant's nonexistent or vague (and potentially self-serving) self-report.

Phenomenological Issues Establishing the Defendant's Experience

The goals included in this section address the defendant's experience including the sequence of events before, during, and following the criminal behavior. Of primary importance is what the defendant was thinking during this period:

1. What was the relationship of his or her thoughts to the emotions he or she was experiencing? Further, what was the relationship, if any, of the individual's emotion to the concomitant behavior?
2. Were there any describable changes in the individual's sensations or perceptions?
3. Were these changes in perceptions related to the defendant's thoughts, emotions, or behavior?

In addressing these issues, the clinician may also observe and employ as a standard of measure the defendant's current perceptions, emotions, thoughts, and behavior to compare with his or her retrospective report for the time of the crime. The goal is a spontaneous uninterrupted account, in as much detail as possible, of what occurred during the several days prior to the criminal behavior, during the criminal behavior, and immediately following the criminal behavior. This account should be followed by a second self-report in which highly specific questions are asked about thoughts, emotions, perceptions, and behavior as well as the interrelationships among these factors. Such a thorough phenomenological examination of the individual will greatly facilitate establishing the psychological state at the time of the offense.

Establishing the Defendant's Motivation

A third goal in criminal responsibility evaluations is to address the defendant's past and current life goals. During the period prior to and during the criminal behavior, what did the defendant want to accomplish?

1. How did the defendant's life circumstances, at that period of time, serve either to fulfill or not fulfill his or her needs? What was accomplished by the crime?
2. If the defendant were to be assessed not on statements but on behavior alone, what are the likely purposes served by the criminal behavior? To what extent was the criminal behavior successful or unsuccessful in reaching its goal?
3. To what extent, if any, are the defendant's goals now different from those held during the period of the criminal behavior?
4. What motivated the defendant during the period of the crime to seek this alternative over other choices?
5. In combining these motivational issues, what is the most parsimonious and demonstrable explanation for the defendant's criminal behavior?

An important factor in assessing the defendant's motivation is the degree of planning and preparation observed in the criminal behavior. A well planned and executed crime may suggest a different motivational structure than an unplanned and random one. Table 5.1 contrasts the degree of planning and preparation for sane and insane defendants.

Establishing the Defendant's Diagnosis

The goals of diagnosis are to identify the presence and severity of psychological symptoms at both the present and the time of the alleged crime.

Table 5.1
Planning and Preparation for the Crime

	Sane (%)	Insane (%)
Detailed planning with general preparation	10.8	6.5
Detailed planning with considerable specific preparation	3.8	1.1
Elaborate planning and preparation extending over a period of a week	0.8	0

This process involves the employment of inclusion and exclusion criteria for establishing the appropriate diagnoses of a mental disorder. Of further diagnostic interest are the onset and course of specific psychological symptoms, particularly those representing psychotic features. This includes the assessment of impairment at the time of the crime and its potential impact on the individual's criminal actions. Finally, as articulated with earlier goals, do these symptoms represent a specific diagnostic entity? Does inconsistency or incongruities in reported symptoms indicate an unreliable self-report?

Establishing the Defendant's Awareness of Criminality

The primary goals concerning the legal issues is the establishment of the defendant's knowledge of his or her alleged criminal behavior and understanding of the concept of insanity. Of particular interest to the forensic clinician is how the defendant now conceptualizes and, if possible, conceptualized at the time of the crime the legal context of this behavior.

1. Does the defendant view his or her behavior as criminal? Further, does this person view it as morally justified?
2. What were the defendant's expectations of the legal system if apprehended for the alleged crime?
3. What does the defendant believe would be fair and just resolution of the current legal situation?

Sane and insane defendants differ widely on their awareness of the criminality of their behavior. As presented in Table 5.2, the great majority of those clinically evaluated as insane show vague or no awareness of the criminal nature of their behavior.

Such issues involve the defendant's volition and desire to enter a plea of

Table 5.2
Degree of Awareness of Criminality

	Sane (%)	Insane (%)
Aware, with some lack of appreciation for the severity	20.8	6.5
Vague	3.2	40.9
None	2	45.2

not guilty by reason of insanity (NGRI). For example, what does the defendant believe it means to be considered legally sane or insane? Does the defendant view him- or herself as a criminal? How does this person believe that insane individuals act? Does, in fact, he or she want to plead NGRI? Examination of such issues allows for a more comprehensive understanding of the defendant's perception of the alleged criminal behavior and his or her role as a willing or unwilling participant in the NGRI plea.

Establishing the Defendant's Self Control

This set of goals involves establishing the defendant's perception of his or her actions and degree of control over them. This particularly complex issue involves establishing what it means for the defendant to be either in control or out of control. Can the lack of control be differentiated from not caring about what happens?

1. What did the defendant perceive to be his or her choices at the time of the criminal behavior?
2. To what extent were these choices forced on the defendant as opposed to being experienced as options?
3. What was the defendant's capacity either to withhold or abort the criminal behavior?
4. Although the defendant may have acted in an explosive or violently unrestrained manner, to what extent did the defendant make choices prior to this behavior with the knowledge that such behavior is likely to occur? This final issue addresses the defendant who may know that his or her presence and/or actions in a particular situation may lead to violence and yet deliberately chooses to be in a situation in which the likelihood is greatly increased.

Available data on loss of behavioral control indicate that such loss discriminates well between clinically evaluated sane and insane defendants. As presented in Table 5.3, major or complete loss of control is experienced rarely by sane defendants in marked contrast to their insane counterparts.

Establishing the Assessment Process

The individual style and temperament of the clinician as well as the idiosyncratic needs of the defendant place great demands on the assessment process to provide a thorough and comprehensive evaluation of the individual's criminal responsibility. This section presents clinical methods that may be employed for a thorough evaluation of the defendant's self-report. None of the clinical methods guarantees the veracity and comprehensiveness of a defendant's report; they serve rather as useful markers for the experienced forensic clinician in gathering as much clinical data as feasible. It should be noted that the spirit of such evaluations should be respectful and professional. There should be no attempt to act in a friendly, or buddy, manner that would minimize the importance of the evaluation and its potentially negative consequences for the defendant. Conversely, the forensic examiner must be respectful at all times of the defendant's right not to respond to specific questions and not to cooperate with the assessment process. Further, the clinician must function as a clinician and avoid, at all costs, an inquisitorial or cross-examination approach to the defendant.

It is often helpful to move from general nondirectional questions to more specific directed inquiries during the clinical interviews. This may assist a clinician in establishing rapport with the defendant and in gathering the defendant's uninterrupted account. This approach may also assist the clinician in avoiding preconceptions and in collecting additional clinical data that might otherwise be missed. Further, such a general account may be used as a reference point in subsequent clinical interviews in establishing the defendant's consistency and veracity. Similarly, the clinician may choose to avoid questioning or challenging the defendant's statements during early interviews, delaying such approaches to later interviews when either better rapport has been established or when such confrontational approaches will not jeopardize the complete evaluation.

Table 5.3
Loss of Behavioral Control at Time of Crime

	Sane (%)	Insane (%)
Moderate	7.2	11.8
Major	3.4	50.5
Complete	0	21.5

Clinicians must be willing to become involved in extensive clinical interviews over multiple time periods to assess criminal responsibility. Separating the defendant's accounts by a several-week interval may assist the clinician in establishing consistency and honesty of the self-report data. Such a format may further assist the clinician in prioritizing the psychological difficulties/symptoms and their relative importance to the defendant during the commission of the alleged crime. In probing the self-account it may be particularly helpful to ask for details and specific examples of symptoms or problems experienced by the defendant. It may also be of some assistance to request that the defendant explain this account using different words, particularly if there is a rehearsed quality to the self-report. This may include asking for explanations of terms used by the defendant. For example, what does the defendant mean when stating that he or she is anxious? In addition, it is often necessary to question whether self-report information is either speculative or plausible as opposed to being an actual memory. It may be necessary periodically to remind the defendant to state only those things he or she clearly remembers. Further questioning in which the same area is covered from different perspectives is often of some assistance in understanding the nuances of the defendant's self-report. For example, questions about sleeping disturbances may be presented directly or indirectly (e.g., through a discussion of dreams).

Comparative questioning, in which the defendant is asked to describe at the time of the alleged crime his or her emotions, behaviors, and perceptions and then subsequently compare them to those of the present time, is often useful. This questioning allows the forensic examiner to calibrate the defendant's reported impairment at the current time with the clinician's observations. For instance, the clinician's perspective of reported depression may be considerably modified by comparative statements that are either much worse or the same as the defendant's current emotional feelings. Further, with intelligent and articulate defendants, it is sometimes helpful to employ a reverse history taking in which the defendant is asked to report sequentially what occurred in reverse order. Clinical inquiry may include what the defendant was doing prior to the crime, what events led up to the crime, and more general questions. Such an approach pushes the defendant to think actively and to remember the sequence of events and diminish the rehearsed or rote quality.

Confrontational methods should be employed parsimoniously and only where clinical data are necessary for completing the forensic assessment. The clinician may, for example, respectfully question inconsistencies in the defendant's self-report. The examiner may further suggest that particular portions of the self-report are either over- or underemphasized. The clinician may also present him- or herself as unconvinced (if this is actually the case) by components of the self-report in an attempt to elicit more information and/or emotional responses. In addition, the examiner may suggest alternative explanations for what is reported to have occurred.

The most difficult area of inquiry is the defendant's formulation of his or her motivation with respect to the criminal behavior. Attempts to have the defendant make connections between emotional and cognitive experiences and the criminal behavior may assist in establishing the extent, if any, to which the reported internal experiences had an impact on the criminal behavior. At times, the clinician may choose to use additional information such as police investigative reports or laboratory studies to confront the defendant's account. Finally, the clinician may choose to disagree directly with the client and state the reasons for this position. The purpose of such a confrontation should not be to argue with a defendant about the self-report but to gather additional clinical data. It is important that the clinician sensitively use a variety of confrontational approaches to avoid grilling the defendant.

DIAGNOSTIC ISSUES

The pivotal issue in most insanity evaluations is the presence and severity of psychotic symptoms. Psychotic symptoms are defined as hallucinations, delusions, and gross disorganization of thinking and/or behavior. The mere presence of psychotic symptoms does not indicate insanity; it is one essential criterion in a multistage decision process. Because of the importance of accurately determining both the presence as well as the impact of psychotic features on behavior, prominent symptoms are examined individually.

Hallucinations

Hallucinations refer to the misperception of external stimuli without stimulation of the appropriate sense receptors. Schizophrenic patients frequently experience auditory hallucinations and rarely have visual, olfactory, or tactile hallucinations. The duration of hallucinations varies widely but usually involves only a small portion of time. Similarly, psychotic individuals use a broad range of coping strategies for ignoring or controlling their hallucinatory activity. Coping strategies frequently involve increased interpersonal contact, physical activity, or other changes in environmental stimulation. Finally, only a small portion of schizophrenic patients reports command hallucinations that consequently have a significant impact on their behavior.

Hallucinations, by their nature, are not directly observable. It is therefore imperative to examine thoroughly the defendant's self-report of any hallucinatory activity in addition to collecting corroborative information. Witnesses or individuals living with the defendant will frequently observe the defendant apparently attending or responding to nonexistent stimuli. In addition, individuals who are hallucinating may occasionally check the veracity of their perceptions with significant others in their environment. It is important for the clinician to distinguish between alien thoughts, those which the defendant may wish to disown, from true hallucinations. Several indicators may be employed in making this differentiation. First, hallucinations have a definite auditory quality in which the defendant can identify the tone, rate, and other speech qualities and other characteristics of the speaker (e.g., age, sex, race, and emotional state). Second, hallucinations are experienced outside the defendant (rarely are they experienced in another part of the body—e.g., a speaking foot) in contradistinction to alien thoughts. Third, hallucinations frequently ask for or elicit an interaction that does not occur with alien thoughts.

Clinical data on the prevalence of hallucinations and their concomitant impact on criminal behavior are summarized in Table 5.4. Clinical data suggest that approximately 40% of those clinically evaluated as insane had definite hallucinations at the time of the crime. These hallucinations varied from those that were unrelated to the criminal behavior to those that had a primary impact on the defendant's criminal conduct. In contrast, individuals evaluated as clinically sane had little hallucinatory activity (approximately 1%), which was apparently unrelated to the criminal behavior.

A detailed examination of the types of hallucinations was available through unpublished Schedule of Affective Disorders and Schizophrenia (SADS) data (Rogers, Thatcher, and Cavanaugh, 1984) on criminal responsibility. These data on seventy eight defendants suggested the presence at the time of the crime of the following types of hallucinations for individuals clinically evaluated as insane: auditory hallucinations (42%), visual hallucinations (16%), olfactory hallucinations (4%), and somatic or tactile hallucinations (7%).

The clinician must be able to establish the overall impact of the hallucination on the individual's day-to-day functioning. This entails a compre-

Table 5.4
Hallucinations at Time of Crime

	Sane (%)	Insane (%)
Not related to the crime	1.2	4.5
Contributed to the crime	0	17
Determined the crime	0	18.2

hensive assessment of the content and occurrence of hallucinations and the individual's response to these phenomena. It further includes an examination of the individual's degree of volition in selecting what behavioral response, if any, was utilized in coping with the hallucination. In addition, the clinician must distinguish between command hallucinations that give direct orders and other intrusive hallucinations that may elicit a coping response from the patient.

The following questions may assist the clinician in determining how relevant the hallucinatory activity was to the issue of criminal responsibility:

1. To what extent do hallucinations intrude on or impede the patient's day-to-day functioning?
2. What coping behaviors has the patient developed in response to these hallucinations?
3. Did the patient experience command hallucinations?
4. From the patient's perspective, what makes these hallucinations command hallucinations?
5. To whom, if anyone, are these command hallucinations attributed?
6. How much authority does the patient place in these hallucinations?
7. Assuming that command hallucinations were not isolated to the period of the alleged criminal behavior, what made the difference for the patient in deciding either to follow or not follow commands on this occasion?
8. To what extent was the content of the hallucinations (i.e., the command) consistent with the patient's wishes?
9. How specific were these command hallucinations and to what extent were they open, from the patient's perspective, to multiple interpretations? For example, an auditory hallucination stating "End it all" might signify a wide range of activities.
10. If the criminal behavior was either preceded by preparation or followed by actions designed to avoid arrest, what is the relationship of such behavior to the intrusive or command hallucinations?

Delusions

Delusions are defined in the *Diagnostic and Statistical Manual of Mental Disorders* (*DSM III*) (American Psychiatric Association, 1980) as reference to any personal beliefs based on misapprehension of external reality and firmly substained in spite of what almost everyone else believes and in spite of what constitutes incontrovertible and obvious proof to the contrary. For defining delusions, the clinician must be sensitive and aware that different subcultures of a religious and/or political nature may have beliefs alien to the mainstream culture. Such beliefs would not qualify as delusions. Distinguishing what constitutes an overvalued idea from an actual delusion often becomes a difficult clinical judgment. Overvalued ideas are observed in areas of greater ambiguity that are usually more open, on the part of the patient, to questioning and re-evaluation. Delusions are frequently manifested with unshakable conviction and are commonly unavailable for re-examination. Further, false beliefs based on lack of knowledge or acculturation do not constitute delusions.

The prevalence of delusional beliefs in defendants evaluated for criminal responsibility is summarized in Table 5.5. Those individuals clinically evaluated as insane have, in a majority of cases, delusions that have a major impact on the observed criminal behavior. This finding is in marked contrast to those individuals evaluated as sane of which are only a small proportion had delusional beliefs, and these exerted no or only peripheral influence on their criminal behavior. The specific types of delusional beliefs have not been examined for any large samples of forensic evaluations. Unpublished data (further analysis of Rogers, Thatcher, and Cavanaugh, 1984) from SADS-based criminal responsibility evaluations found that insane evaluatees had the following types of delusions: ideas of reference (36%), control (22%), thought insertion (9%), persecution (53%), and grandiosity (20%).

The clinical guidelines for establishing the presence and potential impact of delusional beliefs on criminal behavior parallel those considered with hallucinations. Establishing retrospectively the presence of delusions involves a detailed inquiry over multiple time periods to confirm the beliefs that existed and the individual's degree of conviction in these beliefs. The evaluation of this latter issue (i.e., the conviction) is often complex since defendants often have difficulty in differentiating the current degree of belief from their belief at the time of the crime.

Clinical guidelines for the evaluation of delusions include the following diagnostic questions:

Table 5.5
Delusions at Time of Crime

	Sane (%)	Insane (%)
Not related to the crime	1.5	3.3
Contributed to the crime	1.5	21.4
Determined the crime	0	60.9

1. What makes these beliefs delusional? More specifically, to what extent is the clinician convinced of the unusualness of these beliefs in the absence of consensually validated support for these beliefs (i.e., either within the society as a whole or a recognized subculture)?
2. What is the basis or rationale for the belief or belief systems in question?
3. How does the defendant differentiate fanciful ideas from beliefs that carry a strong conviction?
4. How does the defendant respond to a critical questioning of his or her beliefs now and at the time of the crime?
5. Did the defendant, at the time of the crime, recognize that these beliefs were very different from those of most other people? If this awareness of differences did exist, how did the defendant explain it?
6. How permanent were these delusional beliefs at the time of the crime? It is essential that the clinician establish, as closely as possible, when specific delusional beliefs were first recognized and when (if at all) they were subsequently questioned or disregarded. There is no consensus in the literature of a minimal time for which delusional beliefs must exist; however, very transient misbeliefs or misapprehensions, existing for less than several days, rarely reach the diagnostic criteria for a delusion.
7. What influence, if any, did the delusions have on the criminal behavior?
8. To what extent were these influences capable of being resisted?
9. How explicit were the delusional beliefs in relationship to the criminal behavior? If in fact the delusional beliefs were only general (e.g., "I am to serve the will of God"), then how did the defendant reason from such a general statement to the specific criminal behavior?
10. To what extent did the delusion suggest, instruct, demand, or impell the defendant to carry out specific criminal behavior?
11. Did the defendant recognize his or her behavior as criminal? If so, what effect did this recognition have on the behavior?
12. What factors were considered by the defendant, including delusional beliefs, in deciding to engage in the criminal behavior in question?
13. To what extent was the criminal behavior congruent with other nondelusional wishes of the individual?
14. If the delusional beliefs were chronic, how did the defendant select this particular time to engage in the criminal behavior?

Impaired Speech

Gross psychological impairment of speech is typically referred to as incoherence and reflects a marked deficit in an individual's ability to be understood. This lack of comprehensibility involves a disorganization or incompleteness in the individual's speech patterns. Epidemiological data (described in Appendix 1) suggest that some form of speech impairment exists in many defendants who are clinically evaluated as insane. Most specifically, insane defendants manifested peripheral difficulties (mild impairment) in approximately 16% of the cases, some difficulty being understood (moderate impairment) in 20%, and incoherence (severe impairment) in almost 7% of the cases. In contrast, those individuals evaluated as sane manifested mild impairment in 5.7% of the cases and no moderate and severe impairment (Table 5.6).

Bizarre and Disorganized Behavior

Bizarre behavior calls attention to itself because of the unusualness and social inappropriateness within the particular context in which it is observed. Because of its subjectivity, it is important to distinguish bizarre behavior from behavior reflecting a particular subculture or religion, a lack of training or knowledge of prevailing customs, and idiosyncratic behavior. Bizarre behavior goes beyond idiosyncratic behavior in its gross violation of social norms without any logical or understandable reasons (e.g., an individual who dresses up like a chicken and struts about making clucking sounds would not necessarily be considered bizarre if the act were part of a publicity campaign for a family restaurant, but it would clearly be considered so if the person was attending a spouse's funeral). Therefore, any judgment regarding bizarreness must take into account both the context as well as the individual's awareness and intentionality with respect to the behavior in question.

An important consideration in insanity evaluations is whether the criminal behavior should be considered bizarre by itself. More specifically, would sadistic rape, which frequently involves ritualistic cutting or torturing of the victim, be considered bizarre? Further, would an attempt to hijack an airplane with a straight-edge razor be bizarre? Or is a criminal defendant

Table 5.6
Verbal Impairment at Time of Crime

	Sane (%)	Insane (%)
Mild—generally understood	5.7	15.8
Moderate—understood with difficulty	0	19.7
Severe—incoherent	0	6.6

who boils a baby's hand to punish the infant for misbehavior acting in a bizarre fashion? Would any type of pedophilic behavior, by definition, be bizarre? There are certainly no simple responses to these questions. Perhaps the key issue is the examination of the individual's intentions and awareness of his or her bizarre behavior.

An individual who deliberately tortures a hostage as part of an extortion scheme is likely to be operating on entirely different principles than one who is engaging in satanic rites. Further, for bizarre behavior to be evidence of psychotic functioning, there must be concomitant impairment in the individual's perceptions or thinking. Certainly an integral component in the assessment of bizarre behavior is how the defendant expected others to perceive his or her behavior and what the anticipated effect would be on those observing it. The prevalence of bizarre behavior among those clinically evaluated as insane is presented in Table 5.7. It should be noted that those evaluated as insane were fairly evenly divided among those having no bizarre behavior (26%), and those in Table 5.7. with one instance of bizarre behavior, several instances of bizarre behavior, and frequent to continuous bizarre behavior.

The following questions may be helpful in making a detailed clinical examination of a defendant's bizarre behavior:

1. Does the defendant see his or her behavior as bizarre? If so, on what basis?
2. How does the bizarre behavior serve or not serve the defendant's purposes?
3. What is the relationship of the bizarre behavior to the defendant's perceptions, thinking, and emotions?
4. Under what circumstances does the bizarre behavior usually occur?
5. Is the bizarre behavior limited only to this or other criminal acts? If so, how much control does the defendant have over the bizarre behavior?
6. Where in the sequence of criminal behavior does the bizarre behavior occur?
7. Is the bizarre behavior tangential to the commission of the crime?

Table 5.7
Frequency of Bizarre Behavior at Time of Crime

	Sane (%)	Insane (%)
One instance	1.8	16.7
Several instances	0	27.8
Frequent to continuous	0	28.9

8. Did the bizarre behavior facilitate or impede the criminal behavior?
9. What effects, if any, did the defendant observe as a result of his or her bizarre behavior?
10. Was the bizarre behavior observed by anyone else? If so, what was the effect of the bizarre behavior on those observing it?
11. How does the defendant explain the bizarre behavior?

Disordered behavior, reflecting difficulties in carrying out purposeful actions, and satisfaction of self care needs is often comparatively easy to assess (Table 5.8). It is most frequently observed in the disruption of goal-oriented behaviors in which the individual has difficulty either in tracking (i.e., staying with and completing relatively simple tasks) or through psychomotor agitation or retardation that disrupts purposeful behavior. To warrant the determination of disorganized behavior, the defendant must have manifested ineffectual attempts to carry out day-to-day activities that are not the result of voluntary intoxication. Corroborative information is often essential since such defendants frequently have gross memory impairment.

A closely related issue is the absence of responsible behavior within the major spheres of the individual's existence. The individual's capacity and willingness to engage in work or school and to establish responsible and reciprocal interpersonal relations form an important benchmark of psychological functioning. An examination of data on prevalence (Table 5.9) indicates that nearly one-half of those clinically evaluated as insane experienced significant impairment in work or social relationships. Further, it is interesting to note that few of these defendants were grossly impaired; it may well be that individuals with pervasive impairment lack the motivation or capacity to carry out criminal behavior or are currently institutionalized. The clinician may use the individual's capacity for work and social relationships as one of many important indicators in assessing the individual's overall psychological functioning. Again, the important issue is that of capacity as opposed to choice. Therefore, an antisocial individual who chooses not to be employed or an individual who for religious reasons prefers a solitary existence would not necessarily be considered in this category.

Table 5.8
Impairment of Self-Care at Time of Offense

	Sane (%)	Insane (%)
Mild	8.6	31.6
Moderate	2.2	26.3
Severe	0	15.8

Table 5.9
Impairment of Responsible Social Behavior Prior to the Crime

	Sane (%)	Insane (%)
Mild	24	9.3
Moderate	25.2	37.2
Severe	3.6	48.8

Depressive Symptoms

Depressive symptoms are frequently difficult to establish with respect to the legal standard of insanity. The task is complicated by the fact that most defendants being evaluated for criminal responsibility are, at the time of the evaluation, somewhat dysphoric; however, this dysphoria may be unrelated to the psychological state at the time of the crime. Other factors contributing to dysphoric feelings include the effects of incarceration, impending trial, and possible imprisonment; frustration at having been caught; shame or guilt in having committed the criminal behavior; or other intervening events following arrest. It is therefore necessary to examine, as completely as possible, the role of these actions or events in the individual's current dysphoria. Further, it is essential to differentiate what dysphoric state the individual was experiencing at the time of the crime: to what extent was the individual sad, depressed, frustrated, irritable, or angry? Defendants are frequently imprecise and confused when they attempt to describe their negative feelings. The use of the nonleading questions such as How were you feeling? or What was your mood like? is often more helpful than directed questions such as Were you feeling depressed? Having the defendant describe the day of the crime and several days prior, with periodic questions about his or her emotional state, is probably the most helpful in establishing his or her predominant mood. By asking the defendant to recount the time of the crime rather than labeling the mood assists the clinician in providing more extensive clinical data for making his or her judgment regarding the defendant's affective state.

The severity of the depressed mood becomes critical in the establishment of criminal responsibility. Through careful inquiry, the clinician can often establish the duration of the depressed feelings and their onset, course, and severity. Severity is measured in terms of the pervasiveness, hopelessness, suicidal ideation, and degree of impairment of these depressed feelings on day-to-day functioning. Additional symptoms including sleep disturbance, changes in appetite, and psychomotor agitation or retardation are important in confirming the severity of the depression.

The relationship of depression to criminal responsibility is difficult to determine in the absence of gross psychotic features such as delusions or hallucinations. The clinician is required to establish the disorganizing impact emotionally, cognitively, and behaviorally of the depression on the individual's conduct at the time of the crime. What degree of depression is necessary to warrant exculpation? Does a severely depressed woman with intentions to kill herself and her children as an act of altruism qualify clinically as insane? In such an example, perhaps the woman had fully realized what she was doing was criminal and morally wrong yet believed there was no other viable alternative (e.g., I have to save my children from the unremitting pain and horror of continued living, or I am afraid that after I kill myself they cannot possibly live without me). The decisive factor in this and related cases is a conviction of the individual's belief and his or her ability to consider alternatives. In this example, the woman may be approaching a nihilistic delusion or experiencing grossly impaired reality testing in her inability to separate her own phenomenological experience from that of her child. This would not, however, be the case with a person exercising a greater degree of control over his or her homicidal behavior (e.g., a man who murdered his daughter as a form of revenge toward his lover). In such cases, the specific legal standard of insanity may play a determining role in a clinical evaluation of criminal responsibility. Thus, while none of these variations would likely be evaluated as insane under the M'Naghten standard, the first example might meet the volitional prong of the ALI (American Law Institute) standard (ability to conform one's conduct).

From an epidemiological perspective (described in Appendix 1), significant depression was found in approximately 11% of those clinically evaluated as sane and nearly 29% of those evaluated as insane (Table 5.10). The difference lies in the relationship of the depression to criminal behavior with the majority of those found clinically insane in whom depression played a determinative role.

Table 5.10
Depression Level at Time of Crime

	Sane (%)	Insane (%)
Moderate	10.1	12.2
Severe	0.8	12.2
Extreme	0	4.4

Manic Symptoms

Manic symptoms constellate on disturbances in mood, thinking, and behavior. Defendants with a previous manic episode are likely to report a distinct change in mood, becoming either elevated or euphoric; hyperactivity both in the speed and quantity of activities; and changes in their thinking including accelerated speech and pressured thinking. Episodes are defined to last a minimum of one week, with overly positive feelings clearly disproportionate to the individual's situation. Some manic individuals experience episodes of irritability instead of expansive or elevated moods; with such individuals it is imperative to establish whether there were concomitant changes in the individual's level of activity, energy, and rate of speech/thinking. Of particular concern in the assessment of criminal responsibility is the establishment of grandiosity, accelerated thinking, and deficits in judgment. Grandiosity, reflecting an inflated and unrealistically positive assessment of an individual's abilities and attributes, is the most pertinent. As grandiosity reaches a delusional level with blatantly distorted self-appraisal, there is a greater likelihood that the individual was not responsible at the time of the criminal behavior. For example, a manic defendant who believes he or she has the ability to control the stock market and grossly overestimates his or her current assets may violate federal banking regulations because of this disorder. Such an individual may not recognize the criminality of this behavior or grossly minimize actions as a formality or triviaiity. The clinician should follow the clinical guidelines for delusions when examining manic-based grandiose delusions.

The role of accelerated thinking and/or poor judgment within a clinical evaluation of insanity is more problematical. To what extent did accelerated speech or pressured thinking interfere with the individual's ability to understand his or her criminal conduct and, with respect to the ALI standard and revised M'Naghten standard, impair his or her ability to conform or control these actions? Rarely do defendants report, in the absence of delusional material, that the speed of their thinking markedly interfered with the awareness of the criminality/wrongfulness of their behavior. Accelerated thinking may, however, have a disorganizing or disabling effect on the defendant's judgment, rendering him or her nearly incapable of assessing the benefits or risks of a particular course of action. The clinician must assess how the individual chose or did not choose to act in a particular way and to what extent the individual had the capacity to weigh alternatives. Interference with judgment is easier to determine when the irrationality of the decision is obvious from the behavior. For example, an individual who goes on a buying spree and purchases several hundred pairs of children's socks for which he or she has no apparent need is acting irrationally. It is considerably more difficult to assess manic behavior when the object of the buying spree is a luxury sedan or financial investments. In this instance, impulsive behavior must be differentiated from manic behavior with grossly disorganized judgment that rendered the individual incapable of appreciating his or her current needs and financial circumstances. Manic-type symptoms due to voluntary substance abuse would not warrant exculpation of criminal responsibility. In terms of the available epidemiological data (Table 5.11), elevated or euphoric moods were found in approximately 16% of those clinically evaluated as insane and practically none of those evaluated as sane.

As a practical guideline, the clinician must look for several convincing examples of how substantial changes in mood (elevated, euphoric, or irritable) were part of a manic episode and acted significantly on the individual's criminal behavior. Thus, nondirectional questions focused on the time of the crime and immediately preceding that time may be useful in developing a baseline of the individual's mood, speech/thinking, and behavior. As with other symptom constellations, it is frequently of some assistance for the clinician to ask for cross-comparisons between the current observable mood and the mood at the time of the crime. It should be emphasized that it is extremely unlikely that an individual would be manic when the only manifestation of a manic episode is the criminal behavior. Further, manic episodes are usually part of a bipolar affective disorder that requires the presence at some point of a major depressive episode. Further, manically based impulsive behavior can often be verified by family and/or friends if it is intrusive on others or disabling to the defendant. Some individuals with either a counterphobic or adolescent bravado may appear manic because of their impulsive high-risk behavior but lack the requisite symptomatology for such a diagnosis. Therefore, the clinician is cautioned to distinguish between nonpsychopathologically based reckless behavior and that which is manic-based. As discussed earlier, even manic-based behavior must convincingly demonstrate marked deficits in the comprehension of he criminality/wrongfulness of the behavior or, under certain legal standards, in the defendant's ability to conform that behavior before such an individual would be clinically evaluated as insane.

Table 5.11
Elevated or Euphoric Mood at Time of Crime

	Sane (%)	Insane (%)
Mildly elevated	0.4	4.5
Moderate—minor impact on behavior	0.4	2.3
Severe—major impact on behavior	0	9.1

Anxiety Features

It is interesting that, although the retrospective diagnosis of an anxiety disorder is relatively infrequent in insanity evaluations (3.1%), many defendants experience situational anxiety. Such situational anxiety (Table 5.12) is noted more frequently in individuals clinically evaluated as insane (approximately 55%) than in those evaluated as sane (approximately 21%). Some anxiety may reflect an individual's apprehension of the seriousness of the situation and of his or her conduct. It may also be useful to examine anxiety and other symptoms not directly related to the insanity standard as an additional measure of the plausibility of a defendant's self-report.

Depersonalization and Derealization

Defendants, both those clinically evaluated as sane and insane, may frequently experience momentary or brief experiences of depersonalization (e.g., This could not possibly be me, or I feel unreal) or derealization (e.g., This is unreal) during the time of the criminal behavior. These feelings may occur more frequently in an individual's retrospective assessment of his or her behavior as an attempt to make meaning out of what happened. It is quite common for the defendant to look back on the criminal actions as a nightmare or something unreal from the past. It is very rare that the individual will have experienced an actual depersonalization disorder at the time of the crime. In addition, most reported experiences of momentary depersonalization occur after the initiation of the criminal behavior and thus are rarely exculpatory.

Intermittent or Isolated Explosive Personality Disorders

These disorders are marked by loss of control of aggressive impulses in individuals who normally have no difficulties with impulsivity or aggres-

Table 5.12
Anxiety Level at Time of Crime

	Sane (%)	Insane (%)
Moderate	16.2	26.5
Severe	4.4	24.1
Pervasive	0.9	4.8

siveness. The aggressive behavior is grossly out of proportion to any pre-cipitating stressor and is apparently non-goal-oriented. These disorders are frequently associated with nonspecific neurological symptoms with episodes followed by genuine feelings of self-reproach or guilt. The relationship of such a disorder to the issue of criminal responsibility falls on the assessment of the nonpurposefulness of the behavior, the atypicalness of the behavior (absence of general impulsivity and aggressivity), and the individual's doc-umented feelings of reproach or guilt over such behavior. It is essential that the clinician establish the extent to which the individual could control some circumstances antecedent to the criminal behavior and foresee the possi-bility of his or her explosiveness.

This section examined in some detail the psychological symptoms that are critical to retrospective evaluation of criminal responsibility. It assumes that the clinician has a solid foundation in diagnostic interviewing and has comprehensively reviewed all pertinent psychological symptoms.

CONTENT ISSUES

Content issues address the topics investigated through clinical interviews with a focus on what occurred and the defendant's background. This in-cludes a description of the defendant's behavior at the time of the offense and prior psychiatric, criminal, academic, vocational, and family history. This extensive background information provides a contextual basis for evaluating the defendant's motivation and impairment.

The defendant's account of his or her behavior preceding, during, and following the criminal behavior is the sine qua non of an insanity evalua-tion. The time framework will vary from case to case, although as a general guideline it is often helpful to examine the week preceding the criminal be-havior and to gather as much clinical data as possible for the 24-hour period following the criminal behavior. The defendant's account is best gathered in an unstructured manner by simply asking the defendant to report as much as possible about what he or she was feeling, thinking, and doing on each day. Such a systematic approach frequently yields valuable information about the limits of the defendant's memory and establishes a baseline of the defendant's functioning. Further, it is often helpful to discuss the day of the crime in great detail, focusing on each hour and testing the limits of the defendant's memory. Such an exhaustive approach is helpful in detect-ing malingering and other forms of deception since it is frequently difficult for the defendant to remain consistent on details across interviews.

A second content area, addressed in the previous section, is a detailed examination of psychological symptoms preceding and during the time of the criminal behavior as well as at the present time. By systematically reviewing various psychological symptoms, a detailed comparison can be drawn with the defendant's unstructured self-report. Further, a review of current symptoms may be of some assistance in making cross-comparisons between reported disturbances at the time of the crime and current symptomatology.

A third and related content area is the defendant's psychiatric history. This history includes the onset and duration of previously diagnosed mental disorders, types of treatments, and response to treatment. Information on hospitalizations and outpatient treatment may be helpful in corroborating the patient's self-report. It is also helpful to compare the patient's account of prior treatment with the clinical records from treating mental health professionals.

A related topic is a systematic review of the defendant's substance abuse history. This includes clinical information regarding the types of substances, amounts taken, frequency of use, and reactions of the individual to these substances. Such data (see chapter 8) increase the clinician's understanding of the role of substance abuse in the individual's psychological functioning. By collecting this information separately, the clinician can make comparisons between the reported psychiatric disturbances and episodes of substance abuse and verify these observations in subsequent interviews.

A fifth content area is the defendant's antisocial or criminal history. This history includes developmental symptoms (prior to the age of 15) relative to antisocial behavior, with specific deficits in interpersonal functioning and academic performance. As an adult, symptoms include antisocial behavior in which the rights of others have been violated, poor work performance, aggressiveness or criminal behavior, and/or irresponsible functioning as a parent or adult. It is sometimes necessary with less reliable respondents to gather this information chronologically, focusing on each year.

School and work history are also pertinent to criminal responsibility evaluations in assessing the individual's overall functioning and motivation. Although gathered in a brief outline form, this information provides an important measure of the individual's stability. It also serves as a benchmark for assessing specific episodes of a mental disorder and how they may have affected the defendant's productivity and goal-oriented behavior.

Finally, a brief family history addressing its dynamics and the defendant's developmental history may offer some understanding of the individual's personality and psychopathology. Family history may extend from the family of origin, with its concomitant developmental issues, to the individual's current family or living situation. The defendant's account of his or her family and perspective of their interpersonal relationships may give the clinician valuable insight into the various motivations that may have been operating on the defendant at the time of the crime. In addition, a family history may provide clinical data on how the defendant has reacted previously to stress or conflict.

CORROBORATIVE CLINICAL INTERVIEWS

Corroborative clinical interviews often provide invaluable clinical data regarding the defendant's functioning. Except for straightforward cases, the use of corroborative interviews should be established as a standard of practice in criminal responsibility assessments. Such interviews may provide new perspectives on the antecedents and determinants of the criminal behavior. Victims, who often are inaccessible to the clinician either because of homicide or the reluctance of attorneys, have a unique perspective of the criminal behavior from their observations of the dialogue and the defendant's actions. Witnesses also have firsthand information regarding the individual's speech and behavior. With both victims and witnesses, it is important to establish their attitudes toward the defendant and how these attitudes may bias or distort their recall.

Family and friends with whom the defendant was living at the time of the crime may have additional information regarding the defendant's overall functioning and the severity of specific symptoms. Again, it is important to assess these cohabitants' attitudes toward the defendant and the degree of defensiveness or other bias they may possess. Finally, the arresting police officers may be able to provide additional details about what occurred, report details of the crime scene, and remember statements left unreported by defendant and witnesses. All this corroborative information will facilitate an increased understanding of the defendant as well as verify his or her self-report.

An issue raised in conducting corroborative interviews is whose permission or release of information is needed before interviewing. Certainly, if the clinician wishes to interview mental health professionals involved in the defendant's prior psychological treatment, he or she must request a written release from the defendant. Although there is no legal requirement to do so, the clinician may also choose to obtain the defendant's verbal or written permission before interviewing family members or other cohabitants. It may also be necessary to have the state or defense attorney's approval and/or cooperation before contacting victims and witnesses. These individuals are often difficult to locate without the cooperation of an attorney, and clinicians frequently rely on the prosecutor's instructions as to how accessible they will be. Law enforcement personnel are usually quite willing to discuss the particulars of the case with a forensic clinician as long as there is verification of the professional's role and approval by their supervisor.

The content of corroborative interviews is likely to follow this format of focusing on critical topics. It is strongly suggested that the interviews be supportive, particularly of victims and witnesses. It is important to remember that no one in the corroborative interviews is on trial and that these individuals should be treated with considerable respect, both in discussing the respondent's actions at the time of the crime and honoring his or her decision whether or not to be interviewed and the extent to which he or she wishes to go into detail. It is also helpful to ask and occasionally to remind the individual to differentiate between what was observed and what is speculative. This differentiation may be facilitated by asking the individual to give the account with a minimum degree of structure. Further, it is important to question the individual's understanding of the criminal justice process and the role of this interview within that process.

Interviews may provide additional clinical information regarding the defendant and victims. In cases such as homicide or rape, it may be difficult for witnesses to be objective about what they saw or heard occur. Related to this issue is the need for sensitive assessment of interviewee's mental status and current emotional state. With families, its often easy to gather this clinical information while inquiring about family history of mental illness. A final but important issue is whether or not the witness was prepared, or coached, either by the defendant or an attorney. In recapping, the clinician should approach the corroborative interview in a positive and supportive manner and avoid provoking individuals who have already encountered a highly stressful and emotionally upsetting situation.

CONCLUSION

Interviews for the assessment of criminal responsibility are clinically demanding and time consuming. The forensic clinician must be prepared to conduct extensive interviews, often several hours in duration, to develop a full understanding of the defendant's retrospective functioning. The interview process also requires detailed notes on the content and manner of the defendant's account. It is helpful in this documentation of the interviews to include direct quotes of the defendant and clinical observations for preparation of the court report and subsequent testimony.

Integration of interview data requires planning and organization of the assessment process. The forensic clinician may wish to consider his or her goals, and the type of interview to be conducted (e.g., unstructured, diagnostic, or corroborative) for each contact with the interviewee. A careful review of interview material prior to the completion of the assessment will assure that areas of ambiguity or clinical uncertainty are thoroughly addressed.

Chapter 6

Psychological Testing

The relationship of traditional psychological testing to the assessment of criminal responsibility has received scant attention despite the voluminous psychometric literature. The forensic clinician is often placed in the uncomfortable position of attempting to extrapolate from diagnostic studies of current functioning the retrospective psycholegal issue of insanity. This chapter provides a brief review of commonly used psychological tests and their relevance to criminal responsibility.

Discussion of psychological tests is organized into three major content areas. The first component, projective tests, addresses forensic issues as they relate to the Rorschach, Holtzman, and other commonly employed projective procedures [i.e., Thematic Apperception Test (TAT) and human figure drawings]. The second area, objective personality measures, focuses primarily on the MMPI (Minnesota Multiphasic Personality Inventory) and secondarily on the CPI (California Psychological Inventory) and other related measures. The third area addresses intellectual and neuropsychological procedures. This area includes the WAIS-R (Wechsler Adult Intelligence Scale-Revised), Stanford-Binet, Luria-Nebraska, and Halstead-Reitan. The discussion of psychological tests include a brief summary of reliability and validity literature, the capacity of the test to detect malingering and deception, the generalizability of test findings to forensic populations, and the relevance of the psychological tests to criminal responsibility. Before discussing specific psychological tests, several important conceptual issues on the application of psychometric methods to insanity evaluations are discussed.

The forensic standard for the administration and interpretation of psychological tests should meet and probably exceed standards found in clinical practice. The forensic psychologist must rigorously follow standardized procedures (Kahn and Taft, 1983) in the administration of psychological tests. While some flexibility is allowed in clinical practice for the clinician to exercise his or her personal preference, this practice is clearly inappropriate and should be prohibited in insanity evaluations where the clinician must testify to a reasonable degree of psychological or scientific certainty (refer to chapter 1 on clinician's role). Thus, for example, the use of abbreviated test procedures such as the administration of only eight subtests of the WAIS-R or the use of the Mini-Mult instead of the full MMPI is strongly discouraged.

Scoring of the psychological tests requires the same level of care and exactitude as used in their administration. The absence of standardized scoring is found most frequently with projective testing where the majority of psychologists in clinical practice does not stringently apply standardized scoring systems. Thus, Exner and Exner (1972) found that only 16% of the clinical psychologists surveyed systematically scored the Rorschach by one of the standardized scoring systems. Likewise, the TAT is rarely scored; the clinician relies on his or her judgment. While such an approach may be justified in forming psychotherapeutic hypotheses, it has no place in forensic evaluations. This proscription is based on the likelihood of illusory correlations in which the clinician based his or her interpretations on superficially logical assumptions rather than empirical findings (see Chapman and Chapman, 1971). Potential scoring problems also exist in nonprojective tests. These include careless scoring of the MMPI, including the inaccurate computation of the K correction factor; less than rigorous scoring of intelligence tests (e.g., comprehension and vocabulary subtests of the WAIS-R); and use of inappropriate normative data in translating raw scores to standardized scores. It is therefore recommended that the forensic psychologist not rely on the services of a psychometrist but administer and score (with the possible exception of the MMPI) all testing employed in criminal responsibility evaluations.

The interpretation of psychological tests, at one time considered the sanctum sanctorum of psychological practice, has since the 1960s become an area of increased, and at times embittered, controversy. This controversy centers on the issue of verifiability, with one side arguing for validity as congruence with accepted psychological theory and the other side criticizing this approach as self evident and demanding independent and preferably external measures of validity. The polarization between the theory-congruence and the external-empirical groups is clearly observed in insanity evaluations that must address not only the type of impairment but also its severity. Given the present irresolvability of this conflict, it is recommended that the forensic psychologist adopt strict criteria for making psychological interpretations. Such a position would greatly curtail diagnostic conclusions that were either without empirical support or contrary to psychological theory. Studies of locus of control, for example, represent a synthesis of psychological theory and empirical validation.

The most difficult task for the forensic psychologist is to establish a workable model for truth in test interpretation. Such a model would address not only the basis of interpretation but also the degree of certainty in its accuracy. Table 6.1 proposes five levels of interpretation from unsupported to definite. For any interpretation to be labeled definite, it must have a high degree of accurate classification and consistency with accepted psychological theory.

Such an approach would require a thorough housecleaning of the interpretive literature to make probability estimates on the certainty of specific interpretations. While creating great resistance among many clinicians, such a change would likely improve the stature and respectability of psychometric methods in a manner analogous to the impact of the *Diagnostic and Statistical Manual of Mental Disorders* (*DSM III*) on clinical diagnosis. The close connection between test interpretation and external validation is essential to avoid the inevitable arguments regarding faulty inferences and illusory correlations (e.g., Chapman and Chapman, 1971). Without some form of criterion-related validity, test findings may be criticized for not being representative of the defendant's psychological functioning; not ad-

Table 6.1
Descriptive Ranking of Diagnostic Conclusions and/or Interpretations Based on Psychometric Data

Ranking	Proposed Criteria
0: Unsupported	Research findings are nonsignificant or conflicting.
1: Speculative	Conclusions are consistent with accepted theory and/or supported by one or two studies of limited generalizability.
2: Tentative	Research studies consistently show statistical significance in the expected direction but have little or no practical significance in classifying subjects.
3: Probable	Research studies consistently establish statistical significance in which measures of central tendency or a similar statistic accurately differentiate at least 75% of the criterion groups.
4: Definite	Research findings allow for the accurate classification of 90% or more of individual subjects based on extensive cross-validation research and is congruent with accepted theory.

equately measuring, through its scoring schema, the defendant's dynamics or diagnoses; and not having any established relationship between test responses and the defendant's current or retrospective diagnoses. Given the descriptive nature of the current diagnostic system, it becomes imperative that test response may be convincingly related to accepted external measures.

A related issue of great concern with all psychometric methods is the stability of test findings. In the area of criminal responsibility, the stability of test interpretation is particularly important because of the protracted time lapse between the alleged criminal behavior and the forensic evaluation. During this period of time, significant events may occur that cause either a deterioration in the defendant's functioning (e.g., effects of incarceration and stress of the pending trial) or amelioration (e.g., psychological treatment subsequent to arrest). The forensic clinician is left with the arduous task of sorting out not only the type of psychopathology but also its severity at the time of the offense. Thus, in complicated cases involving protracted time periods of more than six months, psychometric methods may be of greater assistance in confirming current functioning and diagnosis and have only modest relevance to the specific issue of criminal responsibility.

PROJECTIVE METHODS

Rorschach

No area in the psychometric literature has received as much attention or controversy as the reliability and validity of the Rorschach Inkblot Technique. Difficulties in test validation are multiplied by the existence of six distinct systems (i.e., Beck, Hertz, Klopfer, Piotrowski, Rapaport-Schafer, and Exner), each with different administration, scoring, and interpretation methods (Exner, 1969). Thus, validation studies on one system have little or no generalizability to the other five Rorschach systems.

Reliability and validity

Establishing reliability of the Rorschach is a multifaceted process that asks the following questions: Are comparable responses obtained by different clinicians? Is there satisfactory interscorer reliability? Is there consistency among interpretations? With respect to the first question, there is some evidence (e.g., Hersen, 1970) that the sex or ethnic background within the examiner-patient dyad may significantly influence the types and numbers of Rorschach responses. Certainly, additional validation studies are necessary, particularly with the more recent systems (e.g., Exner 1969) to measure these influences properly. With respect to the second question, many available studies address the interscorer reliability of the Rorschach. Such reliability (see Jensen, 1972) is highly dependent on the similarity and the training of the examining psychologists. Jensen reported interscorer reliabilities ranging from .64 to .91. Others, like McArthur (1972), point out that reliability coefficients of .80 to .90 may be achieved if the scoring is limited to only commonly occurring categories. Thus, the Rorschach may achieve adequate to exceptionally high interscorer reliability if the examiners are thoroughly trained in the same system and infrequently used categories are discarded from scoring and subsequent interpretation. Toward this end, Blatt and Berman (1984), strong proponents of the Rorschach, have argued for reduction in the number of Rorschach variables to consolidate the test's scoring.

DeCato (1984) recommended for the Piotrowski system (Piotrowski, 1979) a standardized training format for improving interrater reliability. This program involved a series of Rorschach protocols that were systematically analyzed over a 12-week period to standardize and improve interscorer reliability. At the completion of this program, reliability coefficients of .87 for scoring categories and .97 for summary data were achieved. This study suggested that Rorschach systems have the potential to improve interscorer reliability dramatically. It is also encouraging that Exner (1974), in the development of his Rorschach system, routinely checked interscorer reliability of all variables although these studies are limited typically to fifteen to twenty protocols with highly trained Exner clinicians.

Two important problems must be addressed in examining interscorer reliability, particularly as it relates to forensic evaluations. The first issue is that several of the mentioned studies demonstrate optimum interscorer reliability of the Rorschach when employing highly trained clinicians. Such findings may not be comparable to practicing psychologists without such training or with training in a different Rorschach system. The second problem, which is more disturbing, is the fact that the majority of practicing psychologists does not employ any standardized Rorschach system but utilizes either their own idiosyncratic scoring or no scoring. Surveys by Exner and Exner (1972) and Wade and Baker (1977) suggest that only a small minority of experienced psychologists rigorously follow Rorschach scoring. Therefore, in such cases of nonstandardized scoring, clinicians cannot claim any demonstrable reliability in their scoring and subsequent interpretation.

The third question of test reliability is the consistency of Rorschach interpretations. Such interpretations are highly dependent on the consistency of administrative procedures and interscorer reliability. One study with troublesome results in this regard is that of Little and Schneiderman (cited in Ziskin, 1981), which measured the stability of clinicians' interpretations for the same patients' protocols when reinterpreted after a ten day interval. They found only moderate correlations of .74 to .77; these results are particularly disturbing in light of the clinicians' ability to remember his or her earlier interpretations. Jensen (1972), in summarizing reliability research on Rorschach interpretation, found the level of agreement among clinicians to be inadequate. His review of empirical studies yielded reliability coefficients in the .30 range. Packer (1983) completed a meta-analysis of thirty-nine Rorschach studies that appeared in the *Journal of Personality Assessment.* He found that if Rorschach interpretations were strictly limited to those that were unequivocal on the basis of earlier empirical studies, then reliability coefficients for interpretations of as high as .83 could be achieved. This approach is predicated on a thorough knowledge of the empirical basis for specific interpretations and the differentiation of those that are definite from those with lesser degrees of certainty (see Table 6.1).

Additional constraints on the reliability and concomitant validity of Rorschach interpretations have been found in less rigorous test interpretations. It has been demonstrated, for example, that when clinicians based their interpretations on superficially logical assumptions rather than on empirical findings, there is a greater likelihood of misinterpretation of illusory correlations (Chapman and Chapman, 1969; Rosen, 1975). As noted by Dana (1978), examiner bias and expectancy effects are undisputed components of Rorschach interpretations. Clinicians are likely to be biased by the socioeconomic class of the patient and to see lower class individuals as being more maladjusted and less amenable to treatment (Levy and Kahn, 1970; Trachtman, 1970). In addition, Rorschach interpretations are likely to be influenced by other clinicians' perceptions (e.g., Gordon, 1976) and reflect, in part, the personality characteristics of the examiner (Piciucco, 1976). Finally, the context of the evaluation and the immediate emotional state of the evaluatee may seriously influence Rorschach responses and subsequent interpretations.

Researchers attempting to validate the Rorschach have examined a wide array of factors including the relationship of Rorschach interpretation to psychodynamic theory, use of the Rorschach in the identification of certain personality traits, relationship of Rorschach findings to treatment outcome data. Despite encouraging research in other areas, the forensic clinician is primarily interested in validation studies as they relate to diagnosis and concomitant patterns of psychopathology. This has been unfortunately an area of weakness in Rorschach validation that led Dana (1978) to conclude that psychologists no longer attempt to derive clinical diagnoses from the Rorschach.

In an excellent summary of validity research, Klopfer and Taubee (1976) found inconsistent results when attempting to discriminate with the Rorschach between broad classifications of patients (e.g., between schizophrenic and nonpsychotic patients). Further, in cases of positive findings, there were frequently no replication or cross-validation studies. The clinician is therefore strongly cautioned to employ Rorschach interpretations only where there are sound, empirically based, and cross-validated findings in the assessment of criminal defendants. This recommendation represents a radical departure from customary clinical practice in which the Rorschach is seen as a rich, intuitive tool for the development of psychodynamic hypotheses that may be later confirmed or disconfirmed in psychotherapeutic treatment. In contrast, criminal responsibility assessments are retrospective, not prospective, and must address replicated empirical findings. Parker (1983), in his syntheses of Rorschach studies, found that moderate validity coefficients could be achieved (i.e., .45 to .50) if interpretations were stringently limited to empirically verified findings. Such a housecleaning to avoid overinterpretation would potentially increase the value of Rorschach findings to forensic psychology.

Several additional issues are raised in the usefulness of the Rorschach in current and retrospective diagnoses. For example, Potkay (1972) examined the comparative usefulness of personal history data and Rorschach data in determining patients' diagnoses. He found that experienced psychologists were more accurate at rendering psychiatric diagnoses when given only personal history data in comparison to either Rorschach data or Rorschach plus personal history data. Such conclusions suggest that Rorschach data may in some cases confound the diagnostic process.

A second and important issue is the generalizability of the Rorschach to developmentally disabled patients. Talkington and Reed (1969) examined the accuracy of psychotic indicators from Beck, Hertz, and Klopfer systems for differentiating between psychotic and nonpsychotic retardates. These findings, contingent on replication studies, suggest that Rorschach interpretation of psychopathology may be confounded by organic impairment. This point is underscored by the coarse-grained discrimination required in this study (i.e., between psychotic and nonpsychotic in contrast to specific diagnoses). Schartz and Lazar (1979) have argued that it is inappropriate to compare Rorschach interpretations to clinical diagnosis because of the unreliability of psychiatric diagnosis. Such an argument is less convincing given the moderate to high reliability studies found in the latest revision of the diagnostic nomenclature (American Psychiatric Association, 1980).

In conclusion, diagnostic studies with the Rorschach have indicated that the interpretation of such tests to establish either a current or retrospective diagnosis is of limited usefulness. In areas of cross-validated empirical findings, valuable clinical information regarding an individual defendant's psychopathology may be confirmed.

Malingering and deception

Despite more than 5,000 studies of the Rorschach, only a handful of studies has directly examined issues of malingering and deception. Early simulation studies of the Rorschach (summarized in Rogers and Cavanaugh, 1983b) consistently indicated that subjects could, in accordance with experimental directions, significantly modify their responses. Bash (1978; Bash and Alpert, 1980) was able to establish group means for experienced clinicians detecting differences between malingerers and patients with schizophrenic and nonpsychotic disorders on Rorschach protocols that were scored according to the Klopfer system. This study did not, however, address the accuracy of the identification of malingering patients from others. In a second study, Albert, Fox, and Kahn (1980) studied the ability of experts to detect attempts at malingering. The researchers found that individuals without knowledge of paranoid schizophrenia were misclassified by highly experienced clinicians as psychotic in 46% of the cases, while subjects who listened to a 25-minute tape describing paranoid schizophrenia (i.e., its clinical features, not schizophrenic responses to the Rorschach) were misclassified as psychotic in 72% of the cases. Equally important is the absence of studies of patients' ability to respond defensively (i.e., minimize their impairment) or in a random or irrelevant fashion (i.e., not engaged in the test-taking situation). Such research is imperative to establish the frequency with which defensive or irrelevant responders are misclassified as either disturbed or reflecting certain personality characteristics.

Exner (1978) reported two unpublished studies of the Exner system and its ability to detect malingering. The first study, conducted by Exner and Miller in 1974, reviewed Rorschach protocols on thirty convicted males in presentence evaluations. The protocols demonstrated a paucity of responses and an increase in pure F (i.e., form) answers. With confidentiality guaranteed by representatives of the Legal Aid Society, seven patients who had only pure F answers gave a second set of responses with less indices of emotional control (p. 303). This led Exner to the conclusion that the prisoners were attempting to conceal pathology by limiting their responses. Based on the cursory information available, it is difficult to know whether this result reflects examiner bias (were the graduate students employed as examiners blind to the hypotheses?) or is related to situational variables (would other subjects faced with the readministration of the Rorschach after only 10 days have more C [i.e., color] responses?). Finally, no valid conclusions can be drawn from a limited sample of merely seven subjects.

In a second study of malingering, Exner (1978) reported an unpublished 1975 study by himself and Wiley in which twelve graduate students were asked to produce schizophreniclike Rorschach protocols, of whom only one was successful. It is unclear from the brief description who served as examiners, what was the base rate of schizophrenic to nonschizophrenic protocols, and most important, whether or not the Rorschach protocols were controlled with intelligence. Graduate students who are trained in the Rorschach protocol may have well overplayed their part in attempting to appear too schizophrenic. Results from such a limited sample are hardly generalizable to patient populations in general or beyond the diagnosis of schizophrenia. It is unfortunate that Exner (1978, p. 303), based on these meager empirical data concluded that malingering is "probably impossible if the protocol is collected in accordance with standardized procedures." This conclusion is unfounded, considering the paucity of the subjects limited focus of the studies, and absence of requisite cross-validation research.

Applicability to forensic evaluations

Few studies have examined the applicability of the Rorschach to either forensic populations in general or the specific issue of criminal responsibility. Prandoni and Swartz (1978) attempted to establish normative data for adult offenders referred to the forensic psychiatry division. On the basis of 130 usable Rorschach protocols, they distinguished norms for psychotic, organic, and nonpsychotic/nonorganic offenders that showed substantial differences when compared to Beck's adult normative population. Such findings suggest that additional normative studies may be important for insanity evaluatees to identify accurately the psychopathology of this specific subpopulation. Further, data from Edinger and Bogan (1976) suggest that the prognostic signs on the Rorschach may not be generalizable to incarcerated offenders enrolled in a drug abuse program. These two studies underscore a point made by Exner (1978, p. 302) with respect to forensic evaluations, "questions focused on narrow issues, sometimes selected from a broader context, and thus are difficult, if not impossible, to answer from most data."

The specific application of the Rorschach to criminal responsibility evaluations is seriously questioned be Ziskin (1981), who indicated, based on his clinical experience, that different clinicians elicit different Rorschach responses and make conflicting conclusions about these resulting Rorschach protocols. A survey of forensic psychiatrists (Rogers and Cavanaugh, 1983*b*) found that most of those surveyed placed less weight on Rorschach interpretation than on other clinical measures. Further, forensic psychiatrists, while requesting the Rorschach in 28% of the insanity evaluations, tended to overestimate its psychometric properties.

The only study that directly addressed the usefulness of the Rorschach in criminal responsibility evaluations was conducted by Kahn (1967). This study correlated the measure of reality adherence on the basis of F scores with the clinical judgments of sanity/insanity. Kahn does not specify whether the Rorschach data were available to forensic clinicians, thereby contaminating these correlations. Considering this potential limitation, his findings suggest a moderate correlation ($r = .49$) between the overall levels of F and their clinical evaluation of sanity based on the M'Naghten standard. It is interesting that Kahn also found an association between this measure of form level and intellectual functioning ($r = .35$), which raises the issue of whether form level is assessing psychopathology, intellectual abilities, or both.

This relative dearth of empirical studies regarding the appropriateness and usefulness of the Rorschach in criminal responsibility evaluations suggests that forensic clinicians should be very cautious in applying Rorschach interpretations to specific insanity standards. Given the highly specialized nature of criminal responsibility evaluations and the need for retrospective diagnoses, it is recommended that the Rorschach test be limited to providing corroborative data regarding current functioning. It is further recommended that with the Rorschach, as with all psychometric approaches, only interpretations of a probable or definite nature be included in criminal forensic evaluations. By implementing such guidelines, clinicians utilizing the Rorschach may present defensible conclusions based on cross-validated research.

Holtzman Inkblot Technique

The Holtzman Inkblot Technique (HIT) represents a major research effort to integrate the qualitatively rich projective interpretations with more empirically based psychometric methods. The HIT is a result of an extensive investigation of 4,500 original inkblots that, through a series of preliminary studies, were refined to two equivalent sets of 45 inkblots, evoking a wide range of responses on the HIT determinants. The HIT (Holtzman, Thorpe, Swartz, and Herron, 1961) allows only one response per inkblot, which is subsequently scored on twenty-two HIT variables. Validation studies (Hill, 1972) have included diverse samples of several thousand protocols covering a spectrum of mental disorders, chronological ages, and cultural backgrounds.

Reliability and validity

The HIT has demonstrated a high degree of reliability with respect to interscorer reliability, split-half reliability, test-retest reliability, and equivalency of forms A and B. Holtzman (1984b) reported a study of forty schizophrenic patients whose responses were independently scored by two clinicians. The clinicians showed a very high degree of agreement on the individual determinants, with reliability coefficients ranging from .89 to .99. Further, clinicians with only a modest degree of training (i.e., twelve protocols) yielded median reliability coefficients of .86 on a sample of psychiatric patients. In addition, as an index of internal consistency, comparisons of odd versus even responses yielded a high degree of consistency regardless of the population tested (see Holtzman, 1984a). Thirteen of the twenty-two HIT variables had coefficients higher than .80; unsatisfactory internal consistency was found for only one variable (i.e., popular responses).

The test-retest reliability was obtainable because of the equivalent forms of the HIT. These studies (see Holtzman, 1984b) yielded stability coefficients ranging from a level of .36 for popular responses to a high of .82 for location with one week intervals between test administrations. Other studies (in Holtzman, 1984b) of test reliability have been conducted with time intervals of 3 months to 1 year; these studies have found a moderate degree of stability across test administrations.

While the HIT is more systematic in its interpretation than the Rorschach, both through its unidimensional rating of HIT variables and its centralization of clinical interpretive material (Hill, 1972), few, if any, studies have examined the reliability of different clinicians' interpretations. Thus, although the HIT has demonstrated moderate to high levels of test reliability, there are no sufficient studies concerning the consistency of clinical interpretation.

The HIT validity studies, because of their diversity, are difficult to summarize. Holtzman (1984a) has established through a series of validation studies three major factors that have remained consistent across clinical samples. Factor 1, perceptual maturity and integrated ideational activity (i.e., a combination of movement, integration, human, and barrier scores), has been associated with individuals' coping capacity and creativity. Factor 2, perceptual sensitivity (i.e., color, shading, and form definiteness scores), has been related to emotional expression and response to stress. Factor 3, psychopathology of thought (pathognomic verbalization, anxiety, and hostility scores), has been well documented on diagnosis of psychotic thinking and with certain variations of scores with anxiety disorders and aggression. In addition to these major factors, a large number of studies have examined the relationship of individual variables to specific personality types or psychopathology. These are summarized in a comprehensive bibliography by Swartz, Reinehr, and Holtzman (1983).

The majority of validity studies has examined the relationship of one or more factors or variables to personality constellations. Less emphasis has been placed on the relationship of specific variables to either the type or degree of psychological impairment. Thus, highly deviated scores with respect to normative data yield only global impressions regarding the individual's psychological functioning. It may be argued, given the complexity of the HIT, that such finely tuned clinical conclusions are indeed beyond the scope of any projective method. Such an argument carries less weight in forensic evaluations where the burden falls squarely on the clinician to make precise and well-validated diagnostic conclusions.

One primary goal of the HIT is to reduce the amount of contamination through examiner and situational effects. This problem was addressed (Holtzman, Thorpe, Swartz, and Herron, 1961) by limiting the number of responses to one per inkblot, a potential source of contamination of the Rorschach. In addition, the HIT was designed (Hill, 1972) so that inquiry into the determinants of inkblot responses followed each card.

Studies of the HIT show that it is still vulnerable to certain examiner variables. For example, Megargee, Lockwood, Cato, and Jones (1966) found that experimentally modified emotional attitudes of the examiner (i.e., warm, neutral, and cold attitudes) produced significant differences on seven of twenty-one HIT variables, with warm examiners producing more verbal responses. This finding was confirmed by Hamilton and Robertson (1966). An interesting question not asked by these studies was whether these differences in individual variables would have made concomitant differences in examiners' interpretations. An earlier study by Simkins (1960) found that the use of positive reinforcement in the form of nodding or making comments like "That's fine" influenced in the expected direction both the determinants and the content of the responses. This finding was supported through studies by Bienen (1962) and Burke (1963). The HIT may well be vulnerable to subtle extraclinical factors. Unlike the Rorschach, there is a paucity of research regarding Holtzman interpretation and how such interpretations might vary due to the race, sex, or socioeconomic status of the patient.

Several studies have examined how situational variables may influence responses to the HIT. Interestingly, von Rosenstiel (1973) created an environmental situation in which subjects were purposely frustrated (i.e., given a pseudo-IQ test and reported to have a low intelligence) and found an increase in hostility scores on the HIT. Such findings are logical and provided support of the sensitivity of the HIT in the detection of hostility. It poses, however, a somewhat different question in forensic evaluations, which are conducted within an adversarial context and are sometimes frustrating to the defendant. A forensic clinician must be sensitive to the possibility that hostility observed in Holtzman responses may partially reflect the situational characteristics of a forensic assessment.

A second study of interest (Taylor, Altman, Wheeler, and Kushner, 1969) examined the effects of social isolation of HIT protocols. This study required pairs of male subjects to be confined for 8 days in small rooms with only minimal stimulation. Comparisons of pre- and post-HIT administrations demonstrated significant differences for eight variables involving primarily Holtzman's factors 1 and 2. While such findings are not surprising, they suggest that some perceptual disturbances may reflect the effects of social isolation (e.g., being held in detention cells) as a factor independent of a defendant's overall psychological functioning. Thus, several important situational factors must be considered in the overall interpretation of HIT protocols. It may well be advisable not to administer any inkblot technique to an individual who has been held in isolation (correctional or mental health) for several days.

Malingering and deception

No studies have directly addressed the possibility of faking the Holtzman, although it appears that all projective methods are vulnerable to malingering. Although Klieger (1969) found no significant differences in HIT responses for subjects with low and high social desirability, other researchers have observed that subjects may modify their response in relationship to their situational expectations. For example, Krieger and Levin (1976) found that schizophrenics gave less pathological responses when they believed that the examiner was unaware of their patient status.

The length of the HIT may make it difficult for potential malingerers to present a consistent picture of gross psychopathology. The clinician may wish to compare responses from the first half to the second across HIT scoring categories because although schizophrenic patients may show deterioration in their responses, one would not expect dramatic improvements in the quality of their responses. In cases of marked discrepancy or suspected deception administering the other Holtzman set may be justified.

Applicability to forensic evaluations

One advantage of the Holtzman over other projective techniques is the availability of normative data for forensic patients. Mullen (1980) conducted two major studies with forensic patients, including one sample from a Texas maximum security hospital ($N = 269$) and a cross-validation study with patients from Illinois and Massachusetts ($N = 195$). These data suggested that forensic patients differ from other criterion groups (Mullen, Reinehr, and Swartz, 1982), which may facilitate interpretation. Mullen found, however, that the HIT was not effective at discriminating between potentially violent and nonviolent forensic patients (see Mullen and Reinehr, 1982).

No studies have examined the efficacy of the HIT in criminal responsibility evaluations. Its emphasis on psychometric soundness and the presence of forensic norms would recommend its use over other projective methods in the evaluation of sanity. The HIT thus should properly be limited to confirming/disconfirming current psychopathology and not be related to the ultimate issue of criminal responsibility.

Human Figure Drawings

A commonly utilized projective technique is the Draw-A-Person Test, which was developed by Machover (1949). This technique assumes that individuals will project important symbolic representations of their psychopathology onto their drawings of a male and female. Although Machover developed a systematic approach to scoring human figure drawings, most clinicians employ their own idiosyncratic interpretations.

Reliability and validity

Attempts to validate empirically the analytically based interpretations of Machover have largely failed. Swensen (1957) and Roback (1968) systematically evaluated research on human figure drawings and their relationship to Machover's hypotheses. Roback, for example, found three of Machover's interpretations to be supported (i.e., hair, joints, and types of lines), seven to have conflicting evidence (i.e., head, eyes, ears, clothing, size, shading, and sexual treatment), ten to be not supported empirically (i.e., facial expression, lips, nose, eyebrows, head and arms, legs and feet, hips and buttocks, waistline, placement, and erasure), and eleven interpretations had not been tested.

Swensen (1968) did an updated review of human figure drawings. He found in his literature search that clinicians were able to rate the overall characteristics of the Draw-A-Person with a moderate degree of interrater reliability in areas involving the overall drawing quality. He also found several studies that demonstrated small but statistically significant reliabilities for individual signs. He concluded, however, that most of the diagnostic signs of human figure drawings had probably too low reliabilities to make reliable clinical judgments.

Recent research has suggested that human figure drawings assess primarily the artistic ability of the individual being evaluated and not a degree of psychological impairment. In a carefully designed study, Feher, Vandecreek, and Teglasi (1983) found that experienced clinicians could not effectively distinguish between normal and psychotic individuals on the basis of human figure drawings. Independent ratings of the subjects' artistic ability were found, however, to account for much of the variance in clinicians' judgments regarding impairment. More discouraging was the fact that even when experienced clinicians were warned that artistic ability is often a confounding factor, the accuracy of their judgments was not improved. These findings regarding the Draw-A-Person test as primarily a measure of artistic ability have been supported by research (Cressen, 1975).

Applicability to forensic evaluations

The clinical utility of human figure drawings in criminal responsibility evaluations is extremely limited. If a technique cannot make even gross discrimination between normal and psychotic subjects, then it is difficult to imagine its validity for subtler interpretations. Further, considering the adversarial context of insanity evaluations, the degree to which these drawings are under the voluntary control of the defendant needs to be assessed. It is very likely that defendants may grossly distort their human figure drawings to be indistinguishable from those of other apparently impaired individuals. In one notorious case, a clinician made numerous interpretations regarding the primitive nature of a defendant's drawings without realizing that the defendant had made several integrated and normal drawings within the last month.

Variations of the human figure drawings include the house-tree-person test and the kinetic family drawing test. Green and Schaefer (1984) reviewed the validity of these related projective techniques and found, for example, that the house-tree-person test was unsuccessful at making basic discriminations between adjusted and maladjusted subjects. In addition, they conclude that the kinetic family drawings are completely deficient from a psychometric perspective. This latter procedure lacks adequate standardization or data substantiating either its reliability or validity.

In conclusion, there appears to be no justification for the use of human figure drawings or their variations in criminal responsibility evaluations. The absence of satisfactory test-retest reliability as well as these techniques' inability to make even general discriminations militate against their inclusion in the psychometric evaluation of criminal defendants.

Thematic Apperception Test

The TAT was originally developed by Murray in 1943 as a method of exploring personality dimensions focusing on the patient's needs, press (i.e., internal states as they relate to external forces), and thema (i.e., need-press combinations reflecting the individual's motivational trends). Since this early development, attempts have been made to utilize the TAT in psychodynamic formulations, as a diagnostic tool, and as a measure of fantasy and motivational trends. Application of the TAT to forensic evaluations involves primarily its clinical utility in the psychodiagnostic assessment of the defendant.

Reliability and validity

The reliability of the TAT is severely constrained by the absence of standardized administration, ordering and presentation of cards, and an interpretive system. Despite cogent arguments during the development of the TAT (e.g., Tomkins, 1947; Murstein, 1965) for a single standardized procedure, the administration and interpretation of the TAT remain highly individualistic. The obvious question remains, Are any generalized estimates of reliability possible when different clinicians use different cards, different numbers of cards, and in different sequences?

The existing literature suggests that satisfactory levels of interscorer reliability can be achieved when clinicians are trained in the same scoring system. Both the work of Zubin, Eron, and Schumer (1965) and early research on the TAT by Feld and Smith (1958) and Dana (1965) were able to achieve high reliabilities based on their respective scoring systems. Estimates of test-retest reliability have been unacceptably low; Kraiger, Hakel, and Cornelius (1984), in summarizing previous research, report a median test-retest correlation of only .30. It has been argued that such low estimates may be an artifact of the retest instructions. Winter and Stewart (1977) examined the effect of instructing subjects to tell similar or different stories and found a greater degree of consistency among subjects asked to tell similar stories. Kraiger, Hakel, and Cornelius (1984) found correspondingly lower test-retest correlations ($r = .38$) when respondents were given these instructions. It may also be asserted that such instructions tend to overestimate the reliability and may be more a function of the subject's memory than of the stability of the TAT. This finding is supported by Holmes's research (1974) that found only a 35% agreement in the measurement of personality characteristics in a test-retest experiment utilizing a 3-week interval.

Studies have not tended to address the reliability of clinicians' interpretations of the TAT. It should be expected, however, to have a low degree of agreement, considering the obvious constraints on TAT reliability. Although the TAT has the potential for satisfactory interscorer reliability, this may have little bearing on its usefulness in clinical practice. The large majority of clinicians does not utilize any of the available scoring systems but rather opts for their individualistic impressions. Thus, most TAT interpretations have no semblance of standardization and, therefore, no established reliability.

The open-ended approach of the TAT and the diversity of clinical applications militate against the establishment of its validity. Perhaps the most promising validation research has been studies of the TAT and its relationship to certain personality dimensions such as achievement, affiliation, and power. Although these studies (see Eron, 1972) may have practical applications, they do not address the validity of the TAT as a clinical tool. Studies of the TAT and its relationships to other psychometric measures such as the adjective checklist, Edwards Personal Preference Schedule, and the HIT have had limited success. Further, in the area of clinical diagnosis, the ability of the TAT to discriminate between different clinical groups has not been established.

Empirical studies have shown a patchwork (see Klopfer and Taubee, 1976) of positive and negative findings with respect to diagnosis. As a related issue, most of the positive findings have not been cross validated, which raises serious questions regarding the generalizability of these results. This situation has led Swartz (1978, p. 697) to conclude, "when Morgan and Murray constructed the TAT, they thought they provided a method for a psychological investigation that presented subjects with ambiguous stimuli. For the many variations in administration, scoring, and interpretations, it seems that the TAT is equally ambiguous for examiners."

The ability of the TAT to assist in current and retrospective diagnoses of defendants remains equivocal. For example, Eron (1975) studied the TAT protocols of 150 subjects consisting of 25 nonhospitalized neurotics, 25 hospitalized neurotics, 25 hospitalized schizophrenics, a group of other hospitalized patients, and two control groups. He was able to establish group differences in emotional tone, story outcome, and perceptual distortions. However, he was unable to establish any TAT indicators that differentiated one clinical group from the other three. Although successful clinical discriminations have been made between various criterion groups (Eron, 1972) including paranoid and nonparanoid psychiatric populations, brain-damaged patients and controls, and homosexual and nonhomosexual students, none of these findings has been successfully replicated. This result caused Swartz (1978) to conclude that the TAT is not suited for differential diagnosis.

Review papers have conceded that the TAT is influenced by a number of extra clinical-factors. For example, Murstein (1965) reported significant differences in TAT protocols due to the race of the examiner and examinee, sex, and socioeconomic background. Murstein concluded that any TAT study must involve the interaction of the stimuli (i.e., the TAT cards), the patients' background, and the interpersonal characteristics of the examiner-examinee relationship. Others have reported differences as a result of intelligence and possibly verbal reinforcement (Zubin, Eron, and Schumer, 1965), situational cues (Atkinson, 1965), and the sexual attractiveness of the experimenter (Clark, 1965). In addition, Dana (1972) has established that these extra-clinical factors may likewise influence the examiner's interpretation of a TAT protocol. Within the context of criminal forensic evaluations, interpretations made by clinicians of different socioeconomic, racial, and cultural backgrounds than the defendant should be considered suspect in light of these empirical findings.

Malingering and deception

Few studies have directly examined the susceptibility of the TAT to malingering and deception. Holmes (1974), in a well-designed study, asked subjects to complete an abbreviated TAT and directed them to respond honestly an to malinger. In the first experiment, respondents were successfully able to fake a high need for achievement; in a second experiment, the subjects were able to modify significantly their personality characteristics. Consistent with an earlier review by Holmes (1968), abundant evidence indicates that individuals are aware of the personality characteristics they reveal in projective testing. The second component of Holmes's more recent research (1974) involved the evaluation by an experienced clinician of the TAT protocols to identify those subjects who are faking. The clinician, serving as an independent judge, was unable to distinguish malingered from honest TAT protocols.

Eron (1972) reviewed earlier studies that demonstrated that patients' responses were subjected to conscious control and that the TAT was susceptible to faking. His research has shown that nearly all psychometric approaches are vulnerable to malingering and deception (see also Rogers, 1984b). Unfortunately with respect to the TAT, empirical indicators for the detection of deception are lacking. Therefore, it cannot be assumed that the TAT protocol of criminal defendant (particularly considering the adversarial context of insanity evaluations) is an accurate representation of that individual's personality characteristics.

Applicability to forensic evaluations

A major area of research interest with the TAT is aggressive fantasies; many of these studies have included research on violent and nonviolent offenders. The relationship, however, between violent fantasies on a TAT and overt aggressive behavior is unclear. In one study, Purcell (1956) found a positive relationship between aggressive fantasies and three groups of individuals with varying degrees of antisocial behavior. It is interesting that he found that these three criterion groups could not be differentiated simply on the basis of aggressive content but only through a formal scoring system. Considerable research has shown, however, an opposite trend, with violent offenders manifesting lower aggressive fantasies than nonviolent offenders. For example, Keltikangas-Jarvinen (1982) reported an inverse relationship between the violence in TAT stories and offenders' history of aggression. A similar relationship has been found with juvenile offenders (Matranga, 1976) and in a somewhat confounded study of mentally retarded offenders (Silber and Courtless, 1968).

Also germane to forensic evaluations is the research literature examining various personality characteristics of offender populations. For example, Scott (1982) found that violent rapists differed from other violent offenders in their decreased needs for autonomy, dominance, and nurturance. Other research has attempted to differentiate types of aggression (i.e., intropunitive from extrapunitive) with inmate populations (e.g., Inman, 1977). Such research has little direct relevance to forensic assessment.

No research has addressed the clinical utility of the TAT in criminal responsibility evaluations. Considering the psychometric constraints of the TAT with its limited reliability and validity, it is unlikely that the TAT would have any direct relevance to evaluations of criminal responsibility. While TAT cards that bear a resemblance to the criminal behavior in question may have some intrinsic appeal to the forensic clinician, there are no empirical data to support their use. More disturbing has been attempts by psychologists to interpret TAT protocols with respect to the aggressive behavior of a particular defendant. As noted, the relationship of aggressive tendencies on the TAT to violent behavior has not been empirically established, although the preponderance of research would suggest an inverse relationship. Tomkin (1947, p. 20) recommended "a strategic retreat involving temporary abandonment of the clinical applications of the test in favour of a study of the conditions under which valid and invalid inferences may be drawn from the protocol." This recommendation is reaffirmed with respect to the TAT and its specialized application in insanity evaluations.

Hand Test

The Hand Test (Bricklin, Piotrowski, and Wagner, 1978) consists of ten drawings in which nine depict hands in different gestures and the final card is blank. The patient's responses are scored with respect to their content for eleven categories. This test has unfortunately been described by its developers, on the text manual's cover, as having the capacity to predict "potentially aggressive overt behavior." Considering limitations in the normative sample with overlap in scores among criterion groups, limited measures of reliability (e.g., Panek and Stoner, 1979), and the absence of sufficient validation, it is strongly recommended that the Hand Test not be used in forensic evaluations. Studies have yielded mixed results in attempting to utilize the Hand Test to differentiate between aggressive and non-aggressive patients. Although Wagner and Medvedeff (1963) found significant differences between violent and nonviolent samples, more recent research has failed to confirm these results (Drummond, 1966; Himelstein and Grunau, 1981). More important, no research has demonstrated the predictive or postdictive validity of the Hand Test for aggressive behavior.

OBJECTIVE PERSONALITY MEASURES

Minnesota Multiphasic Personality Inventory (MMPI)

The Minnesota Multiphasic Personality Inventory or MMPI was developed by Hathaway and McKinley as an objective method for the routine workup of adult psychiatric patients (see Hathaway, 1946). Early development of the MMPI included an item pool of over 1,000 statements. This was later refined into a 566-item true-and-false test with items included based on their ability to differentiate among clinical groups. This form led to the gradual development (see Greene, 1980) of individual scales that differentiate clinical syndromes. Basic MMPI interpretation is based on three validity scales and ten basic clinical scales that are augmented by numerous additional clinical and research scales.

Reliability and validity

Research on the reliability of the MMPI has demonstrated its stability across time and the internal consistency of its basic scales. Dahlstrom, Welch, and Dahlstrom (1975) have summarized research on the MMPI's test-retest reliability. Utilizing an interval of 1 to 2 weeks, they report an average reliability coefficient of .80 for males and .76 for females, utilizing the three validity and ten clinical scales. Two similar studies (Stone, 1965; Sines, Silver, and Lucero, 1961) with psychiatric patients demonstrated a moderate degree of stability of the MMPI across a 1-year interval; these researchers found an average reliability coefficient of .49 for males and .50 for females.

Dahlstrom, Welsh, and Dahlstrom (1975) summarized four major studies of internal consistency. These studies, while showing some variability, report moderate coefficients for the individual clinical scales, with the majority of reliability coefficients exceeding .60. Finally, research by Goldberg and Rorer (1963) examined the stability of individual MMPI responses over a 4-week interval. Results of the study indicated a high degree of concordance between the two test administrations with high to exceptionally high tetrachoric correlations.

It is difficult to assess, in any overall sense, the test validity of the MMPI. The MMPI has been adapted to such a diversity of mental health, medical, criminal justice, educational, and vocational applications that it is necessary to look at construct- and criterion-related validity with reference to a particular designated topic. Toward this end, the validity of the MMPI with respect to the identification of psychopathology and diagnosis is briefly reviewed. Research in this area, based on an actuarial model, involves a systematic comparison of subjects' MMPI responses with independent judgments by clinicians. Although such studies were limited by the relative absence of standardized measures for clinical judgment, as well as the unreliability of psychiatric diagnosis, basic constellations of personality characteristics were empirically established (see Hathaway and Meehl, 1951). What emerged was the relative inefficacy of employing single-scale elevations for the discrimination of diagnostic classification. Instead, two-point codes emerged as a more effective method in identifying patterns of psychopathology.

Marks and Seeman (1963) conducted a large-scale research effort on the MMPI and its relationship to patient characteristics, including case history, mental status, and treatment outcome. They were able to establish sixteen MMPI profiles that accounted for 78% of their sample's MMPI configurations. These profiles were compared to data on patients' personal history, mental status, critical symptoms, and response to treatment.

A larger and more rigorous validation study was carried out by Gynther and his associates (Gynther, Altman, Warbin, and Sletten, 1972; Gynther, Altman and Sletten, 1973), which involved extensive and replicated research. This study included four samples: Sample 1 had 1,259 patients with both MMPIs and independent clinical evaluations; sample 2 was 1,445 patients with the same standardized clinical evaluations as a replication for sample 1; and samples 3 and 4 involved different independent evaluation forms with a combined total of 1,807 cases. Clinical interpretations were considered valid only if they were supported by replicated research with independent clinical judgment. Seventeen distinct MMPI profiles were identified, accounting for approximately 76% of the patients seen in inpatient and outpatient public mental health facilities.

In addition to large-scale research, hundreds of research studies have examined specific code types with clinical and nonclinical populations. Distillations of these research studies are readily available (Dahlstrom, Welsh, and Dahlstrom, 1972; Graham, 1977; Greene, 1980). At the peril of overgeneralization, these studies have found many patterns of psychopathology that are consistently related to criterion validity. The inherent difficulty with the MMPI, given its voluminous literature, is for the clinician to differentiate empirically established findings from clinically intuitive interpretations.

One potential constraint on the MMPI test validity is the tendency for clinicians to overinterpret MMPI profiles. What is clearly needed is for clinicians to differentiate between replicated actuarial findings and other judgments that must necessarily be considered tentative. This also requires a sensitivity to the validation samples utilized in the development of criterion-based interpretations. For example, the work of Gilberstadt and Duker (1965) was developed on an all-male veteran administration population and is clearly inapplicable to females.

A related issue is the clinical utility of the MMPI in psychiatric diagnosis. Earlier studies based on *DSM II* (e.g., Dahlstrom, Welsh, and Dahlstrom, 1975) or on International Classification of Disorders (ICD 9) (Page, 1982) are not generalizable to more criterion-based diagnostic nosology like the *DSM III* (American Psychiatric Association, 1980). Initial studies have shown that previous configural rules will need to be modified for *DSM III* diagnosis (see Rogers, Wasyliw, and Dolmetsch, 1982). Simple correlations between diagnoses and two-point codes are not likely to be successful. This is exemplified by the difficulties in establishing a modal MMPI profile for the *DSM III* diagnosis of a borderline personality disorder. Various researchers (e.g., Snyder, Pitts, Goodpastor, Sajadi, and Gustin, 1982; Patrick, 1984) found a variety of two-point elevations for borderline patients that typically include an elevation on scale 8. This lack of specificity would suggest the need for multivariate studies of *DSM III* diagnoses with subsequent replications. One fruitful beginning is the research of Vincent (1983) who was able to discriminate common psychiatric diagnoses with MMPI elevations.

In the examination of extraclinical factors, much emphasis has been placed on racial differences. Greene (1980), in examining differences between black and white subjects, found that black subjects had higher elevations on F, 1, 2, 8, and 9. In contrast, white subjects showed greater elevations on scales 3 and 6. Little research has attempted to explain these differences and their relationship to diagnosis. Studies have suggested that blacks may be overpathologized in certain circumstances (e.g., Fowler and Erdberg, 1971) and may give profiles that are difficult to replicate on the basis of clinical correlates (e.g., Gynther, Altman, and Warbin, 1973). These limited data would suggest that clinicians be highly conservative in their interpretations of scales F, 8, and 9 for black patients (see Greene, 1980).

Several larger and more recent studies have questioned whether the MMPI is racially biased. A study by Bertelson, Marks, and May (1982) compared black and white subjects who were matched for a number of crucial variables including sex, age, socioeconomic status, rural or urban residence, employment, years of education, marital status, hospital status, and date of MMPI testing. They found in this study of 231 black and 231 white male and female psychiatric patients no significant effect due to race and no significant differences between blacks and whites on the number of clinical scales greater than 70. They concluded that differences in earlier research may be the result of uncontrolled sociodemographic characteristics. Finally, Butcher, Braswell, and Rainey (1983) found differences between black and white patients but attributed them to true differences in the patients' psychopathology.

Studies of Mexican-Americans have centered on male prisoners and have shown divergent results from those obtained with white prisoners (i.e., lower scores on scales 3, 4, 5, and 6; see Holland, 1979). Other studies, while differing from Holland's research, suggest that Mexican-Americans either experience less psychological distress or are less willing to report it (Greene, 1980).

Research with Chinese and Japanese samples has focused only on college students (Sue and Sue, 1974). These authors found that among individuals requesting treatment at the student health psychiatric clinic, Oriental students had greater elevations on scales L, F, and zero, with male Orientals having additional greater elevations on 1, 2, 4, 6, 7, and 8. It is unclear whether such differences reflect greater psychopathology or whether there are cultural reasons why Oriental students with fewer problems might not seek treatment. In the absence of norms for these minority groups, forensic clinicians should be conservative in their interpretations based on scales in which racial differences have been noted.

Malingering and deception

The MMPI is distinguished from all other psychometric methods by the emphasis placed on the identification of dissimulation and malingering. Within the standard profile interpretation, there are three validity scales for the detection of deception. These include the L scale, including fifteen items whose responses represent unusually laudable behavior that is rarely endorsed by most people; the K scale, consisting of thirty items covering a wide range of psychological adjustment and interpersonal relationships, which is seen as a subtler measure of defensiveness; and the F scale, consisting of sixty-four items that denote unusual psychological impairment rarely observed in or endorsed by psychiatric patients. In addition, the relative elevation of F and K is often considered in the form of the F-K index. This index, devised by Gough (1947, 1950), consists of the raw score of K substracted from the raw score of F. It has been found to be moderately successful in the detection of malingering (Grow, McVaugh, and Eno, 1980) although of questionable usefulness in the detection of defensiveness. While most MMPI interpretations in clinical practice are limited to these four indicators, several additional and perhaps more sophisticated methods are available for the detection of dissimulation on the MMPI.

An effective approach to the detection of dissimulation has been to compare obvious and subtle items. Obvious items (Wiener and Harmon, 1946) are those that are clearly associated with psychopathology in contrast to subtle items. It was expected that individuals attempting to malinger would exaggerate the obvious items in relationship to the subtle items, while those attempting to minimize their psychopathology would suppress obvious items. Research has demonstrated that comparison of obvious and subtle items can be effective at detecting both response sets (Anthony, 1971; Harvey and Sipprelle, 1976). These results were confirmed by Gynther, Burkhart, and Hovanitz (1979), who utilized five categories of item subtlety: very subtle, subtle, neutral, obvious, and very obvious.

Greene (1980) has proposed several clinical guidelines for the detection of dissimulation based on obvious versus subtle items. By utilizing the Weiner and Harmon (1946) subtle and obvious subscales, he established that a 20 or more point difference in the same direction on four or more subscales was indicative of malingering or defensiveness (i.e., if obvious is elevated, the patient is malingering; if obvious is suppressed, then the patient is responding defensively). Further, Greene (1984) has established that an overall difference between obvious and subtle subscales that exceeded 160 meant the patient was definitely overreporting his or her psychopathology. In utilizing either of these procedures, it is necessary to rule out random or inconsistent responses since these may confound the interpretation (see Rogers, 1983).

Other approaches to the detection of dissimulation include Gough's dissimulation scale (Gough, 1957) and the frequency of endorsed critical items (Greene, 1984). Gough's scale, which consists of forty items, has less applicability in criminal forensic evaluations since its goal is to identify those patients who are attempting to simulate neuroticism. Preliminary research (see Anthony, 1971) suggested that the scale might also be effective in identifying male patients with nonpsychotic diagnoses who are attempting to exaggerate their presenting symptoms. Greene (1980, 1984) recommended a cutoff point on Gough's dissimulation scale of T score of greater than 70 for the identification of individuals who are overreporting their psychopathology.

As an additional approach to deception, Greene (1984) recommended an examination of the Lachar and Wrobel (1979) critical item list. He indicated that patients blatantly attempting to malinger will often endorse critical items above the ninety-ninth percentile. Thus, any MMPI profile which exceeds the cutoff score of eighty-three critical items should be strongly suspected of malingering.

Another source of invalid profiles is individuals who respond in a random or irrelevant manner. Such individuals (Rogers, 1984*b*), whether as a result of low reading comprehension, psychotic interference, indifference for the evaluation, or hostility, do not become psychologically engaged in the test-taking situation and give nonmeaningful, often random responses. Although such individuals may be detected through extreme elevations of the F scale (e.g., Colligan, 1976), they may be more accurately identified by two special scales: the test-retest (TR) index and the carelessness scale. The TR index (Buechley and Ball, 1952; Greene, 1979) consists of sixteen pairs of repeated items, which are employed as a measure of the patient's consistency. The carelessness scale (Greene, 1978) utilizes twelve pairs of MMPI items that are judged to be opposite in their content. This latter scale provides a somewhat more sophisticated approach to evaluating the patient's consistency of responding. Rogers and his colleagues (Rogers, Dolmetsch, and Cavanaugh, 1983; Rogers, Thatcher, and Cavanaugh, 1984) have cross-validated various cutoff scores for the detection of irrelevant responding. Two classification rules are: (1) TR index greater than 4 and F greater than 70 and (2) carelessness score greater than 4 and F greater than 70; both rules provide a 95% accuracy in classifying random and nonrandom profiles. Further, Nichols and Greene (1983) have established actuarial tables based on these scales for differentiating between random and nonrandom samples. Finally, Greene (1984) has established that if either TR or carelessness scale scores are above 6 or the sum of both scales is greater than 9, then the profile has highly inconsistent responses.

Applicability to forensic evaluations

There is extensive literature on the use of the MMPI in the assessment of criminal behavior (see Dahlstrom, Welsh, and Dahlstrom, 1975, chapter 3). Studies either frequently examined different types of offenders and their respective MMPI profiles or have attempted to utilize MMPI scales to differentiate between violent and nonviolent offenders. Attempts to typologize offenders' MMPIs by their current offense have been unsuccessful (e.g., Rader, 1977; Langevin, Paitich, Orchard, Handy, and Russon, 1982). More successful have been attempts to classify assaultive offenders on a dimension of overcontrol versus undercontrol. Based on the work of Megargee (1966), several researchers have been able to differentiate types of violent behaviors among offenders (e.g., Henderson, 1983) and forensic patients (Quinsey, MacGuire, and Varney, 1983). Others have employed a variety of strategies including the sum of F, 4, and 9 scores (e.g., Huesmann, Lefkowitz, and Eron, 1978; Mungas, 1984) or a variety of discriminant functions (e.g., Jones, Beidleman, and Fowler, 1981; Chick, Loy, and White, 1984). While such studies are of interest to the forensic clinician, they rarely offer clinically relevant information about the defendant's criminal responsibility.

Several studies have examined forensic patients in pretrial evaluations. Cooke (1969) studied 215 male forensic patients and found only modest differences on MMPI profiles between those judged competent and incompetent to stand trial. In a second study, Holcomb, Adams, Ponder, and Anderson (1984) examined 96 male offenders admitted to the state maximum security forensic unit for a pretrial psychiatric evaluation. They concluded that the MMPI scales, particularly F and 8, did measure psychopathology within this population and that high F scale profiles were often the result of psychopathology. A third study, by Audubon and Kirwin (1982), indicated that NGRI (not guilty by reason of insanity) patients might in posttrial evaluations seriously minimize this psychopathology as compared to pretrial evaluations. Since validity indicators were utilized in differentiating between low and high defensive individuals, their ability to detect such response biases was not studied.

Two studies have examined the MMPI profiles within the context of criminal responsibility evaluations. Kurlychek and Jordan (1980) examined the test's ability to discriminate between sane and insane criminal defendants. They found no significant difference in the comparison of raw scores between the two groups. Although they attempted a chi-square analysis on two-point codes, this analysis, while producing significant results, violated the basic requirements of chi-square through its insufficient sample size. Rogers and Seman (1983) examined MMPI profiles for clinically evaluated sane and insane murderers. The only significant difference between sane and insane evaluatees was on scale 5, which offers little in the way of clinical interpretation.

The absence of significant data in these two small studies does not demonstrate a failure of the MMPI in criminal responsibility evaluations. Much of the research in the criminal justice area has demonstrated that discriminations between criterion groups usually require either specially constructed scales or combinations of clinical scales to establish their accuracy. What these results do indicate is that no MMPI profile should be used to indicate directly responsibility or nonresponsibility. Although several authors (i.e., Whitaker, 1976; Green and Schaefer, 1984) have expressed concern over the potential misuse of the MMPI in forensic evaluations, these concerns are largely unjustified. From a psychometric perspective, the

MMPI provides valuable clinical information regarding the defendant's response style, which is of particular relevance in the area of malingering. Second, the MMPI may provide (see e.g., Gynther, Altman, and Sletten, 1973) carefully replicated clinical data describing the psychopathology of the defendant. For these two reasons, the MMPI is probably the most useful psychometric method in traditional psychological testing of insanity evaluatees. As discussed, the MMPI provides only limited data regarding *DSM III* diagnosis and cannot be directly related to standards of criminal responsibility. Nevertheless, it provides useful ancillary clinical information and should be a component of most insanity assessments.

California Psychological Inventory

The CPI represents one of the more popular objective personality measures and was developed by Gough beginning in 1948 (Gough, 1957). The CPI consists of 480 true-and-false items, ranging from typical behavior patterns to customary feelings, opinions, and attitudes about social, ethical, and family matters (Megargee, 1977). It is intended to provide meaningful descriptions of normal individuals in terms of socially useful personality characteristics and is not a measure of psychopathology. For this reason, the CPI has limited relevance to insanity evaluations because they are predicated on major psychological impairment.

Several studies have examined the usefulness of the CPI in discriminating between delinquents and nondelinquents and in attempting to predict criminal or asocial behavior. Laufer, Skoog, and Day (1982), in a review of sixty-two studies of adult criminals, found that most subject pools had low point codes on social responsibility and socialization. This finding is consistent with Megargee's (1977) review of delinquents and adult prison inmates. Further, research also suggested (e.g., Gough, Wenk, and Rozynko, 1965) that the CPI may be successful at predicting parole violators from non–parole violators. No recent studies were found, however, that utilized the CPI in pretrial forensic evaluations. Since the primary goal of the CPI is to distinguish among criterion groups of the normal population on the basis of interpersonal characteristics, substantial research would be necessary before the CPI could be adapted to criminal responsibility evaluations.

Other Objective Personality Measures

Several other objective personality measures that are not commonly used in clinical practice are available. The Experiential World Inventory (El-Meligi and Osmond, 1970) is a 400-item protocol for measuring distortions in perception, with seven scales measuring disturbances in sensory perception, time perception, body perception, self-perception, perception of others, ideation, dysphoria, and impulse regulation. Although it has not been utilized in forensic evaluations, initial validation research suggested it may be useful in differentiating perceptual changes due to drug and alcohol abuse from functional disorders.

The Millon Inventory (Millon, 1981) is a newly devised objective personality measure for the assessment of personality disorders and classification of patients by *DSM III* diagnosis. Finally, the Jesness Inventory (Jesness, 1966) and the Carlson Psychological Survey (Carlson, 1981) are two psychometric approaches to the classification of delinquents and criminal offenders by psychological impairment and aggressiveness. Since both scales are intended for incarcerated offenders, they were standardized on a population different from that being evaluated for insanity. While of heuristic interest, these latter two measures have little clinical usefulness in insanity evaluations.

INTELLECTUAL AND NEUROPSYCHOLOGICAL TESTING

An underresearched topic with insanity evaluations is the role of intellectual or neuropsychological deficits in the assessment of criminal responsibility. As discussed in earlier chapters, the concept of defect of the mind forms an integral component of each criminal responsibility standard. The following discussion examines in some detail the WAIS-R, the Halstead-Reitan, and the Luria-Nebraska batteries for evaluating organic impairment and mental retardation.

Epidemiological research suggests that there is a low incidence of severe organic impairment and mental retardation among criminal defendants referred for insanity evaluations. These data indicate (Tables 6.2 and 6.3) that while many defendants may show a mild degree of impairment, only 0.4% of the sane and none of the insane evidenced moderate to severe retarda-

Table 6.2
Mental Retardation Level in Insanity Evaluatees

	Sane (%)	Insane (%)
Mild	9.7	4.3
Moderate	0.4	0
Severe	0	0

Table 6.3
Evidence of Neurological and/or Neuropsychological
Deficits in Insanity Evaluatees

	Sane (%)	Insane (%)
Equivocal	17.5	9.9
Definite	1.5	3.3
Severe	0	1.1

tion. Similarly, in a global rating of organic impairment, only a minuscule percentage of defendants was found to have moderate to severe impairment.

Wechsler Adult Intelligence Scale-Revised Edition

The Wechsler Adult Intelligence Scale-Revised Edition or WAIS-R is a 1981 revision and restandardization of the Wechsler scales. The WAIS-R (Wechsler, 1981) was designed as a global measure of intellectual functioning as well as of specific mental abilities. Psychometrically, the WAIS-R demonstrates a high degree of reliability, with split-half correlations for full-scale IQ of .97 and test-retest reliability ranging from .95 to .96. In addition, the WAIS-R has demonstrated a high level of scoring reliability, with clinicians achieving similar scores (i.e., within two points) for the same patient (Ryan, Prifitera, and Powers, 1983).

The validity of the WAIS-R was established primarily through research on its 1955 edition. Validation studies summarized by Matarazzo (1972) indicate that measures of intelligence on the Wechsler correlate with evidence of mental retardation, organic impairment, academic performance, and occupational success. In addition, the WAIS-R has been demonstrated to be highly correlated with its earlier edition ($r = .88$). Despite this high correlation, the WAIS-R yields IQ scores that are typically approximately 8 points lower than those of the 1955 edition (Wechsler, 1981; Lippold and Claiborn, 1983; Smith, 1983).

Traditional use of the Wechsler scales involved the assessment of both intelligence and brain damage. Although studies have consistently demonstrated the relationship of Wechsler scores to organic pathology, new research argues against the use of the Wechsler alone. For example, Goldstein and Shelly (1984) found that the Wechsler alone accurately identified 63% of the brain-damaged patients and 70% of the non-brain-damaged patients. However, when the Wechsler was used in combination with other neuropsychological procedures, the accuracy of classification was substantially improved. In addition, attempts to utilize Wechsler scores or a ratio of Wechsler scores in the detection of hemispheric damage have been only moderately successful (Bornstein, 1983; Lippold and Claiborn, 1983; Bauer, Schlottmann, Kane, and Johnsen, 1984).

The assessment of mental retardation and its role in criminal responsibility cannot be translated into numerical terms; for example, a moderately retarded individual may have a rudimentary awareness and comprehension of his or her criminal behavior and be able to control his or her actions. Further, the forensic clinician should not attempt to translate specific subtests of the Wechsler (e.g., comprehension) into components of the legal standard. In this example, the comprehension of criminal behavior may be very different from the individual's comprehension measured by the WAIS-R. The forensic clinician, therefore, must evaluate intellectual abilities in relation to the defendant's intentionality, purposefulness, and capacity to choose and withhold his or her actions. It is also imperative to assess the defendant's understanding of the wrongfulness or criminality of his or her actions. Retarded defendants, while having a vague awareness of the wrongfulness of their actions, may not be able to appreciate the gravity or magnitude of those actions. Such deficits in thinking and judgment may qualify certain defendants for the ALI (American Law Institute) "appreciate" or the M'Naghten nature and quality of the act elements of the standards to be applied. In cases of severe or profound retardation, it may be necessary to employ the Stanford-Binet intelligence test since the Wechsler scales tend to overestimate low IQs (Green and Schaefer, 1984). Finally, the complexity of the criminal behavior may give some useful indication of the defendant's intellectual comprehension. For instance, if a defendant attempts a sophisticated mail fraud scheme, it would strongly suggest an intellectual awareness of his or her criminal actions.

Research by Heaton and Pendleton (1981) has demonstrated the relationship between mentally disordered patients' Wechsler scores and their capacity for self-care and independent living. This paper, based on earlier research (e.g., Rioch and Lubin, 1959; Pollack, Levenstein, and Klein, 1968), suggested that schizophrenics with a lower intelligence as measured by the WAIS (1955 edition) will have greater difficulty maintaining themselves in independent living situations. The forensic clinician may, therefore, wish to examine closely the relationship of a functional disorder like schizophrenia to impaired intellectual functioning in the evaluation of the criminal responsibility of defendants. It is possible that the combined effect of the intellectual deficiencies and the chronic psychiatric impairment might substantially affect the defendant's ability to appreciate his or her criminal behavior.

Neuropsychological testing has developed since the 1940s as a standardized approach to assess behavioral deficits in neurologically impaired patients. Toward this end, the field of clinical neuropsychology has developed two primary goals (Heaton and Pendleton, 1981): (1) as an ancillary procedure to the diagnosis of organic brain damage and (2), more important, as a measure of the behavioral consequences of cerebral pathology. Of these two functions, neuropsychology has played a prominent role with respect to the behavioral correlates and a less significant role to the diagnosis. Neuropsychological measures are rarely of sufficient accuracy to make a differential diagnosis, by themselves. Unfortunately, the role of neuropsychological testing in criminal responsibility evaluations focuses primarily on its ability to diagnose specific organic syndromes and to evaluate their potential impact on the individual's functioning. The most widely accepted of neuropsychological procedures is a group of subtests organized into the Halstead-Reitan neuropsychological battery.

Halstead-Reitan

The Halstead-Reitan battery originally consisted of ten tests that were developed to discriminate between patients with frontal lobe lesions, those with other lesions, and normal subjects (Reitan and Davison, 1974). The full battery consists of the Category Test, the Aphasia Screening Test, the Tactual Performance Test, the Seashore Rhythm Test, the Speech-Sounds Perception Test, the Finger-Tapping Test, the Grip-Strength Test, and may also include the Trail-Making Test and the WAIS. Reitan developed the impairment index as the number of subtests (out of ten) that exceeded the cutoff scores for the discrimination of brain-damaged patients. In making the simple discrimination between brain-damaged patients and normals, the Halstead-Reitan appears to be successful approximately 75% of the time (see Vega and Parsons, 1967; Goldstein, Deysach, and Kleinknect, 1973). While these findings may appear to be unacceptably low, it should be noted that may neurological procedures have a similar accuracy rate. For example, brain scans correctly identify 80 to 90% of all brain tumors, while electroencephalography has a rate of detection of approximately 70% (see Filskov and Goldstein, 1974). This, of course, further compounds the difficulty of establishing the accuracy of neuropsychological procedures since most validity studies are based on these medical procedures.

Results on the Halstead-Reitan battery are more equivocal when discriminations are attempted between normals, patients with organic disorders, and schizophrenic patients. Studies like those of Lacks, Colbert, Harrow, and Levine (1970) indicate that the Halstead-Reitan may be less accurate than a simple screening procedure, like the Bender-Gestalt. More recent studies (Wedding, 1983*a*, 1983*b*) have attempted discriminations between schizophrenic patients, normals, and brain-damaged patients (i.e., left, right, and diffuse hemispheric damage). They found that a discriminant function utilizing a combination of the Halstead and WAIS accurately discriminated at a rate of 63%. In addition, the procedure developed by Russell (Russell, Neuringer, and Goldstein, 1970) discriminated at a 60% accuracy rate.

Heaton, Baade, and Johnson (1978) completed a comprehensive review of neuropsychological test data as they related to adult psychiatric disorders. They found in a review of a study that the Halstead-Reitan was able to discriminate at a median accuracy of 75% for disorders such as nonpsychotic psychiatric disorders, mixed psychiatric disorders, and various subtypes of schizophrenic disorders. They found that only with chronic schizophrenic disorders was there an unacceptably low classification rate (i.e., 54%). Since in 85% of the studies reviewed there were no neurological assessments of psychiatric patients, it is, therefore, quite possible that the chronic schizophrenic population included a significant percentage of individuals who also had organic impairment. Further, from a diagnostic standpoint, chronic schizophrenic patients may be accurately classified through the use of structured interview and psychometric procedures. Thus, when the current literature is carefully reviewed, it appears that the Halstead-Reitan battery is moderately successful in differentiating brain-damaged individuals from psychiatric and normal populations.

Attempts to utilize the Halstead-Reitan battery in localizing lesions have had equivocal results (Lezak, 1978). As Lezak reported, the battery does elicit differential responses in patients with left and right hemispheric lesions. Such findings have lacked sufficient accuracy and specificity to be utilized in clinical practice, however.

The relationship of neuropsychological deficits on the Halstead-Reitan to individuals' everyday functioning is complicated and difficult to assess. Heaton and Pendleton (1981) found that subtests of the Halstead-Reitan could be related to individuals' everyday functioning and employability. These findings tend to be of a global nature and cannot be directly related to the specific legal standards inherent in criminal responsibility evaluations. It may well be that a neuropsychological evaluation will provide an opportunity to observe individuals' ability to see, organize, and respond to standardized stimuli. It is unlikely that neuropsychological testing will provide pathognomic signs of an individual's nonresponsibility except in those rare cases where the individual is suffering from such pervasive organic damage that it would be immediately apparent to any experienced clinician.

Neuropsychological consultations should be considered by forensic clinicians when there is some evidence of organicity either in clinical presentation, psychological testing, or history. Such consultation should ask for a diagnosis as well as an opinion about the degree of impairment in the individual's day-to-day functioning and judgment. It may be inappropriate to ask a neuropsychologist to respond to the criminal responsibility standard since this is likely beyond his or her area of expertise.

As with all psychometric approaches, the issue of malingering must be evaluated. Heaton, Smith, Lehman, and Vogt (1978) compared sixteen malingerers with sixteen cooperative head trauma patients, utilizing the Halstead-Reitan, the WAIS, and the MMPI. Using a discriminant function, they established on the basis of the neurological test results a high level of accuracy in classifying brain-damaged patients and malingerers (100% for this nonreplicated study). They found most of the differences on subtests of the Halstead-Reitan, including the Category Test, Tactual Performance Test, Speech-Sounds Perception Test, Finger Tapping Test, Finger Agnosia, and Grip Strength. This study is limited by its sample size and focus only on head trauma patients.

Goebel (1983) was able to discriminate between 52 brain-impaired patients, 50 control patients, and 150 malingerers utilizing a discriminant analysis with 90 to 95% accuracy rates. Univariate analyses demonstrated that both the WAIS and the Halstead-Reitan differentiated between patients, controls, and malingerers on nearly all the subtests of the Halstead-Reitan battery.

Lezak (1978) suggested additional neuropsychological tests and procedures that could be easily integrated into a Halstead-Reitan battery. These include simple cognitive tasks for which norms have been established for brain-damaged patients. By employing such tasks, the clinician may differentiate a malingering patient from one who is truly organically impaired.

Luria-Nebraska

The Luria-Nebraska was developed by Golden (see Golden, Hammeke, and Purisch, 1978) as an attempt to standardize Luria's (1973) clinical approach. Golden also adapted many of the diagnostic procedures first developed by Christensen (1975) in the development of a 285-item test battery. The original Luria-Nebraska was divided into ten categories: motor functions, rhythm, cutaneous and kinesthetic functions, visual functions, impressive speech, expressive speech, reading and writing, arithmetic skills, mnestic processes, and intellectual processes. Additional scales were developed (e.g., Lewis, Golden, Moses, Osmon, Purisch, and Hammeke, 1979), including a pathognomonic scale, and right and left hemisphere scales. More recently, McKay and Golden (1979) developed an additional series of factor scales to examine empirically elementary intellectual skills.

Golden, Fross, and Graber (1981) examined the Luria-Nebraska battery's split-half reliability on a mixed population of 338 patients and found very high reliability coefficients for the eleven basic scales (the range was from .89 to .95). As a measure of the internal consistency of the eleven scales, item-scale correlations were computed, and these demonstrated a strong item-scale consistency. No research is currently available on the reliability of the additional thirty factor scales. More specifically, these factors have not been replicated, nor has inter-rater reliability been established. Further, an examination of test-retest reliability for all scales is needed to provide critical information regarding the stability of Luria-Nebraska with various chronically impaired populations.

A primary focus of validity studies on the Luria-Nebraska has been its ability to discriminate between neurological and control patients. The original validation study (Golden, Hammeke, and Purisch, 1978) compared fifty brain-injured patients with fifty control subjects. Of 285 items, 253 discriminated at the .05 level using t tests. In addition, a discriminant analysis employing the 30 most effective items yielded a classification rate of 100%. A second study (Purisch, Golden, and Hammeke, 1978) found that the Luria-Nebraska could discriminate between brain-injured and schizophrenic patients using a one-stage discriminate analysis with a 93% accuracy rate. It should be observed that the two patient groups had significant demographic differences with respect to the chronicity of the disorder, age of onset, and previous hospitalizations, as well as a nearly significant difference in years of education. This lack of comparability between samples constrains the interpretation of these data. The Luria-Nebraska has also been moderately successful in localizing cerebral lesions (Lewis, Golden, Moses, Osmon, Purisch, and Hammeke, 1979; Golden et al., 1981).

Several additional areas have been examined in validation research with the Luria-Nebraska. For example, Golden and his associates (Golden, et al., 1980) examined the clinical utility of the Luria-Nebraska with neurologically impaired chronic schizophrenics. With a small sample of twenty-five brain-damaged and seventeen non-brain-damaged schizophrenics, Golden et al. were able to establish cutoff scores to differentiate between the two groups. It has also been found that the intellectual processes scale of the Luria-Nebraska is strongly correlated with the WAIS providing concurrent validity for the use of this scale (Prifitera and Ryan, 1981; McKay, Golden, Moses, Fishburne, and Wisniewski, 1981). Research has also explored the efficacy of a decision-tree approach to the Luria-Nebraska that was found in two companion studies to be closely related to the fully administered Luria-Nebraska (Webster and Dostrow, 1982).

Attempts to cross validate the Luria-Nebraska by researchers outside Golden's group have not been very successful. Although Sears, Hirt, and Hall (1984) found the Luria-Nebraska highly effective at detecting brain damage, they found procedures for determining the laterality of the lesion less successful. Utilizing the test manual procedures (Golden, Hammeke, and Purisch, 1980), they correctly identified only 56.7% of the correct hemispheres. Further, utilizing the $R*$ − $L*$ difference score yielded an 80% accuracy rate, while the most recent procedure (Golden et al., 1981) resulted in correct identification of 70% of the lesions. Further, Goldstein and Shelley (1984) found that the Luria-Nebraska discriminated brain-damaged from non-brain-damaged patients at approximately the same accuracy as the Halstead-Reitan, 79.8%. They found that augmenting the Luria-Nebraska with the WAIS would significantly increase the accurate classification of non-brain-damaged patients.

These studies underscore a serious methodological problem in the validation of the Luria-Nebraska. Much of the work by Golden and his colleagues is based on a one-stage discriminant analysis that optimizes the differences between criterion groups. What is therefore reported is a series of studies that may well overestimate the discriminability of the Luria-Nebraska. It is essential that two-stage discriminant analysis or subsequent research utilizing the same discriminant function be employed as a more accurate measure of the battery's discriminability.

This point is clearly illustrated by research on the Luria-Nebraska into the identification of multiple sclerosis. Golden (1979) reported discrimination scales that differentiated multiple sclerosis patients from controls with 100% accuracy. Stanley and Howe (1983) attempted to replicate these findings and found that neither of the discrimination scales was successful because none of the multiple sclerosis subjects was correctly diagnosed by either scale using the recommended cutoff scores (i.e., 0% accuracy). Thus, although the Luria-Nebraska appears effective at making broad discriminations like brain-damaged versus non-brain-damaged, much additional research is needed to make fine-tuned discriminations among neurologically impaired groups.

Many criticisms have been raised against the Luria-Nebraska on conceptual grounds. For example, Adams (1980) has questioned whether or not this psychometric approach sufficiently captures the sophistication and flexibility of Luria's idiographic methods. More serious criticisms have focused on the validity of the fourteen basic scales. Spiers (1981) has critically examined the specific items and scoring of six of the basic scales. He concluded that most of the scales are contaminated by items that measure a multiplicity of neuropsychological functions, and this contamination would preclude any meaningful interpretation on the basis of these descriptive scales. Although Golden (see Golden, Ariel, Moses, Wilkening, McKay, and MacInnes, 1982) defended these scales on the basis of factor analytical research, the real controversy focuses not on its factors but the meaning given these factors.

The clinical interpretation of Luria-Nebraska scales has raised much concern. Crosson and Warren (1982) and Delis and Kaplan (1983) have clearly articulated the likelihood of misinterpretation of the Luria-Nebraska scales with aphasic as well as nonaphasic populations. Further, Delis and Kaplan reviewed the low content validity of the Luria-Nebraska as well as the dangers of clinical misuse in devising statistically derived clinical profiles that may well be uninterpretable. Golden's response to these criticisms (see Golden, 1980; Golden, Ariel, McKay, Wilkening, Wolf, and MacInnes, 1982; Golden, Ariel, Moses, Wilkening, McKay and MacInnes, 1982) is to defend the Luria-Nebraska, citing its basic validity and arguing that clinicians should engage in a qualitative as well as quantitative approach to neuropsychological evaluations. This reasoning is not entirely satisfying. To make finer interpretations of the basis of the Luria-Nebraska, the neuropsychologist must be thoroughly trained in brain-behavior relationships and behavioral neurology. Interpretations would, therefore, be based less on statistically derived scales, which ironically are much closer to the original Luria, than their own clinical skill in evaluating cortical functions.

Little has been written on the clinical utility of the Luria-Nebraska in forensic evaluations. Although Golden (1984) described its potential use, primarily in civil cases, he presented no empirical data regarding its effectiveness. With respect to malingering, Golden and his colleagues suggest a readministration of the Luria-Nebraska and a comparison of the two test administrations. In addition, they suggest that the forensic psychologist look for inconsistencies between test behavior and everyday behavior and for test results that do not make neuropsychological sense. Again, no empirical data support the efficacy of these clinical methods (see, e.g., Moses, Golden, Wilkening, McKay, and Ariel, 1983). Finally, research on offenders suggests (e.g., Bryant, Scott, Golden and Tori, 1984) that violent offenders may have serious neuropsychological deficits as measured by the Luria-Nebraska. The authors found in their study that 73% of violent crimes were committed by the brain-damaged group as compared to 28% for nonviolent offenders. They concluded that, although differences were found on the Luria-Nebraska, additional research is needed to understand the complex psychophysiology underlying aggression.

This concise review of the two major neuropsychological test batteries, the Halstead-Reitan and Luria-Nebraska, emphasizes the complexity in both validation and application of neuropsychology to forensic patients. If nothing else, this review underscores the need for competent neuropsychological consultation by a thoroughly trained neuropsychologist when questions are raised regarding potential organicity in a defendant. A second major point of this review is that neuropsychological test batteries are fairly accurate at making gross discriminations (i.e., brain-damaged versus non-brain-damaged) but are considerably less accurate in making fine discriminations. It is, therefore, important to work with neuropsychologists who understand the limits of their clinical methods in accurately localizing and classifying organic impairment and subsequently relating this impairment to behavior. Finally, no specific or general neuropsychological deficits have been related to a loss of comprehension of one's behavior or to uncontrollable violence. The forensic clinician must, therefore, be careful in making any direct statements regarding criminal responsibility on the basis of neuropsychological impairment. Further, deficits in comprehension or volition will most likely extend beyond the criminal act and be corroborated by independent sources. Since most organic impairment is chronic and rarely improves suddenly the forensic clinician may well have opportunities to observe how neuropsychological deficits impair the individual's current cognitive and volitional capacities. Finally, just as schizophrenia cannot be equated to nonresponsibility, neither can specific neuropsychological syndromes.

CONCLUSION

This selective review of traditional psychological testing methods has demonstrated that such test findings do not directly address criminal responsibility. This conclusion does not diminish the importance of testing, however, in providing valuable ancillary information about an individual's psychological functioning and cognitive capacities. Its emphasis has been on how psychological testing, through its standardization, reliability, validity, and generalizability, can be utilized with mentally disordered offenders who are being assessed for criminal responsibility. This focus is toward the forensic applications of each test including reliable under what circumstances and valid for what purposes.

Psychological testing within the forensic context is based on two necessary conditions: (1) the certainty of the clinical data (see table 6.1) and (2) its relevance to insanity evaluations. As long as these two conditions are respected and articulated clearly in the forensic report, the forensic clinician has wide latitude in the types of psychometric methods employed in providing the courts with a comprehensive psychological evaluation. Conclusions regarding the certainty of test findings are possible only when standardized administration and interpretation methods are utilized. Chapter 9 examines the integration of test data with other clinical findings in rendering clinical judgments on criminal responsibility.

Chapter 7

Innovative Approaches to Insanity Evaluations

This chapter examines advances in diagnostic and forensic assessment that are of particular relevance to criminal responsibility evaluations. This includes one general diagnostic method, the Schedule of Affective Disorders and Schizophrenia (SADS), and two protocols designed to address specifically the issue of criminal responsibility: the Rogers Criminal Responsibility Assessment Scales (R-CRAS) and the Mental State at the Time of the Offense Screening Evaluation (MSE). Each assessment approach is described in some detail, including test validation data and practical issues of administration.

A primary concern of the forensic practitioner is the establishment of consistent and valid diagnostic procedures. Based on the work of Murphy, Woodruff, and Herjanic (1974), inconsistencies in diagnostic evaluations may be accounted for by *criterion variance,* the utilization of different standards for what represents clinically relevant data, and *information variance,* clinicians' differences in observing and organizing clinically relevant information and the comparative weighting given to that information. Ward, Beck, and Mendelson (1962) found that 95% of the diagnostic disagreement could be accounted for by information and criterion variance, with only the additional 5% being the result of patient changes (i.e., *patient variance*). Attempts to control this variability have lead to more systematic approaches in the collection of clinical data and the adoption of standardized methods for quantifying observed psychopathology. Each of the three assessment methods described here has attempted to identify relevant symptomatology in systematic and quantifiable approaches.

An additional issue to be considered is the examination of specific decision-making models. Prior to the development of the Research Diagnostic Criteria (described with the SADS in the next section) and their subsequent elaboration in the *Diagnostic and Statistical Manual of Mental Disorders* (*DSM III*), diagnostic evaluations were rather a hit-or-miss proposition with inadequate reliability (see Spitzer and Fleiss, 1974). In contrast, these new approaches have explicit criteria: inclusion criteria (i.e., what constitutes a disorder) and exclusion criteria (i.e., what differentiates this disorder from other disorders). These criteria were formulated as part of the new diagnostic nomenclature. The efficacy of this approach is reflected in the increased interrater reliability estimates found in *DSM III* (American Psychiatric Association, 1980). Studies have also shown that systematic decision models, even if not statistically or empirically based, show significant improvement over clinical judgment. Dawes (1979) demonstrated that entering clinicians' criteria into a decision model, which rated these criteria either equally or according to clinicians' ranking of them, increased the accuracy of the clinician's judgment. Both the presence of inclusion/exclusion criteria as well as explicit decision models are reviewed for each of the three assessment approaches.

SCHEDULE OF AFFECTIVE DISORDERS AND SCHIZOPHRENIA

The SADS (Spitzer and Endicott, 1978) is an extensive semistructured diagnostic interview aimed at eliciting the intensity, duration, and other manifest characteristics of a patient's psychiatric symptomatology. The SADS is designed to minimize information variance by systematically and comprehensively addressing major characteristics of psychopathology. The clinician is involved in three levels of inquiry: (1) general and nondirectional questions that are asked of each evaluatee (e.g., How have you been feeling?); (2) specific probes into the presence, severity, and duration of a particular symptom (e.g., Have you felt depressed? Have you cried or been tearful? How often? How bad is the feeling?); and (3) additional unstructured inquiry with respect to any ambiguous symptomatology (e.g., Were you feeling more frustrated than depressed?). These three levels of inquiry are integrated with collateral information into specific quantifications for each symptom. This quantification employs a five-point scale, with zero representing no information; 1, no symptoms; 2, clinically insignificant symptoms; and 3 to 5, increasing gradations of clinically relevant symptoms. To improve reliability, each of the five levels has descriptive criteria that make clear differentiations between it and other gradations, based on the severity and extent of psychopathology. The SADS is constructed in two major sections: Part 1 examines in detail the patient's last episode with respect to its severest symptomatology as well as the patient's current adjustment; Part 2 provides a historical-developmental orientation that examines discrete periods of past impairment in the patient's functioning for establishing a lifetime diagnoses.

The SADS was constructed to gather systematically clinically relevant information for implementation with the Research Diagnostic Criteria, (RDC). The RDC was designed by Feighner and his associates (Feighner, Robins, and Guze, 1972) to establish the diagnostic validity of specific psychiatric disorders. The validity of each disorder was examined through clinical description, studies of differential diagnoses, outcome studies, and family studies. The outcome of this empirical investigation has evolved into the current RDC (see Spitzer, Endicott, and Robins, 1978). The RDC provides the decision model for the SADS diagnostic interview to reduce criterion variance. Zwick (1983) reviewed much of the current research on the RDC and some limitations for its use with certain disorders (e.g., RDC criteria were unsuccessful at differentiating schizoaffective disorders). As noted by Zwick, many of the RDC studies did not employ a SADS diagnostic interview, and therefore, it is difficult to generalize these results to those that would have been achieved from a SADS-RDC diagnosis.

The SADS examines in detail symptoms of affective disorders, anxiety disorders, substance abuse disorders, antisocial personality disorders, and psychotic disorders. Although symptoms of other types of disorders are presented within the SADS diagnostic interview, the clinician must also be familiarized with *DSM III* diagnostic categories to make additional inquiry with respect to other diagnoses. This is particularly important in areas such as psychosexual disorders, dissociative disorders, and personality disorders. These diagnoses are discussed more extensively later as they relate to SADS evaluations.

The reliability of the SADS was examined through interrater reliability, test-retest reliability, and measures of internal consistency. Endicott and Spitzer (1978) studied 150 newly admitted inpatients who were experiencing primarily affective disorders. These patients independently rated in joint SADS interviews, and exceptionally high interrater reliability was found. The range of intraclass correlations was .82 to .99, indicating nearly perfect agreement. A second study involved an additional 60 newly admitted inpatients who were administered the SADS and retested within a 24-to-72-hour period. Although yielding somewhat lower intraclass correlations (ranging from .49 to .93), the majority of these correlations was greater than .80. Finally, the internal consistency of the SADS summary scales was examined with Cronbach's alpha, yielding moderate to exceptionally high internal consistency for these scales (alpha ranged from .47 to .97). The SADS achieved unprecedentedly high reliability coefficients for both interrater reliability (the mean correlation of .94) and test-retest reliabilities (a mean reliability coefficient of .79). Finally, alpha coefficients, as measures of internal consistency, suggest that eight of the SADS summary scales demonstrate high degrees of internal consistency, with the two measuring anxiety and formal thought disorders having a moderate degree of internal consistency. Subsequent studies of reliability, employing clinicians thoroughly trained in the use of the SADS, yielded a consistently higher level of agreement between raters (D. Clark, personal communication, May, 1985). A series of additional studies (Anderson, et al., 1981; Keller, et al., 1981*a;* Keller et al., 1981*b*) established satisfactory reliability of the SADS diagnostic interview in making longitudinal diagnosis of prior psychiatric episodes.

Validity studies of the SADS have included concurrent validity with other diagnostic measures. This includes examining the relationship of the SADS with Katz Adjustment Scales (completed by both the subject and a relative) and the SCL-90. These correlations suggest a low to moderate relationship between the SADS summary scales and related diagnostic measures. In addition, follow-up studies on the SADS-RDC diagnosis have related its conclusions to outcome criteria primarily involving schizophrenic and affective disorders and, to a lesser degree, other forms of mental disorders. Although the results of these studies are favorable, it is difficult to summarize them briefly since different studies have examined the outcome, laboratory studies (e.g., Spitzer, Endicott, and Robins, 1978), and family studies for different diagnostic groups over different time periods. It is important to note that, because of the high degree of reliability as well as favorable outcome data for SADS-RDC diagnoses, most of its inclusion/exclusion criteria were adopted by Spitzer and his colleagues in the reformulation of the *DSM III.* Thus, an advantage to the empolyment of the SADS is its simple transposition from RDC diagnostic information into the current *DSM III* diagnoses.

Two related studies have examined the discriminability of the SADS diagnostic interview in evaluations of criminal responsibility. The first study (Rogers, Cavanaugh, and Dolmetsch, 1981) examined differences on SADS summary scales for fifteen clinically evaluated sane and thirteen insane defendants. Overall differences were established between the two groups utilizing a MANOVA with canonical loadings primarily on delusions and hallucinations, subjective depression, and associated depressive features. The second study (Rogers, Thatcher, and Cavanaugh, 1984) involved an expansion of the earlier database to include seventy-eight criminal defendants. Similar differences between clinically evaluated sane and insane evaluatees were observed for the period of the crime (Wilk's lambda = 3.70; $p = .002$). Again, differences were noted with respect to delusions and hallucinations, formal thought disorder, associated features of depression, and manic symptoms. The second study also examined the overall degree of psychological impairment at the time of the crime through the

Global Assessment Scale and frequency of observed symptoms. The Global Assessment Scale, which represents a composite rating of psychological impairment on the SADS, differed significantly, with clinically evaluated insane evaluatees demonstrating severe to pervasive impairment (mean = 30.4, s.d. = 13.5) and sane evaluatees showing only mild to moderate impairment (mean = 64.1, s.d. = 9.3). In addition, those individuals clinically evaluated as insane had a much greater frequency of symptoms within the clinical range (mean = 10.7, s.d. = 5.5) than their sane counterparts (mean = 4.8, s.d. = 2.1). These two studies emphasized the importance of psychotic features and overall psychological impairment in differentiating between clinically evaluated sane and insane evaluatees.

The administration of the SADS for a criminal responsibility evaluation (see Rogers and Cavanaugh, 1981a) typically requires 3 to 4 hours of clinical interviews over a minimum of two separate time periods. In addition to the administration of the SADS proper, it is important to gather an unstructured self-report from the patient regarding his or her emotions, thoughts, and behavior at the time of the alleged offense to provide a rough baseline for examining the accuracy and honesty of further statements elicited during the SADS interview. An adaptation of the SADS for criminal responsibility evaluations that has been found helpful is to score the last episode for the time of the alleged offense and the present time for the defendant's current psychological functioning (Table 7.1). This allows the clinician to make systematic comparisons of the defendant's present impairment and reported impairment at the time of the crime.

The SADS is also helpful in developing a highly specific account for the time of the offense and quantification of the individual's psychological symptoms for both time periods for addressing issues of malingering and deception. In addition, it is often imperative that the clinician follow up significant symptoms with detailed probes to establish the presence of specific symptomatology and its relevance to the criminal behavior. For example, with a defendant reporting hallucinations, it is important to establish whether hallucinatory activity was present during the commission of the

Table 7.1
Structure of the SADS in General and Criminal Responsibility Evaluations

Type of Evaluation	Part 1	Part 2
General	Assesses current functioning and functioning during worst period of last episode	Assesses prior functioning
Criminal responsibility	Assesses current functioning and functioning at the time of the crime	Assesses prior functioning

criminal behavior and what impact, if any, it had on the defendant's willingness and deliberateness in engaging in such behavior.

The SADS's extensive format facilitates the clinician's identification of malingering and deception. It is difficult for a defendant to present a consistent and psychologically plausible report of psychological symptomatology over different evaluation periods without becoming either inconsistent or confused. In the test's administration, dissimulating defendants frequently fall into a pattern of endorsing all types of symptomatology at a severe level, including contradictory symptoms. Thus, by taking comprehensive notes and making specific ratings, the clinician has an extensive database with which he or she can address the honesty and completeness of a defendant's self-report.

The forensic clinician must follow through carefully on his or her quantification of psychiatric symptomatology with the SADS. This follow-through frequently involves rechecking critical symptoms from one interview to the next and integrating information from other sources such as collateral interviews and previous psychiatric records. The SADS is also advantageous because of its comprehensiveness, ability to render accurate diagnoses for discrete time periods, and collection of quantified symptoms, all of which may be helpful in the assessment of criminal responsibility. The SADS must be administered by clinicians with substantial training and supervision from senior clinicians trained in this protocol.

Practical guidelines for the administration of the SADS in criminal responsibility evaluations include the following:

1. As decribed, the SADS requires considerable training and supervision to standardize the clinician's administration and ratings. This is of particular importance in criminal responsibility evaluations because of their emphasis on retrospective assessment.

2. The clinician must make a thorough evaluation of all symptoms regardless of their potential role in criminal responsibility. This provides a comprehensive baseline for comparing the presentation of symptoms against corroborative information. Similar care must also be taken in Part 2 of the SADS, which examines previous episodes of mental disorders. Such detailed interviewing may provide additional evidence of malingering or deception as in the case of one defendant who reported 300 to 400 episodes of major depression in contradiction to corroborative information.

3. The relationship of individual symptoms to the criminal behavior must be assessed. More specifically, the forensic clinician must determine the potential impairment on the basis of such symptoms and the effects of the concomitant disorder on the defendant's ability to qualify for the pertinent insanity standard. Toward this end, the clinician must typically focus on the onset and the duration of critical symptoms as well as the degree of severity.

4. Symptoms that are critical to the diagnosis and opinion must be verified with repeated and thorough probes at different evaluation times, compared with unstructured clinical data, and corroborated through other clinical data. In complicated insanity evaluations, the clinician may wish to employ a multiple SADS evaluation. This procedure (described by Rogers and Cunnien, 1986) involves not only the administration of the SADS to the defendant but also corroborative SADS interviews in which witnesses or significant others are independently questioned about the defendant's symptomatology. This may be particularly helpful in establishing the extent of psychological impairment. Through systematic comparisons of quantified observations.

5. The clinician may wish to use as guidelines the Global Assessment Scale (for the time of the crime) or the frequency of clinical symptoms in making his or her determination of criminal responsibility. It is suggested that these guidelines (see Rogers, Thatcher, and Cavanaugh, 1984) be used as a cross-check to alert the clinician to any possible oversight regarding the criminal responsibility standard. More specifically, if the defendant were to be rated 30 or below on the Global Assessment Scale or rated as having ten or more clinical symptoms at the time of the crime, then the clinician should exercise great care if his or her opinion is that the defendant is responsible. Conversely, if the defendant is rated above 60 on the Global Assessment Scale and has fewer than six clinical symptoms at the time of the crime, then the clinician should exercise the same care if he or she decides that the defendant was nonresponsible.

In summary, the SADS presents a systematic and comprehensive approach to diagnosis. It allows the forensic clinician to quantify important symptoms at discrete time periods, including the time of the crime, and provides the basis for opinions regarding retrospective diagnosis and concomitant impairment in the assessment of criminal responsibility.

Additional diagnostic interview formats are available for the forensic clinician. These include the Renard Diagnostic Interview (RDI) (Helzer, Robins, Croughan, and Welner, 1981) and the National Institute of Mental Health (NIMH) Diagnostic Interview Schedule (DIS) (Robins, Helzer, Croughan, and Ratcliff, 1981). Unlike the SADS, these diagnostic protocols were devised for use by nonpsychiatric physicians and lay interviewers; no empirical research has been done on either diagnostic procedure and their applicability to criminal responsibility assessments.

The RDI includes an examination of psychiatric symptomatology, evaluating each symptom for its presence, severity, and etiology. Reliability estimates, based on two or three independent ratings, yielded an average reliability coefficient of .60 for common diagnoses (i.e., alcoholism, depression, phobic disorders, and mania). Further, as a measure of concurrent validity, the RDI was compared in 197 cases with diagnoses from standard interviews. This resulted in an agreement rate of 79% and an error rate of 13% (i.e., missed diagnoses) for the RDI when compared to standard interviews (Helzer, et al., 1981).

The NIMH DIS is an outgrowth of the RDI that was designed for large-scale epidemiological studies. The DIS allows the clinician or lay interviewer to ask questions relating to symptoms on both a lifetime and current basis. Quantified responses can subsequently be computer scored based on various diagnostic decision models (i.e., *DSM III,* Feighner criteria, and RDC). Overall kappa reliability coefficients varied from .62 to .69 for *DSM III* criteria and .70 for Feighner criteria. When nonprofessional interviewers' protocols were computer scored, they yielded an average 72% agreement with psychiatrists' diagnoses. In addition, those interviewers misclassified 6% of their diagnoses for disorders not found by psychiatrists. More recently, the DIS has been applied in large-scale epidemiological research with 12,000 subjects through community interviews and appeared effective at identifying potential disorders (Freedman, 1984; Regier et al., 1984).

Applications of the RDI and the DIS to criminal forensic evaluations have not been explored. It is quite possible that the DIS, in particular, could be adapted for collecting corroborative clinical data on the defendant. Given the lower estimates of reliability of the RDI and DIS and their lack of data regarding the severity of symptoms, it is recommended that clinicians employ the SADS for sanity evaluations.

MENTAL STATE AT THE TIME OF THE OFFENSE SCREENING EVALUATION

Slobogin, Melton, and Showalter (1984) devised the MSE, an interview-based screening protocol for identifying defendants with a potential legal defense of criminal responsibility while screening out defendants for whom there is very little likelihood of sufficient impairment. A potential legal defense must be on the basis of a mental disorder and is defined as an insanity, diminished capacity, automatism, or unconsciousness defense. The important threshold question is whether there are any clinical indicators of a significant mental abnormality, which is operationally defined as any diagnosis that may form the basis of one of the preceding legal defenses because of its impairment and impact on the individual's behavior at the time of the crime.

The MSE is divided into three components: Part 1, history of a mental disorder; Part 2, impairment at the time of the offense; and Part 3, current mental status examination. The three elements of Part 1 hinge on the definition of bizarre behavior, which is operationally defined as delusions, hallucinations, looseness of associations, sudden alterations in consciousness or motor functioning, sudden aggressive affectual discharge, none of which is associated with the use of a psychoactive substance. First, the clinician is asked to consider for defendants with a prolonged history of bizarre behavior the possibility of brain syndromes and various psychotic disorders. Second, the clinician is asked, in cases of brief periods of uncharacteristically bizarre behavior, to consider diagnoses such as brief reactive psychosis, intermittent or isolated psychotic disorders, automatism, and dissociative disorders. Third, the clinician is asked, in cases of episodic uncharacteristically bizarre behavior associated with the use of a psychoactive substance, to consider the diagnoses of substance abuse or withdrawal, delirium, organic delusional disorder, or hallucinosis. Further, the clinician is required to review symptoms for evidence of moderate or severe mental retardation. Finally, the clinician is requested to complete Part 2 even if no positive findings were found in Part 1.

Part 2 of the MSE requires the clinician to address the degree of the defendant's impairment at the time of the crime. This includes the defendant's cognitive perception and emotional response to the offense and a detailed account of the offense including intrapsychic stressors, external stressors, altered state of consciousness, and amnesia. In addition, potential precipitators and postoffense responses (both emotional and behavioral) are addressed. Finally, data from external sources must be considered including court and police reports and witnesses' accounts.

The third part of the MSE is a current mental status examination of which the content and structure are left to the discretion of the clinician. It is somewhat unclear from the instructions whether Part 3 is routinely administered or employed only in cases were ambiguity still exists. Employing Ward's formulation for diagnostic disagreement (described in the introduction to the chapter), the MSE is aimed primarily at reducing information variance. This is accomplished be asking the clinician in Part 1 and Part 2 to address systematically specific topics; it does not, however, address the form or structure of these inquiries or how responses will be quantified. Second, it makes little attempt to address criterion variance. Forensic evaluators are instructed to consider any significant finding as having the potential for a legal defense; no guidelines are presented to outline explicit criteria for a positive finding.

The available validity study (Slobogin, Melton, and Showalter, 1984) utilized twenty-four mental health professionals who were involved in an 8-day training program including the use of the MSE. For the purposes of the study, they were divided into twelve teams of two and performed three evaluations per team for a total of thirty-six evaluations. Each evaluation was jointly conducted by both evaluators and took no longer than 1 hour to complete. Results of the brief MSE assessments were compared to more comprehensive evaluations independently completed by forensic clinicians at Central State Hospital in Virginia.

This validity study unfortunately did not address interrater agreement, and therefore, no estimates are available regarding the MSE's reliability. Comparisons between the MSE and the forensic evaluations by the Central State Hospital staff showed a high degree of accuracy with the respect to sanity (97%) and much less accuracy with respect to mental illness as a potential defense (50%). These findings are consistent with the MSE's intended purpose—that is, to exclude a large number of forensic evaluations where there is a negligible likelihood that the mental state of the defendant would be a pertinent issue. As a screening protocol, the MSE deliberately aims at having a high false-positive rate to achieve its purpose of a very low false-negative rate.

An additional comparison was made in this study (Slobogin, Melton, and Showalter, 1984) between the MSE and the final court disposition. Of the twenty cases in which defendants were rated on the MSE as having a possible mental abnormality, the court agreed in five cases, disagreed in seven cases, and did not address the issue in an additional eight cases in which it did not prosecute. Given the large number of unknown cases, the concordance rate would be somewhere between 42% (five out of twelve) and 65% (thirteen out of twenty). More important, for the fifteen defendants evaluated on the MSE as having no significant mental abnormality, there was 100% agreement between the MSE and the subsequent court disposition. A negative finding on the MSE evidences a high degree of accuracy using as criteria both a comprehensive forensic evaluation as well as the subsequent court disposition. Thus, use of the MSE as a screening protocol may well be efficient because of its high degree of accuracy at excluding those without a significant mental abnormality. Positive findings on the MSE do not suggest the reverse; that is, for those rated as having a possible significant mental abnormality only 50% agreement was found when compared to a more comprehensive evaluation and between 42 and 65% agreement with a legal disposition on the basis of a mental disorder.

Several limitations constrain the present clinical use of the MSE in insanity evaluations. The absence of reliability data and cross-validation seriously limits its potential usefulness to the forensic practitioner. From the perspective of criminal responsibility, the fluidity of the concept of significant mental abnormality, which may refer to a wide range of legal defenses on the basis of a mental disorder, is not comparable to specific insanity standards. Although it is not specified how many defendants were clinically evaluated as sane versus insane, only two were found legally insane. Additional work is needed to establish how well the MSE performs with specific legal standards. Even as a general screening protocol, it is necessary to know how successful the MSE is for each defense (e.g., it may be highly effective with insanity but inadequate with diminished capacity). Slobogin, Melton, and Showalter (1984) report an additional 2-year study with data collected on 207 cases. It is therefore hoped that more precise analyses can be conducted with the respect to criminal responsibility and that estimates of interrater reliability may be obtained.

In summary, the MSE represents an important advance in the assessment of the mental state of defendants at the time of the offense., With additional validation, the MSE may represent a useful and cost-efficient screening protocol for excluding those individuals who had no significant psychological impairment at the time of the crime. It cannot and was not intended to be an assessment device for establishing an individual's impairment at the time of the crime and determining the relevance of that disorder to specific insanity standards.

Practical guidelines for the use of MSE follow:

1. Although the MSE is not recommended as the sole criterion for screening out defendants with potential criminal responsibility defenses, it may be employed as one component of a preliminary evaluation.
2. The clinician utilizing the MSE may wish to transfer its outline (see the appendix in Slobogin, Melton, and Showalter, 1984) onto three or four sheets with space for clinical observations. This procedure would ensure that the MSE is completed systematically.
3. Although Part 3 of the MSE does not specify any particular mental status examination, the forensic clinician may wish to adopt a more structured procedure that would yield more standardized clinical data. Toward this end, the Present State Examination (Wing, Cooper, and Sartorius, 1974) or the Mental Status Evaluation Record (Spitzer, and Endicott, 1974) are recommended both for their standardization and quantification of impairment.

ROGERS CRIMINAL RESPONSIBILITY ASSESSMENT SCALES

The R-CRAS (Rogers, 1984a) was designed as a systematic approach to the assessment of criminal responsibility. This model, paralleling the diagnostic model of the SADS, requires the clinician to quantify significant psychological and situational variables at the time of offense and to apply these clinical data to a hierarchic decision model for sanity/insanity, based symptoms and degree of impairment. The R-CRAS consists of assessment criteria (Part 1A) that rate severity and the potential relevance of critical psychological symptoms to the alleged criminal behavior. Clinical data from Part 1 of the R-CRAS are integrated within a decision model for the ALI (American Law Institute) standard of insanity. This requires the clinician to make judgments regarding malingering, organic mental disorders, major psychiatric disorders, loss of cognitive control, loss of behavioral control, relationship of this loss of control to the mental disorder, and finally, whether or not the defendant meets the ALI standard. Additional assessment criteria and decision models are presented for the examination of the guilty but mentally ill (GBMI) and the M'Naghten standards of insanity. These models, on which only preliminary validity data are available, are presented for research purposes.

A primary focus of the R-CRAS, with reference to Ward's paradigm, is the reduction of criterion variance. This is accomplished on two levels. First, the R-CRAS makes explicit gradations of impairment for each of the assessment criteria. Second, the threshold of what does and does not constitute the elements of a decision model for the ALI standard is clearly articulated. Thus, both the impairment and its relevance to the ALI standard are presented in a systematic and quantifiable manner. Information variance is addressed less comprehensively, with guidelines for the specific parameters of the evaluation delineated in the test manual. Further, the clinician, employing the R-CRAS, is required to follow a standardized approach for the collection of clinically relevant information. This involves a thorough review of all available clinical and police investigative reports, the completion of one or preferable several clinical interviews with the patient/ defendant, and the completion of the R-CRAS immediately following the final clinical interview (Rogers, 1984a). In addition, the clinician is asked to address the defendant's thoughts, emotions, and behavior at the time of the crime and periods immediately preceding and following that time. The R-CRAS specifies content areas (i.e., past medical and psychiatric history, previous criminal history, in-depth questions regarding differential diagnosis, and the patient's account of the criminal behavior). Further, in the areas of diagnostic ambiguity, the clinician is given a standardized approach to collecting relevant clinical information. For example, in cases of suspected retardation, the procedure requires that an individual intelligence test (i.e., the WAIS-R or Stanford-Binet) be administered. As an additional example, in the area of formal thought disorders, the clinician must give examples and specify the subcategory of formal thought disorder. Thus, general guidelines are presented for ensuring a comprehensive evaluation and thereby reducing information variance.

The three validation studies of the R-CRAS (Rogers, Dolmetsch, and Cavanaugh, 1981; Rogers, Seman, and Wasyliw, 1983; Rogers, Wasyliw, and Cavanaugh, 1984) were made from 1981 to 1983 at five forensic centers: the Isaac Ray Center (Chicago, IL), the Nebraska Psychiatric Institute

(Omaha, NB), the Court Diagnostic and Treatment Center (Toledo, OH), the Minnesota Security Hospital (St. Peter, MN) and the Perkins State Hospital (Perkins, MD). R-CRASs were completed by two independent examiners as a measure of interrater reliability on 76 of the 260 defendants. Reliability findings indicated a moderate degree of reliability for the individual variables (mean reliability coefficient was .58) and much higher reliability coefficients for the decision variables (average kappa coefficient was .81). Most important, clinical opinion regarding sanity was in almost perfect agreement, with a 97% concordance rate and a kappa coefficient of .94. In addition, the internal consistency of the R-CRAS summary scales was measured with Cronbach's alpha coefficients and exhibited a moderate degree of internal consistency for all scales (mean alpha was .60) except patient reliability, which has only two items.

The R-CRAS's construct validity was examined through an adaptation of Loevinger's model of construct validation (1957). This model involved the conceptualization of insanity as a theoretical construct, specification of that construct through a series of hypotheses, and the testing of these hypotheses across several validity studies. Results of two-stage discriminant analyses correctly classified a high to exceptionally high percentage of clinically evaluated sane and insane subjects. This multivariate approach demonstrated consistent differences between the sane and insane defendants, with canonical loadings indicating that each of the summary scales made a substantial and unique contribution to the clinical opinion of criminal responsibility. Finally, comparisons were made on 112 cases between the R-CRAS and the subsequent legal disposition; these resulted in an 88% concordance rate.

The generalizability of the R-CRAS was examined for demographic variables including age, race, and sex and legal variables including fitness to stand trial, prior felony or juvenile arrests, and length of time between the most recent arrest and the forensic evaluation. None of these variables made a unique contribution to the clinical determination of sanity/insanity when examined in a stepwise discriminant analysis. Of psychological and developmental variables, only the history of schizophrenia and absence of any close personal relationship had any impact on the final decision regarding criminal responsibility. These two variables, when entered with the R-CRAS summary scales into stepwise discriminant analyses, accounted for only 5 of the 69% of the total variance. The fact that these variables, representing important psychological factors, have a secondary bearing on the clinical decision does not lessen the R-CRAS's generalizability. Finally, the R-CRAS was shown to be generalizable across the five forensic centers (both inpatient and outpatient) and across forensic disciplines (psychiatrists and psychologists).

Validity data (see Rogers, Seman, and Clark, 1985) on additional assessment criteria involving GBMI and M'Naghten decision models were collected at three forensic centers (the Isaac Ray Center in Chicago, IL, Court Diagnostic and Treatment Center in Toledo, OH; and the Center for Forensic Psychiatry in Ann Arbor, MI). Data analysis on 125 subjects suggested that individuals evaluated as GBMI form a distinct group with greater impairment than sane and less impairment than insane defendants. This grouping was demonstrated on comparison of summary scales and through a two-stage discriminant analysis. In addition, the data suggested that the actual application of the M'Naghten standard differs little from the ALI standard with similar findings for construct validity. The data suggested that 88% of those clinically evaluated as insane by ALI were also insane by M'Naghten. As mentioned earlier, further validation research is necessary before these additional decision models of the R-CRAS are available for clinical use.

Many issues in the adminstration of the R-CRAS are addressed either on the R-CRAS protocol or in its test manual. Scoring difficulties occasionally occur in marginal cases or in cases where the composite information from all available sources remains either ambiguous or contradictory. In such cases, the R-CRAS may provide explicit justification for why a clinical opinion regarding criminal responsibility cannot be reached with the requisite degree of medical or scientific certainty. There are several limitations to the R-CRAS, the most important being that it provides no substitution for adequate training and experience in forensic evaluations. The second limitation is, given the small number of subjects with severe organic impairment, care must be given in identifying such defendants and in applying criminal responsibility standards. In spite of the small sample, significant differences were found on two of the three validity studies for organic impairment. Third, the GBMI and M'Naghten standards cannot be applied to clinical evaluations; the presentation of such data to the court would clearly represent a misuse of the R-CRAS.

The most thorough critique of the R-CRAS was completed by Grisso (1984) in his review of psycholegal assessment. Grisso assessed as strengths of the R-CRAS, first, translation process of the legal standard to psychological concepts and operationally defined subclasses of symptoms, behaviors, and affective/cognitive states; second, a high level of agreement between examiners; and third, its generalizability across age, race, gender, education, work history, competence to stand trial, prior felony arrest, and several other legal variables. He described as shortcomings of the R-CRAS the low reliability of three individual criteria and the absence of factor analytical studies for examining statistically the structure of the R-CRAS. (Factor analysis was subsequently addressed in Rogers, Seman, and Clark, 1985.) Grisso (1984, p. 12) concluded that the R-CRAS offers "considerably greater standardization of an insanity assessment process than would be expected for assessments by examiners not employing the system. Yet it also provides sufficient flexibility in the interview to allow the examiners to meet varying circumstances raised by the defendant examinations.''

Practical guidelines for utilizing the R-CRAS include the following:

1. The forensic clinician should familiarize himself or herself with the structure and scoring of the R-CRAS. This may be accomplished through collaboration with or supervision by other forensic clinicians and practice scoring of the R-CRAS with case studies (see Rogers, 1984a, chapter 5).
2. The R-CRAS provides a synthesis of all available clinical and police investigative information. The clinician should secure all available records and sufficient corroborative data prior to completing the insanity evaluation and scoring the R-CRAS.
3. Although the R-CRAS provides for quantification of individual assessment criteria, it would be inappropriate to attempt any numerical translation of individual scores into a clinical opinion regarding criminal responsibility. Expert opinion requires a considered clinical judgment of each element of the insanity standard before rendering a final opinion regarding criminal responsibility. Criminal responsibility requires (see Haney, 1980) an idiographic approach (i.e., What is your opinion of this particular defendant with his or her unique array of mental abnormalities and circumstances?) as opposed to statistically based nomothetic approaches (i.e., What is your opinion of a defendant who falls into a general grouping with respect to mental illness and criminal behavior?).
4. Utilization of the R-CRAS should be based on available self-report and corroborated clinical data. It should never be based on plausibility or logical inferences (e.g., It makes sense that . . .).

CONCLUSION

In summary, there have been advances in the psychological assessment of criminal responsibility. Of the tests considered here, the SADS offers the most comprehensive clinical information regarding an individual's psychological functioning and degree of impairment at discrete time periods, including the time of the crime. The MSE may well be employed on an informal basis or an important component of a preliminary evaluation. From a psychometric perspective, additional validation of the MSE with regard to its reliability, validity, and generalizability must be established before it is implemented in forensic evaluations. Such studies we hope will be forthcoming since the MSE may be very helpful in screening out those individuals for whom a comprehensive evaluation of criminal responsibility is unwarranted. Finally the R-CRAS is a useful protocol for the organization for criminal responsibility evaluations, the quantification of pertinent essential psychological and situational variables for the time of the crime, and the implementation of the ALI standard of insanity.

Chapter 8

Laboratory and Specialized Assessment Techniques: Issues and Methods

This chapter augments earlier chapters on clinical and psychometric assessments of criminal responsibility with a concise discussion of laboratory and other specialized procedures. Since many of these procedures, particularly the laboratory methods, require specialized consultations, this chapter focuses less on the method (e.g., how serum testosterone level is measured) than on the relevance of these approaches to the assessment of criminal responsibility. The chapter is organized around nine topics: (1) laboratory methods with sex offenders, (2) alcohol and drug abuse, (3) chromosomal analysis, (4) E. E. G.'s and criminal behavior, (5) CT Scans and diagnostic imaging, (6) episodic dyscontrol syndrome, (7) drug assisted interviews, (8) polygraph, and (9), forensic hypnosis.

The complex interactions between biology, criminal behavior, and mental illness have been addressed only in a preliminary manner. Research has, for example, established differences (e.g., Goldstein, 1974) between aggressive and nonaggressive behavior on neurochemical, pharmacological, endocrinological, and genetic studies. Little is understood about the relationship of these biological differences for aggressivity and criminality and the biochemical differences noted in many major mental disorders, particularly schizophrenic and major affective illnesses. Explanatory models of both aggressive behavior and mental illness are further confounded by the frequent occurrence of psychoactive medication use and/or substance abuse.

These complexities are well exemplified by genetic studies focusing on twin and familial research. McBroom (1980), reviewing the literature on behavioral genetics, found significant correlates, based on twin studies; for both schizophrenia and affective illness. In addition, she summarized data based on twin and adoptee studies that suggest a genetic factor in criminal behavior. More recently, Mednick and Finello (1983) examined criminality in monozygotic and same-sex dizygotic twins through a review of eight twin studies. They found that identical twins had a much higher likelihood of concordance for criminal behavior than fraternal twins. In addition, they conducted a large-scale adoption study of 14,427 adoptions.

Mednick and Finello (1983) concluded that if both the biological and adoptive parents had a criminal history, then the likelihood of the adoptive sons' being convicted of a criminal offense was 24.5%; if the biological parent had a criminal history and the adoptive parent did not, the rate dropped to 20%; if the adoptive parent had a criminal history and biological parent did not, the rate dropped further to 14.7%; and if neither parent had a criminal history, the rate was approximately 13.5%. These results would strongly support a biological factor in criminal behavior. Further analysis suggests, however, that this relationship exists primarily for property crimes and not necessarily for violent crimes. To complicate matters further, Bohman (1978) examined both alcohol abuse and criminality for 2,000 adoptees. He found that male adoptees were more likely to be convicted of criminal offenses if either of their biological parents had a history of alcohol abuse or alcohol abuse and criminal history combined. An interesting finding was that the biological parents' criminal history alone was apparently unrelated to their sons' criminal history. These findings from both studies did not hold for the female adoptees. Thus, while there appears to be some genetic factor involved in criminal behavior, a clear understanding of this relationship has yet to be explicated.

Many other biological factors have been correlated to criminal behavior. Research by Lewis and Shanok (1979; Shanok and Lewis, 1981) suggested that aggressive delinquents have a greater incidence of respiratory illness, head and face trauma, and accidents and injuries that, in turn, require significantly more outpatient and inpatient medical attention. In addition, delinquent children had a significantly higher percentage of perinatal difficulties than their matched control group.

Other research has suggested that aggressive individuals (Hare and Cox, 1978) may have lower central nervous system arousal with concomitant differences in measures of their electrodermal and cardiovascular activity, as well as a higher incidence of soft neurological signs (Halleck, 1967). An important consideration is a relationship of medical illnesses to the presentation of pseudopsychiatric symptoms; that is, numerous endocrinological and neurological disturbances may present clinically as forms of functional impairment. This latter point stresses the need for thorough medical histories with criminal defendants. In addition, medical and neurological consultations may often be required where presentation or history suggest a physical abnormality. The following sections examine in some detail laboratory methods and other specialized procedures pertinent to criminal responsibility evaluations.

LABORATORY METHODS WITH SEX OFFENDERS

Research has examined the relationship of plasma testosterone levels to aggressive and sexually deviant behavior. (Rada, Kellner, and Winslow, 1976; Rada, 1978; Langevin, Ben-Aron, Coulthard, Heasman, et al., 1985). Research based on animal models have demonstrated a link between elevated testosterone levels in primates and socially dominant and aggressive behavior; several studies of violent prisoners in general offer tentative support to these findings. For example, Kreuz and Rose (1972) found significantly higher plasma testosterone levels in prisoners with violent histories than those without. The study failed to discriminate, however, between those prisoners who were currently engaging in fighting and verbally aggressive behavior from nonaggressive prisoners. Similarly, Ehrenkranz, Bliss, and Sheard (1974) found that twelve prisoners with chronic aggressive behavior (prior to and during incarceration) had significantly higher testosterone levels than nonaggressive patients. In addition, they found that socially dominant patients formed an intermediate group between the chronically aggressive prisoners and the other nonaggressive prisoners.

More germane to forensic evaluations have been studies on the relationship of plasma testosterone level to violent sexual behavior. Early interest in the effects of testosterone level on sexual behavior focused on whether those who engaged in homosexual behavior had lower testosterone levels than heterosexuals. An initial study (Kolodny, Masters, and Hendryx, 1971) suggested this conclusion. More recent research has disconfirmed these findings (e.g., Birk, Williams, Chasin, and Rose, 1973) and even suggested that in some cases male homosexuals may have higher testosterone levels (Brodie, Gartrell, Doering, and Rhue, 1974). With reference to violent sexual behavior, Rada and his associates (Rada, Laws, and Kellner, 1976; Rada, Laws, Kellner, Stivastava, and Peake, 1983) measured the plasma testosterone levels of fifty-two rapists and twelve child molesters. They found that those rapists who are brutally violent and inflicted physical injury had significantly higher testosterone levels (i.e., 852.8 ng/100 ml) than normals (625.2 ng/100 ml), other rapists (595.7 ng/100 ml), and child molesters (501.7 ng/100 ml); all levels were generally in normal limits.

The testosterone levels of sex offenders have been considered primarily by forensic psychiatrists with reference to presentence evaluations. In these evaluations, the forensic clinician might make recommendations regarding the treatability of a violent sex offender through the use of an antiandrogen medication. The fact that antiandrogen (i.e., testosterone depleting) approaches have been moderately successful in the treatment of violent sex offenders (Rada, 1978; Bradford, 1983; Walker, 1978; Money, 1970b), as well as with aggressive patients (Blumer and Migeon, 1975), would lend credence to the role of testosterone in aggressive sexual behavior. Given the wide range of testosterone levels found in normal nonviolent individuals (i.e., from 200 to 1,400 ng/100 ml), it would be difficult to argue that a high testosterone level provided an overpowering impulse that could not be resisted. This finding would, therefore, suggest no direct applicability of plasma testosterone levels in the determination of criminal responsibility; more appropriate applications would be in presentencing evaluations.

Although the radioimmunoassay procedure for analyzing testosterone is apparently quite precise (Rada, Laws, and Kellner, 1976), an individual's testosterone level may be influenced by several factors. According to Rada (1978, 1980), testosterone level may fluctuate because of diurnal effects, chronic abuse of alcohol, and use of psychoactive medication. Rada further suggested that the effects of social isolation and incarceration may likewise deplete androgen levels. Such factors must be taken into account in assessing serum testosterone levels.

A second laboratory procedure involves the measurement of penile tumescence of rapists and other sex offenders through the use of plethysmographic methods. Such approaches measure the sexual arousal of defendants to consenting and deviant sexual material by measuring the degree of erection to various erotic stimuli. Rosen and Keefe (1978) reviewed the currently available plethysmographs. They concluded that a circumferential method (i.e., measuring the circumference of the penis as a measure of its degree of erection) and the volumetric method (i.e., measuring the volume displacement during an erection) were, depending on the specific model, both effective at reliably measuring changes in penile tumescence. In comparing the two procedures, the volumetric approach, utilizing an air-filled penile plethysmograph (see McConaghy, 1974; Freund, Langevin, and Barlow, 1974), appeared to more sensitive to subtle changes in tumescence. Penile tumescence, unlike other physiological measures of sexual arousal, is not confounded by unrelated emotional states such as anxiety or general excitement (Zuckerman, 1971).

The basic procedure for evaluating sex offenders' degree of arousal is to present the defendant, within a laboratory setting, with examples of consenting sex, violent nonconsenting sex, and aggressive nonsexual stimuli. These stimuli are presented by brief audiotape descriptions that have been found to be more effective than visual stimuli in eliciting sexual response (Abel, Barlow, Blanchard, and Guild, 1977). Given the wide variability in sexual arousal, Abel and his associates (Abel, Becker, and Skinner, 1980) have found it necessary to compare an individual's sexual arousal under various conditions. This has resulted in several indices of sexual responsiveness. The rape index (arousal to rape divided by arousal to consenting sex) has been shown to distinguish rapists from nonrapists with a cutoff score of .9. As the rape index increases, there is a greater likelihood that the subject is a sadistic rapist who has committed a high number of rapes.

Based on limited data, Abel, Barlow, Blanchard, and Guild (1977) suggest that a rape index exceeding 2 is likely to be a sadistic rapist who uses far more aggression than necessary to complete the rape. These findings were replicated by Barbaree, Marshall, and Lanthier (1979) and Quinsey, Chaplin, and Varney (1981) although they were not supported in a study of sixteen rapists (Langevin, Ben-Aron, Coulthard, Heasman, et al., 1985). In a similar fashion, Abel and his associates (Abel, Barlow, Blanchard, and Guild, 1977) also developed a pedophiliac index (i.e., arousal to children divided by arousal to consenting adults) and a pedophiliac aggression index (i.e., arousal to physical coercion of a child divided by consenting intercourse with a child). The former index has differentiated between child molesters who are recidivists (average pedophiliac index was 1.81) and those who are not (average pedophiliac index was .50). These indices of sexual arousal have been related to patients' criminal history, age preference, degree of coercion, and frequency.

Concern has been raised regarding the degree of voluntary control that rapists and child molesters might have over their sexual arousal to deviant sexual stimuli. Although Abel and his colleagues conclude that this degree of control is not substantial (Abel, Becker, and Skinner, 1980), particularly with the use of audiotapes (Abel, Barlow, Blanchard, and Mavissakalian, 1975), others like Wydra, Marshall, Earls, and Barbaree (1983) provide experimental data that indicate that rapists can control their arousal even after sexual stimulation.

A related consideration is the role of alcohol intoxication in deviant sexual arousal. Briddell and his colleagues (Briddell, Rimm, Caddy, Krawitz, Sholis, and Wunderlin, 1978) found that normal males who consumed alcohol or believed that they had (i.e., placebo) experienced greater arousal to rape or violent sexual cues. This study, which has been criticized on methodological grounds by Barbaree, Marshal, Yates, and Lightfoot (1983), was not supported in their study of thirty-two male social drinkers. It is, therefore, unclear under what conditions, if any, alcohol plays a significant role in disinhibiting deviant sexual arousal. More germane to this discussion is the need for research on the effects of alcohol on individuals who already demonstrate a deviant sexual arousal. Langevin, Ben-Aron, Coulthard, Day, et al. (1985) found that subjects who had ingested alcohol had greater arousal to mildly erotic materials than controls. In light of these findings, does alcohol play a significant disinhibiting role with sex offenders? Because of these complicated issues, Earls (1983) suggested caution in the interpretation of penile measures with sex offenders.

Measures of penile tumescence as a reliable indicator of sexual arousal have not usually been employed in assessing the criminal responsibility of sex offenders. They may, however, in certain circumstances, provide useful clinical information regarding a defendant's degree of arousal to deviant sexual material. For example, a defendant who claims no sexual interest in children but says he or she acted under command hallucinations from Satan could be evaluated for degree of arousal to sexually aggressive and non-aggressive acts with children. Such an evaluation might provide useful corroborative data either confirming or disconfirming the defendant's reported interest and arousal, but it would not directly address the defendant's intent or criminal responsibility. Similarly, penile measures might provide useful ancillary information on the defendant's arousal and sadistic tendencies involving the crime in question. If a defendant's responses on the plethysmograph suggests a high arousal to deviant behavior, the forensic clinician may wish to discuss these discrepancies with the defendant. Further research is needed on the potential interactions between sexual arousal, major mental illness, and criminal behavior before plethysmographic approaches assume more than an adjunctive role in the determination of criminal responsibility.

ALCOHOL AND DRUG ABUSE

Alcohol Abuse

Numerous studies have examined the relationship of alcohol consumption to criminal behavior. This research has typically found that a majority of individuals convicted of a serious crime had previously ingested moderate to heavy amounts of alcohol. Self-report research of this type is fairly consistent both for homicide (e.g., Wolfgang, 1958; Voss and Hepburn, 1968; Mayfield, 1976) and for aggressive sexual crimes (Rada, 1975; Rada, Kellner, Laws, and Winslow, 1978; Barnard, Holzer, and Vera, 1979) but not crime in general. Such research has several constraints (see Collins, 1981) including no reliable measure of alcohol consumption, no comparison of the base rates for subpopulations or situations, and no measure of the interactions of alcohol with other drugs. An additional issue for those seeking a causal relationship between alcohol and criminal behavior is whether the alcohol consumption prior to the criminal behavior was atypical for the individual. Groth (1979) found, for example, that the majority of rapists had consumed no more that the usual amounts of alcohol.

Experimental research has attempted to elucidate the relationship of alcohol to human physical aggression. This research has typically employed the competition paradox (Taylor, 1967) in which the subject attempts to beat his or her opponent in a reaction time task in administering a shock to the other person. Research with this experimental condition (see Taylor and Leonard, 1983) has shown a positive relationship with subjects who ingest a high level of alcohol utilizing higher shock settings than those who ingest a low amount. In subsequent studies, the subject was led to believe that the opponent planned to administer a strong shock to the subject. Under this condition, the intoxicated subjects were more likely to respond to this perceived threat with increasing levels of shocks than subjects without alcohol. Models for explaining these differences include pharmacological disinhibition (i.e., alcohol weakens superego controls), alcohol-induced arousal (i.e., heightens physiological arousal to aggressivity), and learned disinhibition (i.e., socially inappropriate behaviors are tolerated when intoxicated). Taylor and Leonard (1983), while not endorsing any of these models, conclude that interactive effects of the alcohol and contextual cues increase the likelihood for aggressive behavior.

An area of considerable interest to forensic evaluations is the relationship of blood alcohol level to intoxication. Tinklenberg (1973) examined urine alcohol concentrations and found that individuals arrested for violent crimes tended to have alcohol levels between 0.10 and 0.39. MacDonald (1976) reviewed studies of blood alcohol level and frank intoxication. He found that most individuals were clearly intoxicated with blood alcohol levels of 200 mg although a few individuals did not appear intoxicated with blood alcohol levels of 350 mg. Given this wide degree of individual variability (see Hill, 1981) blood alcohol levels cannot be related to a defendant's intentionality or criminal responsibility. MacDonald (1976) noted that Breathalyzer tests for alcohol may give an accurate measure if there is a minimum of a 15 minute interval between the test and alcohol ingestion or regurgitation. In addition, he observed that severe medical problems or severe hyperventilation might dramatically increase the breath alcohol level. A further complicating factor is the absorption rate of alcohol (averaging 15 mg percent per hour), which also shows considerable variability and significantly influences blood alcohol levels measured at the time of arrest. Given these constraints, forensic clinicians should only consider blood alcohol levels as basic corroborative data for the amount of alcohol ingested.

Voluntary intoxication (Table 8.1) is not a defense accepted under the legal standards of criminal responsibility. Fingarette and Hasse (1979) have noted this inconsistency in the law whereby alcohol addiction may be a

Table 8.1
Effect of Intoxication on Judgment and Actions at Time of Crime

	Sane (%)	Insane (%)
Mild, no significant interference	9.9	5.4
Moderate, peripheral interference	25.2	2.2
Severe, major interference	12.6	5.4

defense against minor crimes (e.g., public intoxication) but not against major crimes. Cases of involuntary intoxication (i.e., forced by others to consume alcohol) are extremely rare and unlikely to be seen in criminal responsibility evaluations. The forensic clinician may also need to address two additional issues: pathological intoxication and toxic psychosis.

Pathological intoxication, referred to in the *Diagnostic and Statistical Manual of Mental Disorders (DSM III)* as *alcohol idiosyncratic intoxication* (American Psychiatric Association, 1980), refers to a marked behavioral change, often aggressive behavior, following the recent ingestion of a small amount of alcohol. The aggressive behavior is seen as atypical for the individual and lasts no more than a few hours in duration. Pathological intoxication has been reported in individuals with neurological abnormalities, unusual fatigue, or debilitating physical illness, although not all of these are necessarily present.

Pathological intoxication is apparently an extremely rare disorder. Bach-Y-Rita, Lion, and Ervin (1970) examined ten patients who were diagnosed as having pathological intoxication. They found that the patients had used alcohol without aggressivity, reported periods of depression and irritability, and demonstrated no aggressivity when administered the equivalent of two to four drinks over a 30-minute period. They suggested that alcohol may be used by these patients as a self-medication for increased irritability, anxiety, or depression. Such individuals would therefore not meet the current diagnosis of alcohol idiosyncratic intoxication. Although Maletzky (1973) was able to elicit uncharacteristic aggressive behavior in a study of twenty-three male patients, questions remain whether this behavior could be accounted for by psychiatric diagnoses other than pathological intoxication.

The forensic clinician must consider several practical issues in establishing the diagnosis of pathological intoxication. First, such a diagnosis requires detailed corroboration of the individual's day-to-day functioning, with particular emphasis on aggressive or assaultive behavior. If the clinician cannot establish that the behavior is clearly atypical for the individual, then a diagnosis of pathological intoxication cannot be made. Second, the diagnosis requires ruling out other mental disorders that could account for the aggressive behavior, such as an intermittent explosive personality disorder or antisocial personality disorder. Third, if the diagnosis of pathological intoxication can be convincingly established, the forensic clinician must address the defendant's awareness of this condition. If the defendant reports a clear pattern of explosive behavior associated with alcohol use, can it be argued that this risk was unforeseeable? This complex issue must be addressed on an individual basis in considering the defendant's awareness and comprehension of drinking and the subsequent likelihood of aggressive behavior.

Alcoholic hallucinosis involves vivid auditory hallucinations following the cessation or reduction of alcohol ingestion in individuals with alcohol dependence (American Psychiatric Association, 1980). Onset typically begins within 48 hours of nondrinking, with unpleasant and disturbing hallucinations. Although the individual may act to defend himself or herself against the voices, rarely do individuals with alcoholic hallucinosis experience command hallucinations. This disorder has its onset in individuals with an extensive history of alcohol abuse and is typically brief in duration (i.e., less than a week).

The forensic evaluation of alcoholic hallucinosis is often straightforward. Individuals with this disorder often have extensive well-documented histories of alcohol dependence including clear-cut patterns of increased tolerance or withdrawal symptoms. In addition, such defendants often require immediate medical attention, which provides considerable documentation of the disorder and auditory hallucinations. Further, there may be considerable evidence from previous episodes of alcoholic hallucinosis of the patient's behavior and response to auditory hallucinations. In addressing the potential impact of alcoholic hallucinosis on the issue of criminal responsibility, the forensic psychiatrist or psychologist should follow the outline on hallucinations in chapter 5.

Drug Abuse

Drug abuse, while posing a myriad of clinical issues, is addressed by the courts in a manner similar to alcohol intoxication. The courts have held (see Brooks, 1974) that a psychotic state that is a result of the immediate influence of a voluntarily ingested drug is not applicable to the defense of insanity. Drug use may lead to a defense of insanity if it is a precipitator of an underlying disorder, with the psychosis and not the drug effects impairing the defendant's cognitive and/or volitional capacities. Further, although drug addiction has been recognized by the courts as something of a compulsive disorder, it has not been used as the basis of an insanity defense. As an additional consideration, a defendant with multiple diagnoses including a functional psychosis like a schizophrenic disorder and a substance abuse disorder must be assessed on the issue of criminal responsibility and what were the relevant contributions of each disorder, if any, on the defendant's criminal responsibility.

The relationship of drug abuse to criminal behavior eludes simple explanation. The majority of drug abusers, by definition, are criminals in the acquisition and use of illicit substances. No simple causal relationship appears to exist between the two (Grinspoon and Bakalar, 1978; Richman, 1985) although each appears to contribute to the other.

The clinical evaluation of drug abusers is further complicated by the illicit status of most abused drugs. The criminal defendant may be reluctant, particularly when faced with minor crimes, to admit to further criminal behavior like the use of illicit drugs that threatens additional prosecution. In contrast, the defendant may purposefully exaggerate the amount of drug abuse when faced with serious charges so it can he used as a mitigating factor. A third and common alternative is that the defendant may not know what drugs he or she is ingesting or their purity. Studies have shown that abusers who have bought mescaline, LSD (lysergic acid diethylamide) cocaine, and THC (tetrahydrocannabinol) may actually be receiving PCP (phencyclidine) as the principal ingredient (Reed and Kane, 1973). A fourth and unknown factor is the presence of adulterants, their effects, and possible interactions with other drugs in affecting the defendant's clinical status.

Other clinical issues include intended or unintended polydrug abuse that may have an additive or potentiating effect. In addition, chronic drug users may develop (see Cox, Jacobs, LeBlanc, and Marshman, 1983) metabolic or central nervous system tolerance or cross-tolerance to abused drugs. In addition, there is a considerable degree of individual variability in drug abusers' response to specific drug dosages, and this variability has been convincingly demonstrated in laboratory studies. All these factors constrain attempts to correlate clinical presentation with self-reported drug use.

Defendants who are hospitalized immediately following arrest may provide a wealth of laboratory studies and medical observations. These data may be of great benefit in establishing the amounts and types of drugs abused and their effect on the clinical presentation of the patient (Shapiro, 1984), and here the issue of individual variability becomes evident. For example, Yesavage and Freman (1978) found that seven of fifteen patients admitted with PCP psychosis (on the basis of self-report, corroboration, and clinical findings) had undetectable levels of PCP in their urine, despite gross disorganization of behavior that necessitated several days of hospitalization.

The following paragraphs discuss classes of drugs frequently abused and relates each of them to both psychosis and criminal behavior. This discussion emphasizes the abuse of PCP and amphetamines because these drugs in particular have been associated with high frequencies of bizarre or unplanned violent behavior.

PCP was developed in the late 1950s as an anesthetic agent in surgical procedures. It was not until 1967 that it was observed in use as a street drug. The drug, which has approximately thirty analogs of which at least six have been used by humans (Domino, 1978), continues to have wide usage in spite of its negative effects. Siegel (1978*b*), from a survey of 319 adult PCP users, noted the following negative effects: perceptual disturbances, restlessness, disorientation, and anxiety. In addition, approximately one-third had experienced paranoid thoughts while others experienced irritability and mental confusion. These negative effects apparently do not outweigh the positive feelings from heightened sensitivity to outside stimuli, increased stimulation, dissociation, mood elevation, inebriation, and relaxation. The unpredictability of this drug experience may add to its excitement (Petersen and Stillman, 1978).

PCP use has been linked both in the lay and professional press to sensational reports of unrestrained violence (e.g., Dellinger, 1978; Dolan, 1978). Empirical investigations of PCP abuse and violence are difficult since most PCP abusers who have become violent have an extensive history of polydrug abuse (Fauman and Fauman, 1979, 1982). These authors have identified four types of aggressive behavior among PCP abusers. First, reality-oriented and goal-directed aggression is often found in chronic PCP abusers. The second is more closely dose related and involves unexpected impulsive aggression involving automobile accidents, some fights, and impulsive criminal acts. The third is unexpected bizarre behavior, often with elements of sadistic aggression or stereotyped behavior; this is very rare in frequency and typically occurs 2 to 3 days after the last drug use. The fourth is severely disorganized behavior, usually uncoordinated and chaotic. This final type is relatively uncommon, probably dose related, and may involve polydrug use. While this classification requires further refinement and replication, it underscores the complexity of PCP-related aggression. Schuckit and Morrissey (1978) found in a study of 355 court-referred adolescents that PCP users more frequently engaged in repeated fights and used weapons. The relationship of PCP use to aggression was not established in this study.

PCP psychosis (Luisada, 1978) is characterized by autistic and delusional thinking and commonly involves global paranoia, delusions of superhuman strength and invulnerability, and delusions of persecution and grandiosity. A formal thought disorder may be present with periods of extreme emotional lability and unpredictable behavior. Luisada, in a study of 200 inpatients with PCP psychosis, established a modal course of impairment including violent psychotic behavior (average of 5 days) followed by restless unpredictable behavior, although more controlled (average of 5 days), that was in turn followed by a rapid disappearance of thought disorder and paranoia (average of 4 days). In addition, the data suggest that patients with a schizophrenic history may be hypersensitive to the adverse effects of PCP. Other research (e.g., Allen and Young, 1978) suggested that a significant proportion of individuals with PCP psychosis may not rapidly recover and continue after 30 days to have hallucinations, tangential speech, and aggressive behavior.

Siegel (1978b) has examined closely the clinical changes of individuals experiencing PCP intoxication. He reports that PCP intoxication can increase aggressive reactions, decrease judgment, occasionally result in hypersexuality, and produce panic reactions and paranoia. While these responses, reflecting the immediate use of PCP, may not be grounds for exculpation, they may, depending on the jurisdiction, be used for diminished capacity in which the abuser's ability to form a specific intent was reduced.

Amphetamines were hailed in the 1930s as a wonder drug, which led to their indiscriminate use in medical practice. Other factors that led to the widespread abuse of amphetamines (see Rawlin, 1968) was their availability during World War II, popularity among truck drivers, and introduction both in pill and intravenous forms into the evolving drug culture. As the medical availability of amphetamines is increasingly curtailed, underground laboratories have been established.

Chronic amphetamine abuse has been implicated in the emergence of psychiatric disorders, particularly amphetamine delusional disorder (American Psychiatric Association, 1980). This syndrome develops following the long-term use of moderate or high doses of amphetamines (not a solitary large dose). It is characterized by persecutory delusions, ideas of reference, aggressiveness and hostility, and anxiety or psychomotor agitation. In addition, individuals experiencing an amphetamine delusional disorder are likely to have distortions of body image and misperceptions of others' faces. Suspiciousness, which may originally be experienced as pleasant, may subsequently lead to aggressive or violent behavior against imagined enemies. Tactile hallucinations of insects crawling on or under the skin may also be observed. Studies of psychiatric admissions (Rockwell and Oswald, 1968) indicate amphetamine use in approximately 15% of the cases through urinalysis, although only one-half of these patients had acknowledged the use prior to drug testing. Hekimian and Gershon (1968) studied amphetamine use in 112 adult inpatients and found that nearly one-fourth of the patients had chronically abused amphetamines (mean duration was 3.4 years). In attempting to establish pre-addiction diagnoses, they found 9 of the patients had prior schizophrenic symptoms and 4 were sociopathic.

Spotts and Spotts (1980) reviewed, as a National Institute of Drug Abuse project, several experimental studies on the relationship of experimentally induced amphetamine psychosis and violent behavior. Several patients, previously nonaggressive, experienced violent impulses that included one assault. Ellinwood (1971), who studied thirteen homicidal amphetamine users, found that seven had paranoid delusions at the time of the offense, four were emotionally labile or impulsive, and two had consumed alcohol. Arrests for the majority of criminal behavior involving amphetamine users (see Greenberg, 1976) appear to involve burglary and robbery. Studies have shown (Allen, Safer, and Covi, 1975) that small to moderate uses of amphetamines, up to 60 mg daily, have not been associated with aggression.

Amphetamine-related aggression appears only to occur in the presence of an amphetamine delusional disorder. Thus, the assessment of aggression in chronic amphetamine users must involve a detailed evaluation of their patterns of usage and psychopathology. Heavy users range from 250 to 300 mg per day although as much as 1,500 mg may occasionally be observed (Cox, Jacobs, LeBlanc, and Marshman, 1983).

Chronic use of cocaine may occasionally lead to increased aggressiveness although this is less likely to be associated with overt psychotic thinking. According to *DSM III*, high doses of cocaine may be associated with transient ideas of reference in paranoid ideation but are usually limited to the period of intoxication (less than 24 hours before recovery). It has been observed that heavy cocaine use (Post, 1975; Busch and Schnoll, 1986) may lead to more chronic psychotic processes, particularly in those patients with preexisting schizophrenic or other disorders.

The abuse of LSD appears to be diminishing and, with it, reports of LSD-related aggressive behavior (Menuck, 1983). Although the early work of Barter and Reite (1969) suggested that LSD intoxication should be considered a true psychosis and grounds for the insanity defense, more recent work (e.g., Brooks, 1974) questioned this conclusion in the context of a recent case law. Although LSD has occasionally been associated with sudden violent behavior, this aggressiveness rarely extends beyond the period of acute intoxication (Cox, Jacobs, LeBlanc, and Marshman, 1983).

Heroin use has long been associated with criminal behavior. Review of research (see Speckart and Anglin, 1985) concluded that chronic heroin users engage in significantly more criminal behavior than nonaddicts. This behavior appears to be income producing to support their addiction and relates primarily, although not exclusively, to property crimes. As noted, addictions, despite their physical dependencies, have not been held to be sufficient grounds for exculpation in insanity defenses. In addition, most criminal behavior observed in heroin addicts is apparently goal oriented—that is, to maintain their drug habit.

Solvents or inhalants are frequently used by adolescent males because of their availability and inexpensiveness. These include glues, cleaning solutions, nail polish removers, lighter fluids, paint and paint thinners, aerosols, and other petroleum products. The high typically lasts 15 to 45 minutes, with feelings of giddiness and lightheadedness. Schuckit (1979) reported symptoms of confusion and disorientation in frequent abusers with occasional violent behavior during acute intoxication.

Controversy surrounds the use of marijuana, and concerted efforts are being made both to decriminalize and recriminalize this drug. Although occasional paranoid ideation has been noted with the use of marijuana, it rarely extends for more than a few hours and typically has little effect on the individual's behavior toward others. As noted by Cox, Jacobs, LeBlanc, and Marshman (1983), these mild paranoid reactions rarely lead to abusive or violent behavior.

The majority of criminal defendants assessed for criminal responsibility have done at least some experimenting with psychoactive drugs prior to their arrest. Rogers and Zibarg (1985) found no significant differences in the history of drug experimentation of forty-five defendants legally adjudged insane and twenty-one found guilty (Table 8.2). Possibly because of the limited sample size, little significant drug abuse was reported for the time of the offense, and only one criminal defendant warranted the diagnosis of a drug psychosis.

A forensic psychiatrist or psychologist must be thorough in his or her evaluation of a defendant's drug use and its potential role in establishing criminal responsibility. The following is a list of clinical inquiries that can be used in such an evaluation:

1. If the defendant was significantly impaired, was there any prior drug use that might explain his or her presentation?
2. If there has been significant drug use, what clinical differences are reported by the defendant and corroborated by others between periods of drug use and abstinence? If drug use does not appear to alter significantly the defendant's clinical presentation, particularly at the time of the offense, then the forensic clinician may wish to shift his or her emphasis to address other disorders that may account for the criminal behavior.
3. If the defendant's thinking and behavior appear to be significantly influenced by drugs, are these results of the immediate response to the drug intoxication or prolonged effects existing far beyond the active presence of the drug? Although the majority of cases is likely to

Table 8.2
History of Drug Use among Defendants Legally Adjudged Insane and Guilty

Types of Drugs[a]	Insane (%)	Sane (%)
Narcotics	17.8[b]	23.8
Amphetaminelike substances	24.8	23.8
Cocaine	22.2	05.8
Sedatives, hypnotics, and tranquilizers	28.9	19
Cannabis derivatives	40	38.1
Hallucinogens	15.6	23.8
Solvents	11.1	4.8

[a]Significant usage by RDC criteria.
[b]All chi-square values comparing insane and sane defendants are nonsignificant.

be clear cut (either immediate or prolonged), there may be marginal cases (e.g., detection of PCP in urinalysis 5 days after ingestion). In such cases, there would be no clear demarcation when intoxication stops and legally defined fixed psychosis begins. One solution to these marginal cases is to present these clinical data to the court for its decision in a particular case regarding the intoxication-psychosis dichotomy.

4. Where there is both a major mental disorder and significant drug use, would the criminal behavior have occurred without the drugs? This is a particularly complex issue since many schizophrenics also experiment with drugs and may be particularly vulnerable to their adverse effects.

The thrust of these four inquiries is the exclusion of drug-intoxicated defendants, whose behavior is a result of the intoxication, from being clinically evaluated as not responsible for their actions. In marginal cases, it is recommended that the forensic clinician consult with an addiction specialist or psychopharmacologist about drug interactions and their behavioral correlates in criminal defendants. In cases or prolonged impairment of psychotic proportions, diagnosis (whether organic or functional), while important, is less critical than establishing the relationship of this disorder to the criminal behavior. For example, a chronic PCP delusional disorder may be indistinguishable from a PCP-precipitated schizophrenic disorder, although either could play a significant role in the assessment of criminal responsibility.

CHROMOSOMAL ANALYSIS: THE XYY

The XYY karyotype was first reported in 1961 and was soon linked, on the basis of questionable statistical data, to aggressive criminals. Research at Carstairs Hospital (Jacobs, Brunton, Melville, Brittain, and McClemont, 1965; Price, Strong, Whatmore, and McClemont, 1966) indicated that nearly 3% of 342 mentally retarded patients had an XYY karyotype. Research on XYY karyotypes has proceeded from case studies to specific research on various populations and finally to overall incidence rate. The first two approaches, which form the bulk of the XYY research, contained an inherent sampling bias (Owen, 1972) in selecting subjects on the basis of known XYY characteristics. In addition, Owen indicated that caution is needed in accepting XYY diagnoses found i earlier research; he concluded that some subjective judgment may have entered into earlier karyotyping procedures and that some subjects diagnosed as XYY were actually XXYY or XXY. Owen found in his review a much lower rate than previous research for both hospitalized patients (10 XYY cases in 8,500 patients) as well as in prisons (55 XYY cases in 17,500 inmates). Hook (1973) provided an exhaustive review of chromosomal abnormalities in psychiatric and prison settings. Larger studies varied from 0 to 4% of XYY cases in both populations; this wide variability again suggested problems in sampling procedures. Hook concluded that an increased prevalence rate might be associated with differences in height (i.e., seen as more threatening) or in intellectual abilities. In addressing these issues, Witkin and his associates (Witkin et al., 1976) performed a chromosomal analysis on 4,139 tall Danish males. Although 5 of the 12 XYY subjects had criminal convictions, these were for minor offenses with mild penalties. The researchers also found that XYY individuals had lower intellectual functioning and fewer years of education. They concluded that this greater incidence of petty offenses was related to the lower intellectual abilities, and because of the nature of the offenses, the likelihood of apprehension was greater. They found no relationship between XYY individuals and violent behavior.

Many attempts have been made to relate the XYY karyotype to criminal responsibility. Owen (1972) cites a considerable literature in the 1960s of cases where the XYY karyotype was raised as a component of a psychiatric abnormality in an insanity defense. These cases (Craft, 1978) were often dramatic and occasionally led to insanity acquittals. Recent research (Theilgaard, 1983) provided no causal models for chromosomal abnormalities, including other variations (see Money, 1970a) for XYY and criminal responsibility. Although a higher incidence of property crime is noted among XYY individuals, there is no empirical evidence to suggest that such individuals lacked either cognitive or volitional capacity in the commission of these petty offenses. Although evidence of chromosomal abnormalities may have some influence on the triers of fact, it has no practical value in the assessment of criminal responsibility. Thus, a defendant of limited intellectual abilities should be assessed on the relationship of this possible retardation to the commission of the offense, regardless of the specific etiology of intellectual deficits.

THE EEG AND CRIMINAL BEHAVIOR

The relationship of electroencephalograms (EEGs) to antisocial behavior has sustained considerable interest since the 1940s. Stafford-Clark and Taylor (1949) studied five groups of murders: incidental killings, clearly motivated murders, apparently motiveless murders, sex murders, and homicides committed by individuals unfit to stand trial or not guilty by reason of insanity (NGRI). They found the highest incidence of EEG abnormalities for the motiveless and insane groups. Hill and Pond (1952) replicated this research with 105 homicide cases and yielded similar results. Such early findings are difficult to interpret in light of more recent research that has suggested that individuals with behavior disorders, psychopaths, and schizophrenics have high rates of EEG abnormalities (Tucker, Detre, Harrow, and Glaser, 1965). The criteria varied from study to study since what constitutes an abnormal EEG was not standardized. This point is exemplified in a study of Ostow and Ostow (cited in Halleck, 1967) that found an extremely high prevalence of abnormal EEGs in diverse groups (i.e., 80% of the schizophrenics, 65% of the conscientious objectors, and 56% of the homosexuals).

Tucker and his colleagues (Tucker, Detre, Harrow, and Glaser, 1965) examined EEG abnormalities by diagnostic groups and compared clinical descriptions of patients with normal and abnormal EEGs; they found other patient groups likewise evidenced a substantial percentage of abnormal EEGs, including depressive, neurotic, and organic mental disorders. Researchers generally accept (see MacDonald, 1976) that EEG abnormalities, by themselves, are not reliable indicators of either mental disorder or organically based criminal behavior. The following discussion examines in detail 14 and 6 per second spikes on the EEG and its relationship to epilepsy.

Gibbs and Gibbs (1951) identified the 14 and 6 per second positive spikes as a particular EEG pattern found in 6% of epileptic and 2% of normal cases. This pattern was different from that of psychomotor epilepsy because of a higher incidence of assaultiveness that they characterized as directed and skillfully executed. They reported a few cases of rage reaction, which is found with other types of epilepsy. This finding generated considerable enthusiasm, particularly in the study of behavior disorders in adolescence. Schwade and Geiger (1956, 1960) reported a high proportion (73%) of 6 and 14 per second positive spiking with aggressive adolescents. Unfortunately, these studies suffer from several methodological problems including a sampling bias (only those with suspected organicity were referred) and a lack of adequate statistical comparison with a control group. Pathological behavior is described (Schwade and Geiger, 1956, p. 307) as "impulsivity, inability to establish controls, in some no memory or no awareness of the act, varying degrees of violent action without demonstrable feeling tone, and with inability to change the direction of the act until it is completed." The authors further suggest the uncontrollability of behavior (1960, p. 617) in "response to a deep, undeniable, inner need, and extreme sort of compulsion which cannot be redirected." Most of the patients studied were of average intelligence and yielded no abnormal studies with respect to spinal fluid or pneumoencephalograms.

Despite the enthusiasm for these earlier studies (e.g., Woods, 1961), more recent research has failed to corroborate these findings. Weiner (1966), for example, failed to find any significant differences in a controlled study of delinquent and nondelinquent adolescents. Further, MacDonald (1976) reviewed numerous studies that suggest that the 14 and 6 per second positive spiking may be found in normal as well as behaviorally disordered adolescents. Such variability in findings would suggest the need for large-scale multivariate research under standardized conditions to establish the relationship of this EEG abnormality to both mental impairment and criminal behavior.

Interest in the relationship between psychomotor epilepsy and unrestrained violent behavior has persisted since the 1800s (Walker, 1961). Indeed, the early belief that epilepsy was a causal agent in aggressive behavior led to the institutionalization of many epileptic patients. Research by Gunn (Gunn and Fenton, 1969; Gunn and Bonn, 1971) indicates a higher prevalence of epilepsy in prison inmates than in the general population. His research suggested 7.10 per 1,000 inmates are epileptic in comparison to 4.45 in the general population. He concluded that four factors may contribute to this difference: (1) inmates may have greater disturbances of personality and behavior; (2) some epileptics react to social isolation and rejection with criminality; (3) deprived early environments that are common for criminals may expose children to a greater risk of brain damage and subsequent epilepsy; and (4) criminally prone individuals may take greater risks and increase the likelihood of cerebral injury, eventuating in epilepsy. He found that epileptics engaged in proportionately less violent behavior than other prisoners and that there was no difference among the types of epilepsies for the degree of aggressiveness shown in their most recent crime.

Lewis (Lewis, 1976; Lewis, Pincus, Shanok, and Glaser, 1982) found symptoms of psychomotor epilepsy (i.e., not all subjects met strict criteria for epilepsy) in 6% of the 285 adolescents referred to her clinic from juvenile court. Of these, 14 had engaged in aggressive behavior, and 16 reported paranoid ideation. In subsequent analysis Lewis et al. (1982) concluded that 5 subjects had committed violent acts during seizure activity; no precise criteria were offered for how these determinations were made.

Recent research has reported little or no ictal or postictal aggression associated with psychomotor epilepsy. Rodin (1973) found no such examples among 150 patients; Knox (1968) found only 1 case in 434 epileptic patients. Further, King and Ajmone-Marsan (1977) described 9 of 199 patients who behaved aggressively during a seizure. Their action consisted of pushing, flailing, and throwing objects with no evidence of directed or complex aggressive behavior. Ashford, Schultz, and Walsh (1980), in reviewing these data, conclude that destructive behavior is always self-limited, of 1 to 2 minutes in duration, stereotyped, and nondirected.

An international review of aggression and epilepsy was conducted under the aegis of the Epilepsy Foundation of America. This panel (Delgado-Esceuta et al., 1981) identified 19 patients from a group of 5,400 epileptics who had engaged in violent behavior during seizures. The clinical diagnosis of epilepsy was unquestionable in 13 of the 19 patients. Videotapes of their aggressive behaviors were viewed by the panel, who then made quantified ratings of the degree of aggressiveness. They found that 6 of the 13 engaged in nondirected aggressive motion such as kicking or hitting movements not directed at any particular individual or object; 4 utilized force to destroy inanimate objects; 2 engaged in threatening behavior toward others such as shouting or spitting; and 1 engaged in mildly aggressive behavior— namely, attempting to scratch another person. In further examination of past behavior of these patients, 5 had previously expressed mild violence toward another person such as pushing and shoving without bodily harm. An important point is that the researchers found many characteristics that identified aggression during seizure behavior including sudden onset, no evidence of planning, and episodes averaging 29 seconds; and that aggressive behavior was undirected, fragmentary, and unsustained. These findings confirm the rarity of directed aggressive behavior as is typically found in criminal responsibility evaluations. Gunn and Bonn (1971), in their examination of forensic patients at Predmore, a maximum security hospital, found only two cases in which the violent behavior was probably committed during a seizure.

Forensic clinicians should carefully review criminal defendants' past medical and psychiatric history for evidence of epilepsy. Significant findings of seizure behavior require careful investigation including consultation from a neurologist with expertise in epilepsy. Delgado-Escueta et al. (1981) recommended that forensic evaluations utilize the following procedures: establishment of the diagnosis by at least one neurologist with special competence in epilepsy, documentation of epileptic automatisms on videotape with simultaneous EEGs, verification of agression during episodes through videotape and EEGs, elicitation of patterns of aggressive behavior with seizures, and utilization of neurological consultation into the possibility that the crime was part of a seizure. The panel expressed concern at the frequency of cases in which epileptic automatisms had been used as part of a diminished responsibility or insanity defense, given the weight of the earlier described clinical evidence.

MacDonald (1976) warned of the possibility of simulated epilepsy in forensic evaluations; he suggested that several criteria may be clinically employed to differentiate between simulated and actual epilepsy. These include an absence of motive, absence of premeditation and planning, no attempt to conceal the crime, and partial or complete amnesia. Finally, Bacon and Benedek (1982) raise the possibility of psychosis versus automatism following an epileptic seizure. While psychosis has clearly been demonstrated in some epileptics, the possibility of brief psychosis immediately following a seizure of such severity that it contributes to criminal behavior without sequelae is very unlikely.

CT SCANS AND DIAGNOSTIC IMAGING

The development of computerized tomographic (CT) scans has heralded a new generation in diagnostic radiology. CT scans provide a three-dimensional examination of structural abnormalities in psychiatric and neurologic patients. There is some debate over the degree to which CT scanning should be employed in the evaluation of psychiatric patients who do not present neurological symptoms. For example, Owens, Johnstone, Bydder, and Kreel (1980) randomly selected 136 chronic schizophrenic patients for CT scans. They found 10 patients who had conditions that were either potentially remediable or influenced by the diagnosis. Other researchers have argued (e.g., Tsai and Tsuang, 1981) that clinical and psychometric approaches should be employed first in screening out those patients with a low probability of organic brain damage. As a middle ground, Weinberger (1984) suggested the use of CT scans with psychiatric patients who were experiencing confusion and/or dementia of unknown cause, first episode of a psychosis of unknown etiology, movement disorder of unknown etiology, anorexia nervosa, prolonged catatonia, or first episode of a major affective disorder or personality change after the age of 50. This clinical decision model attempts to optimize the use of the CT scan in those cases where an organic condition might go undetected on the basis of a neurological evaluation.

Roberts and Lishman (1984) conducted an important study of the diagnostic usefulness of the CT scan in identifying undetected organicity. The study examined the CT scans of 201 clinical and 122 research referrals. They found that a history of organic symptoms missed approximately 40% and neurological exams missed approximately 60% of patients with abnormal CT scans. Subsequent analysis suggested that CT scans were of considerable importance in evaluating the prognosis of patients (i.e., in 18 cases) and less frequently resulted in changes in diagnosis (i.e., 4 diagnoses were changed to psychogenic and 2 diagnoses were changed to organic) or changes in treatment (i.e., 1 case). Data from the research sample indicated that normal CT scans may be useful in ruling out organic psychosis but that equivocal or definitely abnormal scans may be found with a wide range of disorders including schizophrenia, affective disorders, personality disorders, and anxiety disorders.

Tsai and Tsuang (1981) found similar results to the preceding study in that neither a mental status nor neurological examination was particularly accurate at classifying abnormal CT scans. They found, however, that a combination of a mental status examination, neurological evaluation, Bender-Gestalt with Canter's background interference procedure, and EEGs could correctly screen out patients with normal CT scans. Thus, normal findings on these procedures (either the Bender-Gestalt or EEG could be abnormal) would effectively screen out patients for whom organicity might be suspected. This offers the forensic clinician an alternative procedure to basic questions of differential diagnosis.

Initial research has been completed on CT abnormalities with various functional disorders. Findings suggested (e.g., Weinberger, Wagner, and Wyatt, 1983) that schizophrenics may have several nonspecific CT abnormalities including increased ventricular size and cortical atrophy. Alcoholics also differ from normals (Ron, 1983) with larger ventricles, wider cerebral sulci, and wider Sylvian and interhemispheric fissures. Although these findings are exciting, they have not been refined to the point of diagnostic usefulness.

No published studies were found on the use of CT scans in the assessment of criminal forensic populations. Langevin, Ben-Aron, Coulthard, Heasman, et al. (1978) found 50% of 20 sex offenders (presentence and incarcerated) to have abnormal CT scans in comparison to 39% of a matched group of nonsex offenders. In an informal survey of criminal forensic evaluations at the Metropolitan Toronto Forensic Service, approximately sixty-one CT scans were performed in a 24 month period. Of these, an estimated 45% resulted in abnormal scans; these scans were valuable in several cases in confirming the diagnosis, although they caused no change in diagnosis or psycholegal opinion.

CT scans, along with consultation with experienced neurologists, represent a useful clinical procedure in cases of suspected organicity. The forensic clinician may wish to use both the clinically oriented rule-in procedures of Weinberger (1984) and the rule-out procedures of Tsai and Tsuang (1981) in determining which cases are appropriate for CT scans. In addition, the forensic clinician must consider the relevance of structural abnormalities to the specific issue of criminal responsibility. For example, in the case of a grossly psychotic defendant whose actions were dictated by persecutory delusions, less relevant to the question of insanity is whether there was an additional or underlying organic component to this impairment. With this example, the forensic clinician may wish to proceed with a CT scan for issues beyond criminal responsibility, such as prognosis or treatability.

Several additional diagnostic imaging procedures have been developed that utilize sophisticated methods in conjunction with two- or three-dimensional computer simulations (Lentle, 1983). These include the PET scan (positron emission tomography), the BEAM EEG (brain electrical activity mapping system), and NMR imaging (nuclear magnetic resonance). Insufficient research and normative data on these techniques have been collected to recommend their clinical application in forensic evaluations. PET scans employ radioactively labeled glucose to measure cerebral blood flow and oxygen metabolism in various clinical populations. Initial research suggests that PET scans may at some point be clinically useful in investigating mental disorders like schizophrenia (e.g., Sheppard et al., 1983) although the controversy continues regarding the accuracy and reliability of its measurements (Fox, 1984).

The BEAM EEG developed by Duffy in 1981, involves the use of a 20-lead EEG with computer-synthesized results (see Friedman, 1982). Although this procedure may prove useful in localizing organic abnormalities, the procedure is in the experimental phase of development.

NMR imaging (Pykett, 1982; Lentle, 1983) utilizes radio frequency pulses within a static magnetic field that is able to detect the presence of hydrogen, spatially recording its presence and constructing images of body parts through mathematical algorithms. This method (Bydder, 1983) appears to have advantages over the CT scan because it provides a high level of grey/white matter contrast, particularly in subcortical regions of the brain, and is able to identify in greater detail structural differences. This technique may soon be sufficiently refined and available for use in applied research on psychiatrically impaired individuals.

EPISODIC DYSCONTROL SYNDROME:
A SPECIAL CASE

Episodic dyscontrol syndrome has received considerable attention as an explanatory model for aggressive criminal behavior. Mark and Ervin (1970, p. 126) described four characteristic symptoms: histories of (1) physical assault, (2) pathological intoxication, (3) impulsive sexual behavior, and (4) repeated traffic violations and automobile accidents. In addition, they found that approximately one-half of the individuals studied experienced altered states of consciousness, warning states preceding aggressive attacks, and EEG abnormalities.

Monroe (1970) attempted to develop further the concept of episodic dyscontrol in terms of clinical, psychometric, and EEG correlates. Despite extensive empirical and conceptual work, the results have been discouraging. Self-report data collected on the Monroe Dyscontrol Scale, while having face validity, presuppose the complete honesty of participating patients, which is a severe limitation in forensic research. The scale is found to correlate with a number of psychiatric history variables including a number of emotional problems, behavioral problems, health problems, sexual problems, social problems, and a history of family violence and disease.

Monroe's work (1970) also evidenced small but significant correlations with neurological variables and EEG activation (i.e., correlation with theta frequency counts was .23). Its correlations with the MMPI (Minnesota Multiphasic Personality Inventory) validity scales would raise the index of suspicion regarding malingering with a positive correlation to the F scale (.35) and negative correlations to the L and K scales ($-$.31 and $-$.38 respectively). In addition, correlates of theta and delta waves with clinical variables had even smaller correlations, which rarely exceeded .30 for neurological, psychiatric history, and dyscontrol behavior variables. Such modest correlations between clinical, psychometric, and EEG data, while suggesting that some of the subjects may have organic impairment, provide little evidence that the enumerated symptoms form the clinical entity known as episodic dyscontrol syndrome.

All research in this area suffers form the same methodological problems. Studies by Bach-Y-Rita and his associates (Bach-Y-Rita, Lion, Climent, and Ervin, 1971) and Maletzky (Maletzky, 1973; Maletzky and Klotter, 1974) found that violent individuals often have a greater than expected number of soft neurological signs and EEG abnormalities. Their findings stress the heterogeneity of these individuals as well as psychodynamic issues. Monroe (1970) and Harbin (1977) stress the cultural and family contributions to violent individuals who may show such abnormalities. Further, the interrelationships between such abnormalities and psychiatric disorders have not been thoroughly explored.

The most recent revision of the diagnostic nomenclature (American Psychiatric Association, 1980) subsumed this syndrome under intermittent explosive personality disorder. This disorder was defined in terms of its phenomenological characteristics, and neurological findings were considered associated features.

Because of the emphasis of episodic dyscontrol syndrome in explaining aggressive criminal behavior, this concept has been introduced into evaluations of criminal responsibility. Ratner and Shapiro (1978) advocate the use of episodic dyscontrol syndrome in insanity evaluations to explain explosive uncontrollable behavior. In contrast, Feldman (1981) questioned its application to criminal responsibility because of difficulties in defining involuntariness and whether such a syndrome would be recognized as a mental disease or defect under various legal standards.

The forensic clinician is urged to exercise extreme caution in attempting to utilize this loosely defined constellation of features. The syndrome has an inherent attractiveness to attorneys because of the concept of dyscontrol.

To relate this concept to the issue of criminal responsibility, the clinician must do more than establish the existence of this syndrome. The clinician must be able to relate the neurological and EEG abnormalities to the loss of volition. Given the presence of these abnormalities in both normal as well as nonaggressive patients, their mere presence is insufficient to qualify under any legal standard. Extensive inquiry, as discussed in chapter 5 on clinical interviews, is essential in establishing the uncontrollability of the behavior and its unforeseeability. Even proponents of this syndrome agree that assessment is a multidetermined process involving nonspecific neurological abnormalities, psychodynamic issues, and interpersonal factors. The assessment of such symptoms, perhaps better under the rubric of intermittent explosive personality disorder, is similar to that of other functional disorders that often have neurological and biochemical abnormalities.

DRUG-ASSISTED INTERVIEWS

The use of barbiturates in clinical interviews, after strong initial interest, has been the subject of considerable controversy. Lindemann (1932) studied the effects of sodium amytal on thirty patients and six normal individuals. He concluded that the drug allowed the expression of previously repressed thoughts and had possible treatment benefits (see also Bohn, 1932). Only recently have double-blind experimental designs been utilized in the study of sodium amytal interviews.

Several double-blind studies were conducted at the University of Virginia School of Medicine (Hain, Smith, and Stevenson, 1966; Smith, Hain, and Stevenson, 1970; Stevenson, Buckman, Smith, and Hain, 1974) and compared the effects of sodium amytal to hydroxydione, an anesthetic, methamphetamine, and a placebo of saline solution. They found no significant differences across conditions for either the amount of speech or new material uncovered during the interview; patients on amytal tended to be more coherent than those under other drug conditions and experienced somewhat less anxiety. They found no evidence of abreaction although the expression of affect and suppressed material did correlate with indicators of improvement. Two important limitations of this research are, first, the studies were not truly blind (i.e., clinicians frequently detected the type of drug interview based on the clinical presentation) and, second, all patients received what was described as a standard conservative dose of amytal (400 mg).

Another study (Dysken, Kooser, Haraszti, and Davis, 1979) suggested that the value of drug interviews is in obtaining additional clinical information from the patient. These authors concluded that this benefit may be related to several nondrug factors including the patients' expectations. These studies focused on the possible diagnostic and therapeutic effects of sodium amytal interviews and suggested only modest success in achieving these goals. No systematic studies have been conducted on the clinical usefulness of sodium amytal interviews in forensic evaluations. Anecdotal data suggested that better integrated individuals may be able to fabricate convincingly during drug-assisted interviews (Redlich, Ravitz, and Dession, 1951). Adatto (1949) utilized drug-assisted interviews with fifty forensic patients (twenty unfit to stand trial, eighteen NGRI, ten transfers from state prison, and two others) with favorable results. He found the technique helpful in the recall of amnesiacs and the assessment of fabrication. More recently, Zonana (1979) utilized a sodium amytal interview in the case study of an insanity evaluatee. Since the defendant, who was blatantly psychotic, claimed no involvement in the alleged criminal behavior, a sodium amytal interview was conducted. It is interesting that his repressed memories did not become available under the sodium amytal but were subsequently recalled under hypnosis. Thus, there is no extensive literature on the relative efficacy of sodium amytal interviews in amnestic or suspected malingering forensic cases. MacDonald (1976) recommended the use of sodium amytal interviews in insanity evaluations for examining defendants who are mute or have suppressed or repressed pertinent data regarding the alleged crime.

Dosages of sodium amytal are clinically titrated to ensure a deep state of relaxation. Clinical signs include a thickening and slurring of speech, skipping numbers in counting backward from 100, drowsiness, and nystagmus (Naples and Hackett, 1978; MacDonald, 1976). It is important with criminal defendants that the questioning move gradually from neutral topics to more sensitive ones. Questioning should always be nondirective to minimize contaminating the defendant's recall. One effective approach (American Academy of Psychiatry and Law, 1979) is for the defendant to recall his or her behavior prior to, during, and following the criminal behavior. It is often helpful to have the defendant tell his or her story several times at appropriate intervals as a measure of the consistency of the self-report. Finally, it is important that the forensic clinician observe the facial expressions and gestures of the defendant since these may provide useful qualifying information in evaluating the defendant's description.

Sodium amytal interviews might best be conceptualized as a challenge test in cases of suspected elective mutism, reported amnesia about the offense, or suspected malingering since a minority of electively mute or malingering defendants may provide strong confirming data regarding either of these two options. A defendant who spontaneously confesses to a different version of his or her criminal behavior should be questioned closely about this discrepancy in a nondrug interview following the sodium amytal. The absence of inconsistencies in a defendant's account under sodium amytal is not demonstrable evidence of his or her honesty, however, given the fact that many patients have the capacity to fabricate during a sodium amytal interview. As with all procedures, forensic clinicians must obtain informed consent before utilizing sodium amytal in insanity evaluations.

POLYGRAPH TECHNIQUES

Use of the polygraph, or lie detector, became increasingly popular during the 1930s and 1940s as a method of criminal investigation (Lykken, 1984). Polygraphs typically record three channels of physiological data: galvanic skin response (GSP), cardiovascular responses (pulse and blood volume), and respiration (rate and volume) (Lykken, 1974). Recent claims (Bartol, 1983) have asserted its accuracy at greater than 90% in ascertaining the truthfulness of criminal defendants. Such claims have not been supported by empirical research in which laboratory studies commonly achieve an accuracy rate of between 70 and 85% (Lykken, 1974). In addition, an examination of these rates suggests that the polygraph is biased against honest subjects. For example, Barland and Raskin (1975) report an 81% rate of accurate classification; closer analysis, however, reveals approximately 88% accuracy in the detection of deceptive subjects and only a 78% rate for honest subjects. This bias, confirmed in other research (Szucko and Kleinmuntz, 1985), is one of the most troublesome aspects of polygraph techniques.

Polygraph techniques are administered by individuals with only modest training in polygraphy and no other professional training in psychological principles or clinical practice. Such individuals are typically trained in the control question technique, which compares the subject's physiological responses to control questions, unrelated to the crime, to questions concerning the crime. Such an approach is less sophisticated than the guilty knowledge test or GKT (Lykken, 1974), in which details known only to the perpetrator are embedded in a multiple choice format. For example, an innocent armed robbery suspect should show no great arousal to the name of the robbed bank or the picture of a particular teller. By increasing the number of items in a GKT format a high degree of accuracy can be achieved (Lykken, 1981). More recent studies involving the commonly used control question and better trained polygraph examiners (e.g., Hoivath, 1977; Kleinmuntz and Szucko, 1982) have established an approximate 70% accuracy rate with a bias against innocent subjects.

The few studies of polygraphy as it relates to forensic evaluations have been nonexperimental in nature. Lynch (1979; Lynch and Bradford, 1980) examined patients for suspected malingering and amnesia. One interesting finding was the wide degree of variability in polygraph findings by different psychiatric diagnoses. This result would suggest the need for further research on the physiological responses of different diagnostic groups within the framework of standard polygraphic examinations before any interpretations are drawn regarding the honesty or dishonesty of a criminal defendant. Further, a case study by Mutter (1979) suggested the possibility that polygraph responses can be significantly altered through the use of hypnosis, although the use of hypnosis to beat the polygraph has not been empirically explored.

In summary, the scientific unreliability and consistent bias against honest subjects militate against any clinical application of polygraph techniques to insanity evaluations. The admissibility of polygraph evidence (see Adelman and Howard, 1984) is greatly circumscribed because of its lack of scientific reliability; only five states allow polygraph evidence admitted without the prior stipulation of both the defense and prosecution.

FORENSIC HYPNOSIS

The use of hypnosis for legal purposes has been controversial. Proponents of forensic hypnosis are aligned into two camps: those who advocate its use for memory enhancement within the context of police investigation and those who advocate a broader role including the adversarial evaluation of defendants.

Kline (1979), while acknowledging some of the constraints of forensic hypnosis, advocated its selective use in permitting the expert witness to have a comprehensive picture of the defendant's psychodynamic composition and to uncover elements related to the etiology of the defendant's behavior that may relate to the issue of criminal responsibility. He suggested that it may be particularly relevant in the evaluation of psychotic murderers who were partially or totally amnestic to the period of the alleged offense. He has utilized extensive sessions and had defendants focus on the sensory and verbal associations, attempting to facilitate revivifications (i.e., an emotional reliving of the event) as a method of addressing the defendant's repressions and distortions. He further recommended videotaping the entire hypnotic session and having the defendant's attorney present but not participating in the evaluation. Others (e.g., Packer, 1981) have cautiously endorsed the use of hypnosis with psychogenically amnesiac defendants although not as a test of their truthfulness.

Orne (1979) has argued cogently against the use of hypnosis in the assessment of defendants' veracity by pointing to his earlier research (1971, 1972) that supported the possibility of individuals who feign hypnosis or of deeply hypnotized subjects who intentionally fabricate (1961). In addition, defendants may unintentionally confabulate, supplementing their memory with pseudomemories. The pseudomemories become indistinguishable from actual memories for both the defendant and the examiner, thus confounding the defendant's self-report. Indeed, the demand characteristics of the hypnotic situation may encourage the defendant through his or her hypersuggestibility to have more memories (confabulated or not) and greater belief in these memories. Several research studies (Putnam, 1979; Zelig and Beidleman, 1981) have found in experimental studies that hypnotized subjects are more vulnerable than nonhypnotized subjects to leading questions. Thus, the hypnotized criminal defendant may be saying what the forensic clinician wants to hear.

Even the more circumscribed use of hypnosis in police investigation work has come under question. Reiser (1974; Reiser and Neilson, 1980) has strongly encouraged the use of hypnosis in criminal investigation. He reported that police officers with training in hypnosis were able to achieve at least a light trance in 92.5% of the cases and elicited additional information that was considered valuable in approximately two-thirds of these cases. Further, he reported, where corroboration was possible, that hypnotically enhanced memories were accurate in approximately 90% of the cases.

These findings may be criticized on many grounds (e.g., Roberts, 1982), given the lack of experimental design in collecting self-report data from vested police officers; for example, it would be hard to imagine, within a context of program evaluation, that police hypnotists would rate their own contributions as unhelpful. Others (Hilgard and Loftus, 1979; Kroger and Douce, 1979; Spiegel and Spiegel, 1984) have advocated stricter control over investigative hypnosis, utilizing highly trained professionals, videotaping sessions and establishing the parameters for independent verification. With such safeguards, sufficient independent evidence may be collected in occasional cases for the apprehension and conviction of perpetrators.

In summary, forensic hypnosis has no direct role in criminal responsibility evaluations. The forensic clinician should be aware of the possibility, particularly in controversial cases, that the defendant may have been hypnotized earlier by a forensic psychiatrist or psychologist. Such information would be of critical importance in the assessment of the criminal defendant since it might contaminate the defendant's self-report. In these infrequent cases, it is imperative that the forensic clinician review notes and, if possible, recordings of the hypnotic session to assess its scope and detail. This is of importance both in the assessment of malingering and in evaluation of patients' reported psychological state at the time of the offense.

CONCLUSION

A variety of laboratory and other specialized techniques may contribute to our understanding of defendants assessed for criminal responsibility. These methods, often with consultation from specialists, may support or question our clinical conclusions regarding the retrospective diagnosis and sanity of a particular defendant. In addition, this chapter has critically reviewed the questionable validity of several specialized approaches (e.g., forensic hypnosis and polygraphy), limitations in promising laboratory methods (e.g., NMR imaging), and controversial clinical entities (e.g., episodic dyscontrol syndrome and epileptoid aggression). An awareness of such limitations may assist the forensic clinician in appreciating the true value of specialized techniques and avoiding their misuse.

Chapter 9

Clinical Synthesis

This chapter examines the process of integrating the psychological information gathered in the formulation of a retrospective diagnosis and opinion of criminal responsibility. Applied research (Meehl, 1954; Dawes, 1970) has indicated that mental health professionals are much more effective at making clinical observations than in combining these observations into clinical decisions. Without some type of explicit structure, the clinician becomes more vulnerable to overvaluing certain clinical information or otherwise distorting the decision process.

Gauron and Dickinson (1966) attempted to observe the diagnostic decision process of twelve psychiatrists in their evaluation of case studies. Perhaps most revealing was the heterogeneity of styles (six distinct styles were identified) that varied from a highly structured inclusion/exclusion approach to an unstructured intuitive approach. Despite the many variations, most clinical decision making may be conceptualized within either a hypothesis testing model or a linear best fit model.

The hypothesis testing model is probably the most commonly used approach to insanity evaluations (Fig. 9.1). The forensic clinician develops near the onset of the evaluation a hypothesis about the defendant's criminal behavior and diagnosis. Such hypotheses may range from "a paranoid schizophrenic with systematized persecutory delusions" to "a long history of drug abuse in an antisocial personality disorder." The decision process then focuses on confirming or disconfirming this hypothesis. In cases where the hypothesis is disconfirmed, a second hypothesis is created, and a similar process is followed. The final decision is reached when a hypothesis has appreciably greater confirming than disconfirming evidence.

The linear best fit model involves a standardized collection of clinically relevant material, irrespective of clinical hunches or hypotheses (Fig. 9.2). This model is best typified by the Schedule of Affective Disorders and

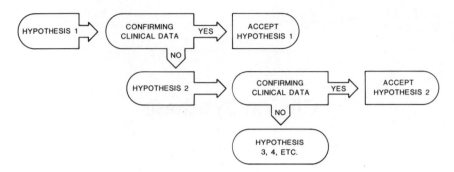

Figure 9.1
Hypothesis testing model.

Schizophrenia (SADS) in which clinical symptoms are comprehensibly reviewed for all patients. This constitutes an atomistic approach to collecting clinical observations prior to the decision process.

Neither the hypothesis testing nor the linear best fit model exists in pure form in either clinical or forensic practice. A comparison of the two approaches is, however, instructive. A major disadvantage of the hypothesis

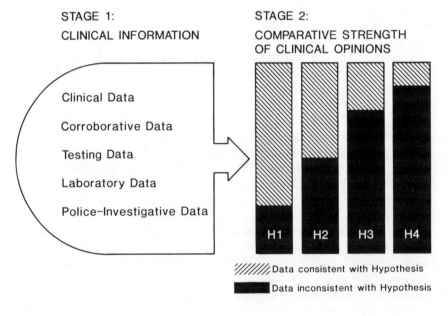

Figure 9.2
Linear best fit model.

testing model is that the forensic clinician is attempting both to observe and decide simultaneously. This dual process necessarily limits the amount of clinical information that may be considered by the diagnostician. In addition, the hypothesis testing model runs the risk of prematurely accepting a hypothesis because it is confirmed by available data, thus limiting the types and amounts of clinical information reviewed. In one unfortunate case, an experienced clinician became firmly convinced on the basis of an initial clinical interview and police reports of his working hypothesis that the defendant had a severe schizophrenic disorder and was nonresponsible; a doctoral student, who was carefully reviewing prior psychiatric records, found numerous examples of the defendant's capacity to malinger. This situation led to a considerably more extensive evaluation of the defendant and eventually a complete reformulation of the diagnosis and opinion.

The linear best fit model attempts to divide the assessment process into clinical observations and subsequent decisions. It is less efficient than the hypothesis testing model in that much of the information is not directly employed in the decision process. For instance, a SADS evaluation of criminal defendant may take 4 hours to complete although only 1 hour may have direct relevance to the defendant's criminal responsibility. The advantage of such an approach is that it optimizes clinical observation because it is unencumbered by hypothesis testing. The second stage of this model requires the clinician to review the clinical findings with respect to several hypotheses. This allows for a direct comparison among hypotheses with respect to confirming and disconfirming data. Because of these advantages, the linear best fit approach is recommended for insanity evaluations.

COMPONENTS OF FORENSIC DECISION MAKING

The decision process in criminal responsibility evaluations involves four primary areas involving the defendant's conduct and psychological impairment. These include what happened, its intended purpose, degree of impairment, and relationship of the intended purpose with both the impairment and the legal standard of insanity.

What Happened?

It is essential in every insanity evaluation that the forensic clinician closely focus on the defendant's actions prior to, during, and immediately following the criminal offense. This focus includes an examination of the defendant's interactions with the victim as well as with others. It further includes an exploration of relevant environmental and situational factors in addressing the circumstances of the offense. Sources of information about what occurred include the defendant, witnesses, and police officers. Although the defendant should be asked to describe what happened in detail on at least two separate occasions, this should not be the sole basis of assessment; it is critical (McGarry, 1980) that the defendant's account be corroborated by independent sources. As discussed in the chapter on clinical interviews, collateral interviews with witnesses or family members who observed the defendant at the time of the offense may be invaluable. Police reports are particularly helpful when they include either statements made by the defendant or verbatim reports of what the defendant said. In addition, police reports may be helpful in confirming a defendant's eccentric or bizarre behavior; the absence of such observations, however, cannot be construed as the absence of such symptoms. Police, for a variety of reasons, may be unaware of or choose not to describe unusual or crazy behavior.

What Was the Intended Purpose?

What did the defendant hope to accomplish by engaging in criminal behavior? This inquiry entails more than the obvious. While a defendant may rob a bank for financial gain, he or she may have a myriad of goals for engaging in such behavior, ranging from supporting a drug habit to acting as a CIA operative in a covert operation. It is, therefore, important to assess the defendant's short-and long-range goals for engaging in criminal behavior. This assessment often involves a heavy reliance on the defendant's self-report although it may sometimes be inferred by the defendant's actions or statements at the time of the offense. In the bank robbery example, the defendant may make statements from which it may be inferred what he or she intends to do with the money. The clinician must be careful to assess in detail the defendant's stated goals and their plausibility when compared with corroborative data. Intended goals must not be confused with culpability: whether a defendant wants to play Robin Hood and give the stolen goods to the poor has only an indirect bearing on the issue of criminal responsibility.

How Psychologically Impaired Was the Defendant?

Three facets of this issue must be considered: (1) What was the defendant's diagnosis? (2) How severe was this disorder? (3) What was its impact on the defendant's criminal behavior? Diagnosis provides useful information on the authenticity of the disorder and its probable course and impact on the defendant. Similarly, the severity of a particular disorder is important to understanding the defendant and may be relevant in determining the impact of the disorder on criminal behavior. For example, a defendant who is blindly obedient to command hallucinations (criminal or otherwise) is likely to be more impaired than many ambulatory schizophrenics with the same diagnosis. While severity is a measure of the overall disabling impact of the disorder on the defendant, the forensic clinician in an insanity evaluation must look more closely at the specific relationship of the disorder to the criminal behavior.

A wide range of evaluative methods is available in the assessment of a defendant's psychological impairment. Diagnostic and corroborative interviews are essential in addressing the three subcomponents of psychological impairment. In addition, traditional psychological testing may be of considerable assistance, particularly in cases where the evaluation is conducted soon after the commission of the offense. Further, specialized assessment methods such as the SADS and Rogers Criminal Responsibility Assessment Scales (R-CRAS) may be particularly useful in assessing the severity of the impairment and its relationship to the criminal behavior. Laboratory approaches like drug level measures may also assist in making differential diagnoses, although they are less likely to be useful in assessing the severity of the disorder.

Does the Defendant Meet the Standard of Criminal Responsibility?

This final content area addresses the interrelationship between existing mental disorders and the defendant's actions and intentions. As described in earlier chapters, the mental disorder or defect must play the major role in disrupting the defendant's cognitive or, in some jurisdictions, volitional capacities at the time of the offense. Integration of SADS data with clinical and corroborative interviews will assist in this determination, although this decision point is highly dependent on the other three content areas and their respective clinical observations. In jurisdictions utilizing the ALI (American Law Institute) standard, the forensic clinician may wish to employ the R-CRAS in the formulation of his or her final opinion.

Given the complexity of criminal responsibility evaluations, forensic clinicians must employ explicit decision models in their assessment of insanity. Such models have been explicated with respect to differential diagnosis in the *Diagnostic and Statistical Manual of Mental Disorders* (*DSM III*) (American Psychiatric Association, 1980, appendix A) through the development of decision trees and the formalization of specific inclusion and exclusion criteria. Employing these two methods, the forensic clinician may examine prominent clinical features and determine the relevant psychiatric diagnosis. Another effort (Dubovsky, Feiger, and Eisman, 1984) offers a wide array of decision trees for the diagnosis and treatment of psychiatric patients.

The purpose of such decision trees is to make operational these subcomponents of a clinical issue and, where possible, offer a logical sequencing of these subcomponents. This ensures that the forensic psychiatrist or psychologist does not overlook elements of the criminal responsibility evaluation. With respect to insanity, four general factors emerge: first, how accurate is the defendant's presentation (Is the patient deliberately attempting to manipulate his or her self-report or malinger? Are there involuntary constraints on the defendant's self-report, such as psychotic interference, repression, or amnesia?)? The second factor involves the establishment of retrospective diagnoses for the time of the crime. The third factor is the evaluation of the defendant's cognitive and volitional capacities (Did the defendant know what he or she was doing? that these actions were wrong/criminal? Did he or she choose to engage in such behavior?). The fourth factor is assessing the relationship between loss of cognitive or volitional capacity and the mental disorder (Do other variables, like intoxication, account for this incapacity?). The application of these four components to specific standards of criminal responsibility was articulated in chapter 2.

The primary limitation of these decision models is that they do not allow for a numerical or statistical quantification of each component and its relationship to insanity standards. The following section briefly describes statistical models of prediction in their potential application to criminal responsibility evaluations.

APPLICATION OF STATISTICAL MODELS
TO INSANITY EVALUATIONS

Applications of statistical models to the fields of mental health and medicine have included a variety of multivariate analyses and a Bayes theorem. The purpose of these methods is to assess elements of a decision process in terms of its sensitivity (how often does it correctly identify impaired individuals?) and specificity (how often will it exclude patients without impairment?). Statistical decision models (McNeil, Keeler, and Adelstein, 1975) examine the accuracy of classification based on the presence or absence of clinical data for test results. Such models (Elstein, 1976) avoid the clinical tendency to overpredict and typically increase the accuracy of classification and/or predictions.

Most statistical models of clinical decision making are based on Bayes theorem (see Weinstein and Fineberg, 1980). This theorem (Kraus, 1972) is based on a combination of prior probabilities (i.e., the likelihood of a dis-

ease or condition existing in a specific population) and conditional probabilities (i.e., the likelihood of a given symptom or test finding being found
with this condition or impairment). These two probabilities are combined
to measure for each symptom or test finding the likelihood of the presence
of a specific disorder. Although this model has been primarily applied to
medical diseases, initial studies have examined its efficacy with alcoholism
(Reich, Robins, Woodruff, Taibleson, Rich, and Cunningham, 1975),
depression (Roberts, 1978), and suicide risk (Kraus, 1972).

Several constraints on the use of the Bayes theorem in insanity evaluations include the absence of large-scale studies reporting the frequency of
clinical symptoms for sane and insane defendants (see also Grove, 1985,
for a discussion on the constraints of Bayesian approaches to *DSM III* diagnoses). Further, unlike medical studies where the condition can be con-
clusively determined (e.g., autopsy), insanity as a psychological construct
and legal standard lacks this definiteness. The legal disposition, for example, may include many artifacts unrelated to the defendant's mental condition at the time of the offense (e.g., plea bargaining, sympathy, or
punitiveness of the triers of fact). A final factor militating against the use
of the Bayes theorem is the strong emphasis placed by the law on idiographic elements of knowledge; that is, with a particular defendant, what
are the particular and unique elements of the case, in contradistinction from
social science's nomothetic approaches (see Haney, 1980).

The research presented throughout this book on the clinical characteristics of not guilty by reason of insanity (NGRI) defendants provides initial
data in a Bayesian approach on the likelihood of specific symptoms in the
clinical evaluation of sane/insane defendants. In problematic cases the forensic clinician may wish to consult these tables to provide ancillary information about a defendant's clinical presentation. These data cannot be used
as the primary basis in clinical decision making for criminal responsibility.

An alternative approach that has not been sufficiently explored with respect to insanity evaluation is the presence of positive or adaptive factors
and their relationship to sanity/insanity. From this perspective, an individual's ability to form intimate relationships and perform successfully in
school or at work might also be assessed employing the Bayes theorem.
Preliminary data suggest that an emphasis on adaptiveness might well complement the current emphasis on psychopathology and dysfunction.

CONTRADICTORY AND DISCREPANT FINDINGS

The insanity case, which presents a fairly consistent picture both from
self-report and corroborative data, poses much fewer difficulties than cases
with contradictory or markedly discrepant findings. In these latter cases,

the forensic psychiatrist or psychologist must critically evaluate these inconsistent findings before reaching any diagnostic or forensic conclusions. For the purposes of this discussion, the term *discrepant findings* is used to describe marked inconsistencies in the severity of symptoms—for example, mild dysphoria versus pervasive depression. The term *contradictory findings* is reserved for complete disagreements over the presence of some behavior or symptom.

Contradictory findings in a defendant's self-report bring into question the reliability of this information and the possibility of malingering. The ordering of such contradictory findings is also important. In some cases, there appears to be no particular direction between initial and subsequent interviews regarding the degree of psychopathology. In other cases, the defendant may report discrepant or contradictory findings that over time are consistently in the direction of greater psychopathology. Particularly in those cases where the defendant suddenly remembers psychotic symptoms, like hallucinations, the forensic clinician must carefully address the issues of malingering and deception.

Contradictory findings between the defendant's self-report and corroborative interviews pose several additional issues. It cannot be assumed that the information from the corroborative interview is necessarily accurate or complete. In conducting corroborative interviews, a forensic clinician must assess the accuracy of the individual's recall as well as his or her motivation for participating in the assessment. In one unusual case (Rogers and Cunnien, 1986), an obviously disturbed defendant claimed that the Mafia had murdered the victim and continued to affirm his mental health. Two corroborative interviews with his mother presented a sympathetic picture of her psychotic son, although she had had minimal contact with him in the year prior to the offense. In contrast, a corroborative interview with his schizophrenic girlfriend presented an equally sympathetic view, this time attempting to normalize his bizarre behavior. Neither the defendant nor the two informants were deliberately attempting to distort their perceptions, although together they yielded contradictory findings. Further, the forensic clinician cannot assume anything about the motivation of victims, witnesses, or family members. In one case, a superficially caring mother presented an extremely negative account (out of proportion with all other corroborative information) of her adolescent daughter. If the forensic clinician concludes which of two contradictory reports is more accurate, he or she must be able to defend this decision on the basis of more than his or her clinical judgment. Such a decision must take into account the memory, recall, scope of the corroborative information, and honesty and motivation of each interviewee. In some insanity evaluations, the unreliability of both the defendant's and the corroborative information will necessitate a no opinion.

Contradictory or discrepant findings may also occur between the defendant's self-report and psychological test findings. One particular problem occurs when there is no evidence of malingering throughout the clinical interviews although evidence of malingering is found on the MMPI (Minnesota Multiphasic Personality Inventory). This raises the important question of whether the defendant was not actually malingering throughout the evaluation. The forensic clinician may wish to conduct further interviews, incorporating critical items from the MMPI, in an attempt to assess these apparent contradictions. In addition, a readministration of the MMPI may also be justified. Although no evidence of malingering can be disregarded, the forensic clinician should be cautious about making a definite determination on the basis of a single test finding. Where MMPI validity indicators are the only evidence of malingering, the terms *limited reliability* or *suspected malingering* are more appropriate (refer to Table 3.2).

Contradictions may also be found between self-report and test results with respect to the presence of psychotic material. It occasionally occurs that the only evidence of psychotic thinking is found on projective testing. How much weight should these findings be given? Considering the vulnerability of projective testing to both malingering on the part of the defendant and multiple interpretations by the examiner, it is important that these findings be confirmed. Confirmation would involve further test administration: in the case of the Holtzman, administration of its alternate form; in the case of the Rorschach, administration of the Holtzman. In addition, it is preferable that the accuracy and strength of the interpretations be reviewed in these cases by an independent consulting psychologist. The consistent presence of reliable indicators of psychotic thinking must be addressed in relationship to retrospective diagnosis in criminal responsibility. It is unlikely that such findings would allow any definitive conclusions regarding the second of these two issues. They may, however, provide essential information about why no definite conclusion can be reached on the issue of criminal responsibility.

Contradictory or discrepant findings may also exist between psychological tests. The forensic clinician must assess the validity of each test finding and the relevance of these findings to the issue of criminal responsibility. Specific test interpretations often represent only the modal clinical formulation or diagnostic grouping, and alternative explanations may also exist. These issues, while important for the clarity and comprehensiveness of the insanity evaluation, rarely have direct bearing on the issue of insanity.

Contradictory and discrepant findings are also observed between interview data and laboratory studies. Such discrepancies most frequently questioned the reliability of the defendant's self-report. As noted in chapter 8, marked discrepancies in blood alcohol levels and the defendant's self-report may raise questions about the defendant's reliability. This is less true with respect to illegal drugs since the defendant may not know which drug or how much of it he or she has ingested. Laboratory procedures may also be employed to assess a defendant's degree of arousal to either specific groups (e.g., children, the aged, or homosexuals) or the use of violence (e.g., sexual sadism). While these measures show the degree of sexual arousal, they are considerably less effective at assessing past sexual behavior. A defendant claiming no sexual interest in children might well be confronted with discrepancies found on phallometric procedures. Finally, the use of drug-assisted interviews may assist in establishing the presence of malingering with a particular defendant. In summary, laboratory procedures, while assisting the assessment of the defendant's reliability, usually play only a secondary role with respect to diagnosis.

NO OPINIONS

One of the more difficult decisions for the forensic clinician is that of giving a no opinion. Some forensic psychologists and psychiatrists have a feeling of defeat when there is either contradictory of insufficient clinical data to render an opinion on criminal responsibility. While this situation runs contrary to the expectations of legal professionals, a no opinion decision may occasionally be the only ethical opinion. When serious questions remain about the four basic issues listed earlier, then the forensic clinician has the responsibility of openly addressing these limitations and of determining whether an opinion can be reached. As noted in chapter 1, the concept of psychological or medical certainty implies a strong probability and not a more-likely-than-not opinion.

The decision to render a no opinion is an individual one. The mental health professional must decide his or her degree of certainty and whether an expert opinion can ethically be given. This opinion, like all other opinions, should not be assisted or influenced by either the prosecuting or defense attorney. Likewise, it should also not be a group decision made by the evaluation team since this may introduce a host of additional extraneous factors (e.g., relationships among the team members and their persuasibility).

Some forensic psychologists and psychiatrists have never rendered a no opinion, either in their forensic reports or subsequent testimony. This situation might occur because of a lack of training or experience in forensic mental health, motivation by extraneous factors, or simply overconfidence in one's clinical abilities. It is surprising, however, that this absence of no opinions is rarely used by attorneys to impeach expert witnesses. It is inconceivable that anyone could always be certain about so complicated an issue as a retrospective assessment of criminal responsibility. Carefully prepared cross-examination or rebuttal testimony might raise legitimate doubts about the credibility of overly certain experts.

A no opinion conclusion must be organized and presented as carefully as any other decision. The forensic clinician must present the insufficient or contradictory information and the multiple explanations suggested by the data. Finally, the clinician must show how the absence of comprehensive and consistent clinical information prohibits him or her from reaching a conclusory opinion of criminal responsibility. A well-documented and well-reasoned argument may increase the expert's credibility and minimize the amount of antagonism engendered by this apparent side stepping of the final issue.

FORENSIC REPORT

As a result of this clinical synthesis, the clinician summarizes his or her results in the form of a forensic report. The process of writing this report and articulating both clinical decisions and the basis of these decisions forms a critical final step to the integration of clinical data. Elements of the report include the referral, description of the evaluation, the defendant's behavior at the time of the offense, clinical description of the defendant, consultations with other professionals, conclusions, and the expert opinion regarding criminal responsibility.

Referral

Every forensic report should briefly describe the circumstances under which the criminal responsibility evaluation was conducted, including the referral source and for whom the evaluation was performed—that is, the defense attorney, prosecuting attorney, or the court. In addition, the forensic psychologist or psychiatrist should clearly articulate what referral question or questions were posed as the purpose of this evaluation. With respect to the issue of criminal responsibility, the expert must make explicit what specific opinion was asked—that is, insanity, guilty but mentally ill, (GBMI), and/or diminished responsibility. Further, the forensic clinician may be asked to address other criminal forensic issues such as competence to understand Miranda warnings, competence to stand trial, and alternatives to incarceration. An argument has been made that these latter issues should be presented in a different report so they do not unduly bias the judge. This strategy is preferable since statements regarding the defendant's treatability or dangerousness might influence the judge's perception of the defendant and possibly the legal outcome.

Description of the Evaluation

It is advisable that each criminal responsibility evaluation include a detailed description of what clinical procedures were used and their purpose. This description should enumerate the dates of evaluations, the types of clinical methods used (e.g., interview, corroborative interview, testing), and their duration. This attention to detail not only clarifies for the court the thoroughness of the evaluation but also helps in preparing for courtroom testimony. Since neither the legal professionals not the jurors are likely to have specialized knowledge of psychiatric or psychological assessment procedures, it is often helpful to describe briefly the rationale for the evaluative procedure or selection of specific diagnostic tests. For example, "because of his poor academic performance and amnesia for the time of the offense, I referred the defendant for a neuropsychological consultation."

The description of the evaluation should also include additional information received from sources other than the defendant. Three common sources of such information are (1) police reports and prior clinical records, (2) corroborative interviews with witnesses or family members, and (3) specific consultations with other mental health or medical staff. Each of these should be described in similar detail. Finally, the forensic clinician should include a statement about the Miranda-type warning given at the onset of the evaluation and the clinician's judgment of the defendant's understanding of this warning.

Defendant's Behavior at the Time of the Crime

It is helpful to include in the forensic evaluation a concise description of the defendant's behavior prior to, during, and immediately following the criminal behavior. This information allows the forensic expert to relate what happened to the defendant's degree of impairment and thus to form an opinion of criminal responsibility. Unless the descriptions of the defendant's behavior are highly consistent, each source of information should be summarized separately. This summary should always include the defendant's self-report with detailed descriptions of his or her thoughts, feelings, behavior, and perceptions. Since this information should be reviewed on several occasions, the forensic clinician should be careful to note discrepancies in the defendant's account across interviews. Separate sections of the report should include descriptions of the defendant's behavior as summarized in police reports and statements made by the defendant and corroborative sources.

It is sometimes useful to include direct quotes from the defendant or other sources that capture the defendant's attitude or thinking prior to and during the offense. Such careful preparation may lessen the likelihood of the expert's being strenuously cross-examined with "what-is-the-basis. . . ." type questions.

An important consideration is whether the forensic report in an insanity evaluation should include a description of previous criminal history or other unreported crimes. The relevance of reporting prior criminal history must be decided on a case-by-case basis, although it usually has little bearing on the issue of criminal responsibility. Possible exceptions might be a defendant who has a recent pattern of crime similar to that in question or who has been diagnosed as having an antisocial personality disorder. While information regarding unreported crimes may be relevant, with appropriate warnings, to several forensic issues including civil commitment and duty to warn, there is no justification for its inclusion in a criminal responsibility evaluation. The forensic clinician is asked to be a consultant on a specific psycholegal issue—namely, criminal responsibility. To play investigator is to confound one's professional role and potentially to bias the court against the defendant. As a guideline, it is preferable for the forensic clinician to address only the criminal behavior for which the insanity defense is being raised.

Clinical Description

Much attention should be paid to providing an accurate and comprehensive description of the defendant's psychological functioning both at the time of the offense and at the current time. Presentation of clinical material for both time periods facilitates the assessment process and may make comprehensible to the triers of fact why a defendant, who looks relatively unimpaired at the present time was severely disturbed at the time of the offense or, conversely, why a defendant, who looks obviously impaired at the present time developed these symptoms following his or her incarceration.

The clinical description typically includes the defendant's mental status and a clear description of past and current symptomatology. It further entails a description of the defendant's functioning in interpersonal relationships and at work. It is also helpful to provide, when possible, a description of the severity of the symptoms and their apparent impact on the defendant's overall functioning. For example, the term *depression* may provide little valuable information about the defendant to the criminal justice system, while a more precise description of "a pervasive depression with periods of crying, hopelessness, and recurrent thoughts about suicide" would better assist the court in understanding both the depression and its severity.

The forensic clinician may wish to refer to chapter 5 on clinical interviews for a detailed outline of how the clinical description may address specific psychiatric symptoms.

Consultations

There is some divergence of opinion on how forensic psychologists and psychiatrists report consultations made at their request in insanity evaluations. Some experts both summarize the evaluation and append the consultative report to their own report. Others, without appending the report, attempt to provide a thorough summary of the consultant's findings including findings that are not directly germane to the issue of criminal responsibility. Still others, without including the report, are highly selective in the type of information they report even as it pertains to the defendant's sanity. Of these three general approaches, the third is particularly troublesome. It has been observed that many experts who were highly selective in their summary of consultant's reports had a tendency to oversimplify the reports' conclusions and to minimize conflicts between the consultant's findings and their own. Such summarizing of a consultant's reports could be construed as deliberate misrepresentation or, in extreme cases with courtroom testimony, as perjury. For example, it is inexcusable for a forensic psychiatrist to neglect to mention a psychologist's findings of limited intellectual abilities or for a forensic psychologist to overlook a neurological report of an abnormal CT scan.

It is incumbent on attorneys to subpoena consultant's records when they are not appended to the forensic report. Although there is nothing inherently wrong with a forensic clinician's providing a thorough summary of a consultant's report, it may be simpler to append the report and highlight areas of agreement and disagreement. This would further minimize the possible temptation towards oversimplification. When a summary is made with the report appended, the forensic clinician should focus on the report's major findings and its relevance to the issue of criminal responsibility. In addition, the clinician should clearly articulate areas of disagreement and the reasons for this disagreement. Certainly those familiar with the workings of the criminal justice system realize that it does not expect unanimity on every point in a criminal forensic evaluation.

Clinical Conclusions

Every forensic report on criminal responsibility should include specific statements about the defendant's retrospective as well as current diagnosis. The diagnosis should include a description of the onset, course, and duration of mental disorders and the *DSM III* inclusion and exclusion criteria that indicate the presence of a specific disorder in this particular defendant. When possible, descriptions should include statements about the severity of the disorder and its overall impact on the individual's functioning.

Clinical conclusions should also address the relationship of these mental disorders at the time of the offense to the defendant's criminal behavior. It is important to relate to the defendant's psychological impairment how the criminal behavior was carried out and its circumstances (e.g., extreme provocation or intoxication). It has been cogently argued by Pollack, Gross, and Weinberger (1982), that forensic mental health professionals must present alternative explanations and their judgments about these alternatives as determinants of criminal behavior. This is a fairly demanding standard that would require the forensic clinician to evaluate critically several possible explanations and provide well-reasoned arguments for the acceptance of one of these explanatory models. This degree of organization and thoroughness is rarely seen in either clinical or forensic evaluations, but it may be a useful model for clarifying clinical judgments as well as the underlying logic.

Exploration of the factors leading to the criminal behavior involves a careful integration of relevant information from the defendant's behavior and clinical description sections of the report. It should address how psychological constructs do or do not contribute to the understanding of the defendant's criminal behavior.

Opinion

The forensic clinician should address individually each component of the relevant criminal responsibility standard. In applying the M'Naghten standard, the clinician should address the concepts of disease of the mind, defect of reasoning, nature and quality of the act, and wrongfulness. With the ALI standard, the clinician must address mental disease or defect, lack of substantial capacity, criminality or wrongfulness, and ability to conform conduct. These opinions may be stated precisely since the reasoning and clinical data were presented in the clinical conclusion section. Similar approaches should be utilized with the GBMI standard, the M'Naghten-irresistible impulse standard, and the ALI cognitive-only standard.

It is the expert's decision whether or not to render a final conclusory opinion of the defendant's criminal responsibility. As noted in chapter 1, the impact of such a statement is the subject of ongoing debate. If a conclusory opinion is given, it should be clearly identified as such, "it is my opinion . . . " that the defendant (meets/does not meet) the relevant criminal responsibility standard. Another option is to make a conclusory statement of no opinion. Such a conclusion would require sufficient explanation for why an opinion cannot be reached within a reasonable degree of medical or psychological certainty.

CONCLUSION

This discussion of clinical reports addresses the complexity of insanity evaluations and the individual styles of forensic psychiatrists and psychologists. There are other readily available outlines for organizing criminal responsibility evaluations and their subsequent reports. These include discussion of potential content areas (Gutheil and Applebaum, 1982; Ruzicka, 1979) as well as exhaustive outlines (Lawrence, 1978) of what details and issues might be included in a criminal forensic evaluation. For those clinicians operating in an agency setting, Keilitz (1981) provides very good systematic models for data acquisition and flow in the context of forensic evaluations. Forensic clinicians may wish to adapt these and other sources in constructing their outlines for forensic evaluations.

Clinical synthesis in the context of criminal responsibility evaluations is both complicated and time consuming. Professionals who wish to specialize in the evaluation of criminal responsibility bear a singularly difficult responsibility in understanding the evolving legal and clinical contexts of such evaluations.

Appendixes

Appendices

Appendix I

Database on Criminal Responsibility Defendants

Data on the clinical symptomatology of criminal responsibility defendants is presented throughout the text in the form of tables. Each table addresses the severity of a psychiatric symptom by two criterion groups: those clinically evaluated as sane and insane. This book represents the first large-scale effort to examine systematically the clinical characteristics of insanity evaluatees. These tables summarize the analysis of symptom severity for 385 criminal defendants from seven forensic centers.

The bulk of the clinical data was gathered as part of the validation studies for the Rogers Criminal Responsibility Assessment Scales (R-CRAS) (see chapter 7). For each case, an experienced forensic psychologist or psychiatrist would review pertinent police reports and psychiatric records, administer or have access to psychological test findings, and conduct at least one and typically several clinical interviews. Following the last clinical interview, the forensic clinician would complete the R-CRAS as a method of quantifying the presence and severity of symptoms for the time of the offense. The data reported here represent a reanalysis of these validity data with a cross-tabulation of clinically evaluated sane and insane defendants by symptom severity. Such an analysis is justified on the basis of the R-CRAS's adequate interrater reliability.

This current database included R-CRAS validation studies ($N = 260$) and a more recent study of the M'Naghten and guilty but mentally ill (GBMI) standards ($N = 125$). The three major sites for data collection were the Isaac Ray Center in Chicago, IL; the Court Diagnostic and Treatment Center in Toledo, OH; and the Center for Forensic Psychiatry in Ann Arbor, MI. Smaller samples were gathered from the Minnesota Security Hospital in St. Peter; a forensic team at Nebraska Psychiatric Institute in Omaha; a combined sample from Perkins State Hospital and the Court Clinic in Baltimore, Maryland; and the Forensic Clinic at the University of Cleveland. These insanity cases were evaluated over a 5-year period from 1979 to 1984.

219

Canadian Standard of Criminal Responsibility

The Canadian courts, during the nineteenth century, relied on the criminal law of the United Kingdom, which following the celebrated 1843 trial
was based on the M'Naghten standard. Its most controversial application
in the nineteenth century was in the highly politicized trial of Louis Riel.
As reported by Verdun-Jones (1979), Riel was charged for his participation
in the Saskatchewan rebellion of 1885. Riel's attornies, over his objections,
raised the defense of insanity, with expert testimony asserting that the defendant suffered from megalomania, although it was suggested in the testimony of Dr. Clark from the Toronto Asylum that he could distinguish
between right and wrong (Markson, Greenland, and Turner, 1965). When
Riel was allowed to speak in his behalf, he spoke eloquently for more than
an hour, which was highly inconsistent with the defense's arguments of a
"poor confirmed lunatic." Despite the jury's plea for clemency, he was
eventually executed for treason.

The Canadian Parliament and legislatures, seeking uniformity in their
criminal law, passed the 1892 Criminal Code, which made provisions for
the defense of insanity. The Canadian standard differed from M'Naghten
on several grounds. First, it deleted the concept of defect of reason as a
condition of insanity. Second, it substituted the word *appreciate* for the
more restrictive term *know*. These changes apparently reflected (Verdun-
Jones, 1979) the thinking of one of its drafters, Sir Fitz Jameson Stephen,
who wished to broaden the M'Naghten standard to include emotional and
volitional elements. As noted by the Canadian Royal Commission on the
Law of Insanity, these modifications of the M'Naghten standard do not
appear to have made an appreciable difference on Canadian courts, which
continue to rely heavily on British authorities and make little distinction
between the words *appreciate* and *know* (McRuer, 1956).

The current standard of criminal responsibility reflects minor changes introduced in the 1954 revision of the Criminal Code of Canada. Section 16 of the code states:

1. No person shall be convicted of an offense in respect of an act or omission on his part while he was insane.
2. For the purposes of this section, a person is insane when he is in a state of natural imbecility or has a disease of the mind to an extent that renders him incapable of appreciating the nature and quality of an act or omission, or of knowing that an act or ommission is wrong.
3. A person who has specific delusions, but is in other respects sane, shall not be acquitted on the ground of insanity unless the delusions caused him to believe in the existence of a state of things that, if it existed, would have justified or excused his act or omission.
4. Everyone shall, until the contrary is proved, be presumed to be and to have been sane.

Interpretation of the Canadian standard differs in many respects from the U.S. versions of the M'Naghten test. Subsequent paragraphs briefly describe the key components of the Canadian standard.

DISEASE OF THE MIND

Martin (1981) has defined the legal term, *disease of the mind,* as any medically recognized disorder that may render a defendant incapable of understanding the nature and quality of his or her actions or knowing that those actions were wrong. This concept has on occasion been broadened to encompass even antisocial personality disorders (Greenspan, 1978). It is felt that the type of mental disorder is less significant than the consequences or level of impairment of the disorder in determining the defendant's criminal responsibility.

The current definition of "disease of the mind" is found in a Supreme Court decision [*Cooper v. The Queen* (1980) 1 S.C.R. 1149] as "any illness, disorder or abnormal condition which impairs the human mind and its functioning excluding however, self-induced states caused by alcohol or drugs, as well as transitory mental states such as hysteria or concussion" (p. 1159). It goes on to state that the severity of the disorder and its effect on the individual's ability to appreciate are the determining factors in deciding criminal responsibility.

APPRECIATE

Since the McRuer report of 1956, there has been an intensified interest in the definition of the term *appreciate* and its relevance to the insanity defense. McRuer, in the case of *R. v. O.* [1959, 3 Crim. L.Q. 151 (Ont. H.C.T.)], defined "appreciate" as a capacity of "forseeing and measuring the consequences of her act or of estimating aright or perceiving the full force of her act" (p. 153). Martin (1981) has affirmed that the capacity to appreciate must reflect more than the absence or inappropriateness of the defendant's emotional response. Thus, the defendant's lack of feelings toward the victim or remorse for the crime are not sufficient to address the component of appreciation. In the earlier cited case of *Cooper v. The Queen,* the concept of appreciate is delimited as "inability to perceive the consequences, impact, and results of a physical act" (p. 12).

A more recent Supreme Court of Canada decision, *Kjeldsen v. The Queen* [(1982), 64 C.C.C. (2d) 161], affirmed this definition of appreciate to be limited to the physical actions and the consequences of these actions. Thus, if the defendant had an awareness that his or her actions might eventuate in the death of the victim, then this person would meet this more circumscribed definition of appreciate.

WRONGFULNESS

Canadian courts have traditionally held that the concept of wrongfulness could be either moral or legal. This interpretation may well have been the intent of the original drafters of the 1892 Criminal Code (see Verdun-Jones, 1979). More recent Supreme Court decisions have limited this definition to legal wrongfulness. Martin (1981, p. 21), in citing *Schwartz v. The Queen* [(1976) 29 C.C.C. (2d) 1, S.C.R. 673] defined the term *wrong* as "contrary to law in that a person knows that he is committing a criminal act must be taken to know that the act is wrong within the meaning of s.16(2)." As noted by Greenspan (1978), the criterion is that of being incapable of knowing in contrast to not knowing or ignorance.

The concept of legal wrongfulness is seen as more restrictive than that of moral wrongfulness. As discussed in chapter 2, a psychotic individual may act on divine demands while recognizing they are contrary to the criminal law. Such individuals would not qualify under the current interpretation of the Canadian standard.

OTHER CONSIDERATIONS

The concept of natural imbecility is defined as a cogenital defect or a natural decay in the functioning of the brain (Greenspan, 1978). Although it may reflect a distinct entity, it is usually subsumed under the more general concept of disease of the mind.

One component of Section 16, which specifies that the delusion must alter the defendant's perceptions to the extent that his or her actions would be justified or excused, has yielded little appellate comment. Despite the argument raised by Verdun-Jones (1979) regarding the disorganizing impact of any delusion, this principle that the delusion must be connected to the criminal behavior in question is reasonable. Whether the delusions are grandiose (e.g., "I am a special envoy of the prime minister") or persecutory (e.g., "They were poisoning my drinking water"), such a connection can be demonstrated.

INSANE AUTOMATISM

Automatism has been defined as unconscious involuntary behavior over which the defendant has no control. Automatisms that are the result of internal factors like a dissociative disorder would qualify as a disease of the mind and be labeled "insane automatism" (Martin, 1981). More common applications of automatism are a result of external causes such as concussions, medical administration of drugs, and hypoglycemia. In the case of *R. v. Rabey,* Verdun-Jones (1979) defined the concept of disease of the mind in relationship to automatism:

"Any malfunctioning of the mind or mental disorder having its source primarily in some subjective condition or weakness internal to the accused (whether fully understood or not) may be a disease of the mind if it prevents the accused from knowing what he is doing, but transient disturbances of consciousness due to certain specific external factors do not fall within the concept of disease of the mind.

There is no empirical data on the use of the defense of insane automatism in Canadian courts. The difficulty of establishing the concept of unconsciousness or the degree of unconsciousness is very problematical, both on conceptual and diagnostic grounds. In the absence of specific external etiology, it is doubtful that the authenticity (see Campbell, 1981) or the degree of unawareness of a defendant could be reliably determined in a retrospective evaluation as insanity. Further, the interrelationship between apparently purposeful behavior and unconsciousness poses a further dilemma. The presence of amnesia or neurologic or neuropsychological abnormalities is of little assistance in making the determination of insane automatism. Further, machinelike or robotlike behavior, while possibly indicative of a dissociative disorder, may be unrelated to the degree of voluntariness in the defendant's actions.

The Canadian standard of criminal responsibility shares a common origin with U.S. standards but differs significantly in both its criteria and subsequent case law. Awareness of and experience with these differences is essential both in a comparison of research studies and in the application of criminal responsibility standards in clinical practice. While statutory changes are anticipated in the Canadian standard (Sharpe and Richter, 1984), these will most likely emphasize modernization of the language with little or no substantive change. Forensic clinicians, with their awareness of the evolving Canadian standard, should find the discussion of clinical issues and clinical methods relevant to their assessment of insanity.

References

Abel, G. G.; Barlow, D. H.; Blanchard, E. B.; and Guild, D. (1977). The components of rapists' sexual arousal. *Archives of General Psychiatry, 34*, 895–903.

Abel, G. G.; Barlow, D. H.; Blanchard, E. B.; and Mavissakalian, M. (1975). Measurement of sexual arousal in male homosexuals: Effects of instructions and stimulus modality. *Archives of Sexual Behavior, 4*, 623–629.

Abel, G. G.; Becker, J. V.; and Skinner, L. J. (1980). Aggressive behavior and sex. *Psychiatric Clinics of North America, 3*, 133–151.

Abrams, N. (1979). Definitions of mental illness and the insanity defense. *Journal of Psychiatry and Law, 7*, 441–456.

Adams, K. M. (1980). In search of Luria's battery: A false start. *Journal of Consulting and Clinical Psychology, 48*, 511–516.

Adatto, C. P. (1949). Observations on criminal patients during narcoanalysis. *Archives of Neurology and Psychiatry, 69*, 82–92.

Adelman, R. M.; and Howard, A. (1984). Expert testimony on malingering: The admissability of clinical procedures for the detection of deception. *Behavioral Sciences and the Law, 2*, 5–20.

Albert, S.; Fox, H. M.; and Kahn, M. W. (1980). Faking psychosis on a Rorschach: Can expert judges detect malingering? *Journal of Personality Assessment, 44*, 115–119.

Allen, R. M.; and Young, S. J. (1978). Phencyclidine-induced psychosis. *American Journal of Psychiatry, 135*, 1081–1083.

Allen, R. P.; Safer, D.; and Covi, L. (1975). Effects of psychostimulants on aggression. *Journal of Nervous and Mental Diseases, 160*, 138–145.

American Academy of Psychiatry and the Law. (1979, October). *Memory dysfunction and the law: Special investigative techniques.* Course presented at the annual meeting of the American Academy of Psychiatry and Law. Baltimore, MD.

American Bar Association, Standing Committee on Association Standards for Criminal Justice. (1983). *Criminal justice and mental health standards,* First draft. Chicago: American Bar Association.

225

American Law Institute. (1962). *Model penal code, Proposed official draft.* Philadelphia: Author.

American Psychiatric Association. (1980). *Diagnostic and statistical manual of mental disorders* (3rd ed.). Washington, D.C.: Author.

American Psychiatric Association. (1983). American Psychiatric Association statement on the insanity defense. *American Journal of Psychiatry,* **140**, 681–688.

American Psychological Association. (1981). Ethical principles of psychologists. *American Psychologist,* **36**, 633–638.

American Psychological Association. (1974). *Standards for educational and psychological tests.* Washington, D.C.: Author.

American Psychological Association (1984). Text of position on insanity defense. *APA Monitor,* **15**, 11.

Andreasen, N. C.; Grove, W. A.; Shapiro, R. W.; Keller, M. B.; Hirschfield, R. A.; and McDonald-Scott, M. A. (1981). Reliability of lifetime diagnoses. *Archives of General Psychiatry,* **38**, 400–405.

Anthony, N. (1971). Comparison of client's standard, exaggerated, and matching MMPI profiles. *Journal of Consulting and Clinical Psychology,* **36**, 100–103.

Arboleda-Florez, J. (1978). Insanity defence in Canada. *Canadian Psychiatric Association Journal,* **23**, 23–27.

Ashford, J. W.; Schultz, S. C.; and Walsh, G. O. (1980). Violent automatism in a partial complex seizure: Report of a case. *Archives of Neurology,* **37**, 102–122.

Atkinson, J. W. (1965). Thematic apperceptive measurement of motives within a context of a theory of motivation. In B. I. Murstein (Ed.), *Handbook of projective techniques* (pp. 433–456). New York: Basic Books.

Audubon, J. J.; and Kirwin, B. R. (1982). Defensiveness in the criminally insane. *Journal of Personality Assessment,* **46**, 304–311.

Bach-Y-Rita, G.; Lion, J. R.; Climent, C. E.; and Ervin, F. R. (1971). Episodic dyscontrol: A study of 130 violent patients. *American Journal of Psychiatry,* **127**, 1473–1478.

Bach-Y-Rita, G.; Lion, J. R.; and Ervin, F. R. (1970). Pathological intoxication: Clinical and electroencephalographic studies. *American Journal of Psychiatry,* **127**, 698–703.

Bacon, P. D.; and Benedek, E. P. (1982). Epileptic psychosis in insanity: Case study and review. *Bulletin of the American Academy of Psychiatry and Law,* **10**, 203–210.

Barbaree, H. E.; Marshall, W. L.; and Lanthier, R. D. (1979). Deviant sexual arousal in rapists. *Behavior Research and Therapy,* **17**, 215–322.

Barbaree, H. E.; Marshall, W. L.; Yates, E.; and Lightfoot, L. O. (1983). Alcohol intoxication and deviant sexual arousal in male social drinkers. *Behavior Research and Therapy,* **21**, 365–373.

Barland, G. H.; and Raskin, D. C. (1975). An evaluation of field techniques in detection of deception. *Psychophysiology,* **12**, 321–330.

Barnard, G. W.; Holzer, C.; and Vera, H. (1979). A comparison of alcoholics and non-alcoholics charged with rape. *Bulletin of the American Academy of Psychiatry and the Law,* **7**, 432–440.

Barter, J. T.; and Reite, M. (1969). Crime and LSD: The insanity plea. *American Journal of Psychiatry,* **126**, 531–537.

Bartol, C. R. (1983). *Psychology and American Law*. Belmont, CA: Wadsworth.

Bash, I. Y. (1978). Malingering: A study designed to differentiate schizophrenic offenders and malingerers. *Dissertation Abstracts, 39*, 2973-B.

Bash, I. Y.; and Alpert, M. (1980). The determination of malingering. *Annals of New York Academy of Sciences, 347*, 86-99.

Baskett, G. D.; and Freedle, R. O. (1974). Aspects of language pragmatics and social perception of lying. *Journal of Psycholinguistic Research, 3*, 117-131.

Bauer, C. A.; Schlottmann, R. S.; Kane, R. L.; and Johnsen, D. E. (1984). An evaluation of the digit symbol component of the Russell, Neuringer, and Goldstein average impairment rating. *Journal of Consulting and Clinical Psychology, 52*, 317-318.

Beis, E. B. (1984). *Mental health and the law*. Rockville, Md.: Aspen Publication.

Berlyne, N. (1972). Confabulation. *British Journal of Psychiatry, 120*, 31-39.

Bertelson, A. D.; Marks, P. A.; and May, G. D. (1982). MMPI and race: A controlled study. *Journal of Consulting and Clinical Psychology, 50*, 316-318.

Bienen, S. M. (1962). Verbal conditioning of inkblot responses as a function of instructions, social desirability, and awareness. (Doctoral dissertation, University of Maryland, 1961) *Dissertation Abstracts, 24*, 379.

Birk, L.; Williams, J. H.; Chasin, M.; and Rose, L. I. (1973). Serum testosterone levels in homosexual men. *New England Journal of Medicine, 289*, 1236-1238.

Blair, D. (1977). The medical/legal aspects of automatism. *Medical Sciences and the Law, 17*, 167-182.

Blatt, S. J.; and Berman, W. H. (1984). A methodology for the use of the Rorschach in clinical research. *Journal of Personality Assessment, 48*, 226-239.

Bloom, J. D.; Rogers, J. L.; and Manson, S. M. (1982). After Oregon's insanity defense: A comparison of conditional release and hospitalization. *International Journal of Law and Psychiatry, 5*, 391-402.

Bloom, J. L.; and Bloom, J. D. (1981). Disposition of insanity defenses in Oregon. *Bulletin of the American Academy of Psychiatry and the Law, 9*, 93-100.

Blumer, D.; and Migeon, C. (1975). Hormone and hormonal agents in the treatment of aggression. *Journal of Nervous and Mental Diseases, 160*, 127-137.

Bohman, M. (1978). Some genetic aspects of alcoholism and criminality. *Archives of General Psychiatry, 35*, 269-276.

Bohn, R. W. (1932). Sodium amytal narcosis as a therapeutic aid in psychiatry. *Psychiatric Quarterly, 6*, 301-309.

Bonnie, R. J. (1977). Commentary: Criminal responsibility. In Bonnie, R. J. (Ed.), *Diagnosis and debate*. New York: Insight Communications.

Bornstein, R. A. (1983). Verbal I. Q.-Performance I. Q. discrepancies on the Wechsler Adult Intelligence Scale-Revised in patients with a unilateral or bilateral cerebral dysfunction. *Journal of Consulting and Clinical Psychology, 51*, 779-780.

Bradford, J.M.W. (1983). The hormonal treatment of sex offenders. *Bulletin of the American Academy of Psychiatry and Law, 11*, 159-169.

Bradford, J. M. W.; and Smith, S. M. (1979). Amnesia and homicide: The Padola case and a study of thirty cases. *Bulletin of the American Academy of Psychiatry and the Law, 7*, 219-231.

Bricklin, B.; Piotrowski, Z. A.; and Wagner, E. E. (1978). *The hand test*. Springfield, IL: Charles C Thomas.

Briddell, D. W.; Rimm, D. C.; Caddy, G. R.; Krawitz, G.; Sholis, D.; and Wunderlin, R. J. (1978). Effects of alcohol and cognitive set on sexual arousal to deviant stimuli. *Journal of Abnormal Psychology, 87,* 418-430.

Brodie, K. H.; Gartrell, N.; Doering, C.; and Rhue, T. (1974). Plasma testosterone levels in heterosexual and homosexual men. *American Journal of Psychiatry,* **131,** 82-83.

Bromberg, W. (1979). *The uses of psychiatry in the law: A clinical view of forensic psychiatry.* Westport, CT: Quorum Books.

Brooks, A. D. (1974). *Law, psychiatry, and the mental health system.* Boston: Little, Brown.

Brooks, A. D. (1980). *Law, psychiatry and the mental health system: 1980 supplement.* Boston: Little, Brown.

Bryant, E. T.; Scott, M. L.; Golden,. C. J.; and Tori, C. E. (1984). Neuropsychological deficits, learning disability, and violent behavior. *Journal of Consulting and Clinical Psychology, 52,* 323-324.

Buckhart, B. R.; Christian, W. L.; and Gynther, M. D. (1978). Item subtlety and faking on the MMPI: A paradoxical relationship. *Journal of Personality Assessment, 42,* 76-80.

Buckhout, R. (1974). Eye-witness testimony. *Scientific American, 6,* 23-31.

Buechley, R.; and Ball, H. (1952). A new test of "test validity" for the group MMPI. *Journal of Consulting Psychology, 16,* 299-301.

Burke, M. (1963). The control of response choice on projective techniques. (Doctoral dissertation, University of Denver, 1962). *Dissertation Abstracts, 24,* 2119-2120.

Bursten, B. (1982). What if antisocial personality is an illness? *Bulletin of the American Academy of Psychiatry and the Law, 10,* 97-102.

Busch, K. B.; and Schnoll, S. (1986). Cocaine abuse and the law. *Behavioral Sciences and the Law.*

Butcher, J. N.; Braswell, L; and Rainey, D. (1983). A cross cultural comparison of American Indian, Black, and White inpatients on the MMPI and presenting symptoms. *Journal of Consulting and Clinical Psychology, 51,* 587-594.

Bydder, G. M. (1983). Clinical nuclear magnetic resonance imaging. *British Journal of Hospital Medicine, 30,* 348-356.

Campbell, K. L. (1981). Psychological blow automatism; a narrow defence. *Criminal Law Quarterly, 23,* 342-368.

Carlson, K. A. (1981). A modern personality test for offenders. *Criminal Justice and Behavior, 8,* 173-184.

Cavanaugh, J. L.; and Rogers, R. (1982). Convergence of mental illness and violence: Effects on public policy. *Psychiatric Annals, 12,* 537-541.

Cavanaugh J. L.; Rogers, R.; and Wasyliw, O. E. (1981). Mental illness and antisocial behavior. In W. H. Reid (Ed.), *Treatment of antisocial syndromes* (pp. 3-19). New York: Van Nostrand Reinhold.

Center for Forensic Psychiatry, (1974, June). *Evaluation of Guilty-but-mentally ill.* Seminar at Center for Forensic Psychiatry, Ann Arbor, MI.

Chapman, L. J.; and Chapman, J. P. (1969). Illusory correlation as an obstacle to the use of valid psycho-diagnostic signs. *Journal of Abnormal Psychology,* **74,** 271-280.

Chapman, L. J.; and Chapman, J. P. (1971). Associatively-based illusory correlation as a source of psychodiagnostic folklore. In L. D. Goodstein and R. I. Landon (Eds.), *Readings in personality assessment.* New York: Wiley.

Chick, G. E.; Loy, J. W.; and White, W. E. (1984). Differentiating violent and nonviolent opiate-addicted reformatory inmates with the MMPI. *Journal of Clinical Psychology,* **40,** 619–623.

Christensen, A. L. (1975). *Luria's neuropsychological investigation.* New York: Spectrum.

Clark, R. A. (1965). Projective measurement of experimentally induced levels of sexual motivation. In B. I. Murstein (Ed.), *Handbook of projective techniques,* (pp. 561–574). New York: Basic Books.

Cole, W. G., and Loftus, E. S. (1979). Incorporating new information into memory. *American Journal of Psychology,* **92,** 413–425.

Colligan, R. C. (1976). Atypical response sets in the automated MMPI. *Journal of Clinical Psychology,* **32,** 76–78.

Collins, J. J. (1981). *Alcohol use and criminal behavior.* Washington, D.C.: National Institute of Justice.

Cooke, G. (1969). The court study unit: Patient characteristics and differences between patients judged competent and incompetent. *Journal of Clinical Psychology,* **25,** 140–143.

Cox, T. C.; Jacobs, M. R.; LeBlanc, A. E.; and Marshman, J. A. (1983). *Drugs and drug abuse.* Toronto: Addiction Research Foundation.

Craft, M. (1978). The current status of xyy and xxy syndromes: A review of treatment implications. *International Journal of Law and Psychiatry,* **1,** 319–324.

Cressen, R. (1975). Artistic quality of drawings and judges' evaluations of the DAP. *Journal of Personaltiy Assessment,* **39,** 132–137.

Criss, M. L.; and Racine, D. R. (1980). Impact of change in legal standard for those adjudicated not guilty by reason of insanity, 1975–1979. *Bulletin of the American Academy of Psychiatry and Law,* **8,** 261–271.

Crosson, B.; and Warren, R. L. (1982). Use of the Luria-Nebraska neuropsychological battery in aphasia: A conceptual critique. *Journal of Consulting and Clinical Psychology,* **50,** 22–31.

Cunnien, A. J. (1986). Alcoholic blackouts: Phenomenology and legal relevance. *Behavioral Sciences and the Law,* in press.

Dahlstrom, W. G.; Welsh, G. S.; and Dahlstrom, L. E. (1972). *An MMPI handbook: Clinical interpretation.* Minneapolis: University of Minnesota Press.

Dahlstrom, W. G.; Walsh, G. S.; and Dahlstrom, L. E. (1975). *An MMPI Handbook, Volume II: Research Applications.* Minneapolis: University of Minnesota Press.

Dana, R. H. (1972). Thematic Apperception Test. In O. K. Buros, (Ed.), *Mental measurements yearbook* (6th ed.) (pp. 492–495). Highland Park, NJ: Gryphon Press.

Dana, R. H. (1978). Rorschach. In O. K. Buros (Ed.), *Eighth mental measurements yearbook* (pp. 1040–1042). Highland Park, NJ: Gryphon Press.

Davidson, H. A. (1952). *Forensic psychiatry.* New York: Ronald Press.

Davidson, H. A. (1965). *Forensic psychiatry* (2nd ed.). New York: Ronald Press.

Dawes, R. M. (1979). Robust beauty of improper linear model in decision making. *American Psychologist*, 34, 571–582.

DeCato, C. M. (1984). Rorschach reliability: Toward a training model for inter-scorer agreement. *Journal of Personality Assessment*, 48, 58–64.

Deiker, T. E. (1974). A cross validation of MMPI scales of aggression on male criminal criterion groups. *Journal of Consulting and Clinical Psychology*, 42, 196–202.

Delgado-Escueta, A. V.; Mattson, R. H.; King, L.; Goldensohn, E. S.; Spiegel, H.; Madsen, J.; Crandall, P.; Dreifuss, F.; and Porter, R. J. (1981). The nature of aggression during epileptic seizures. *New England Journal of Medicine*, 305, 711–716.

Delis, D.; and Kaplan, E. (1983). Hazards of a standardized neuropsychological test with low content validity: Comment on the Luria-Nebraska neuropsychological battery. *Journal of Consulting and Clinical Psychology*, 51, 396–398.

Dellinger, R. W. (1978). High on PCP. *Human Behavior*, 7, 38–45.

Delman, R. P. O. (1980). Participation by psychologists in insanity defense proceedings: An advocacy. *Journal of Psychiatry and Law*, 9, 247–262.

DePaulo, B. M.; and Rosenthal, R. (1979). Telling lies. *Journal of Personality and Social Psychology*, 37, 1713–1722.

DeVito, R. A. (1980). Some new alternatives to the insanity defense. *American Journal of Forensic Psychiatry*, 1, 38–51.

Diamond, B. L. (1959). The fallacy of the impartial expert. *Archives of Criminal Psychodynamics*, 3, 221–236.

Diamond, B. L. (1961). Criminal responsibility of the mentally ill. *Stanford Law Review*, 59, 82–83.

Dickinson, R. L. (1984). Indiana court condemns mentally ill man to die for murder. *Mental Health Reports*, 8, 1–2.

Dickey, W. J.: Remmington, S. J.; and Schultz, D. (1980). Law, trial judges, and psychiatric witnesses: Reflection on how a change in legal doctrine has been implemented in Wisconsin. *International Journal of Law and Psychiatry*, 3, 331–341.

Dix, G. E. (1971). Psychological abnormality as a factor in grading criminal liability: Diminished capacity, diminished responsibility, and the like. *Journal of Criminal Law, Criminology, and Police Science*, 62, 313–334.

Dix, G. E. (1984). Criminal responsibility and mental impairment in American criminal law: Response to the Hinckley acquittal in historical perspective. In D. N. Weisstub (Ed.), *Law and mental health: International perspectives* (pp. 1–44). New York: Pergamon.

Dolan, M. (1978). PCP: A plague whose time has come. *American Pharmacy*, 18, 22–29.

Domino, E. F. (1978). Neurobiology of phencyclidine—an update, In R. C. Petersen and R. C. Stillman (Eds.), *Phencyclidine (PCP) abuse: An appraisal* (pp. 18–43). Rockville, MD: National Institute on Drug Abuse.

Drummond, F. (1966). A failure in the discrimination of aggressive behavior of undifferentiated schizophrenics with the Hand Test. *Journal of Projective Techniques and Personality Assessment*, 30, 275–279.

Dubovsky, S. L.; Feiger, A. D.; and Eisman, V. (1984). *Psychiatric decision-making.* Philadelphia: B. C. Decker.

Dysken, M. W.; Kooser, J. A.; Haraszti, J. S.; and Davis, J. M. (1979). Clinical usefulness of sodium amobarbital interviewing. *Archives of General Psychiatry,* **36,** 789–794.

Earls, C. M. (1983). Some issues in the assessment of sexual deviants. *International Journal of Law and Psychiatry,* **6,** 431–441.

Edinger, J. D.; and Bogan, J. B. (1976). The validity of the Rorschach prognostic rating scale with incarcerated offenders. *Journal of Clinical Psychology,* **32,** 887–890.

Ehrenkranz, J.; Bliss, E.; and Sheard, M. H. (1974). Plasma testosterone: Correlation with aggressive behavior and social dominance in man. *Psychosomatic Medicine,* **36,** 469–475.

Ekman, P.; and Friesen, W. V. (1969). Non-verbal leakage and clues to deception. *Psychiatry,* **63,** 88–106.

Ekman, P.; and Friesen, W. V. (1974). Detecting deception from body or face. *Journal of Personality and Social Psychology,* **29,** 288–298.

Ekman, P.; and Friesen, W. V. (1975). *Unmasking the face.* Englewood Cliffs, NJ: Prentice-Hall.

Ellinwood, E. H. (1971). Assault and homicide associated with amphetamine abuse. *American Journal of Psychiatry,* **127,** 1170–1176.

El-Meligi, A. M.; and Osmond, H. (1970). *Manual for the clinical use of the experiential world inventory.* New York: Mens Sana Publishing.

Elstein, A. S. (1976). Clinical judgement: Psychological research and medical practice. *Science,* **194,** 696–700.

Emery, P. E.; and Emery, O. B. (1984). *A case study of the New Hamsphire rule.* Unpublished manuscript, Dartmouth Medical School, Dartmouth, NH.

Endicott, J.; and Spitzer, R. L. (1978). A diagnostic interview: The schedule of affective disorders and schizophrenia. *Archives of General Psychiatry,* **35,** 837–844.

Eron, L. D. (1965). A normative study of the Thematic Apperception Test. In B. I. Murstein (Ed.), *Handbook of projective techniques* (pp. 469–509). New York: Basic Books.

Eron, L. D. (1972). Thematic Apperception Test. In O. K. Buros (Ed.), *Mental measurements yearbook,* (pp. 460–462). (7th ed.). Highland Park, NJ: Gryphon Press.

Exner, J. E. (1969). *The Rorschach system.* New York: Grune and Stratton.

Exner, J. E. (1974). *The Rorschach: A comprehensive system.* New York: Wiley.

Exner, J. E. (1978). *The Rorschach: A comprehensive system. Vol. 2: Current research and advanced interpretation.* New York: Wiley.

Exner, J. E.; and Exner, D. E. (1972). How clinicians use the Rorschach. *Journal of Personality Assessment,* **36,** 403–408.

Exner, J. E.; and Miller, A. S. (1974). *Protocols of newly admitted prison inmates* (Workshops Study No. 200). Rorschach Workshops: Unpublished manuscript.

Fauman, B. J.; and Fauman, M. A. (1982). Phencyclidine abuse and crime: A psychiatric perspective. *Bulletin of the American Academy of Psychiatry and the Law,* **10,** 171–176.

Fauman, M. A.; and Fauman, B. J. (1979) Violence associated with phencyclidine abuse. *American Journal of Psychiatry,* **136,** 1584–1586.

Feher, E.; Vandencreek, L.; and Teglasi, H. (1983). The problem of art quality in the use of human figure drawing tests. *Journal of Clinical Psychology,* **39,** 268–275.

Feighner, J. P.; Robins, E.; Guze, S. B.; Woodruff, R. A.; Winokur, G.; and Munoz, R. (1972). Diagnostic criteria for use in psychiatric research. *Archives of General Psychiatry,* **26,** 57–63.

Feld, S.; and Smith, C. P. (1958). An evaluation of the objectivity of the method of content analysis. In J. W. Atkinson (Ed.), *Motives in fantasy, action and society.* Princeton, NJ: Van Nostrand.

Feldman, R. S. (1976). Nonverbal disclosure of teacher deception and interpersonal affect. *Journal of Educational Psychology,* **68,** 807–816.

Feldman, W. S. (1981). Episodic cerebral dysfunction: A defense in legal limbo. *Journal of Psychiatry and Law,* **9,** 193–201.

Filskov, S. B.; and Goldstein, S. G. (1974). Diagnostic validity of Halstead-Reitan neuropsychological battery. *Journal of Consulting and Clinical Psychology,* **42,** 382–388.

Fingarette, H.; and Hasse, A. F. (1979). *Mental disabilities and criminal responsibility.* Berkeley: University of California Press.

Fisher, C. M.; and Adams, R. D. (1964). Transient global amnesia. *Acta Neurologica Scandinavica,* **40,** 46–72.

Fox, J. L. (1984). PET scan controversy aired. *Science,* **224,** 143–144.

Freedman, D. X. (1984). Psychiatric epidemiology counts. *Archives of General Psychiatry,* **41,** 931–933.

Freedman, L. Z. (1983). *By reason of insanity: Essays on psychiatry and the law.* Wilmington, DE: Scholarly Resources.

Freedman, L. Z.; Guttmacher, M.; and Overholser, W. (1961). Mental disease or defect excluding responsibility: A psychiatric view of the American Law Institute's model penal code proposal. *American Journal of Psychiatry,* **118,** 32–34.

Freund, K.; Langevin, R.; and Barlow, D. (1974). Comparison of two penile measures of erotic arousal. *Behaviour Research and Therapy,* **12,** 355–359.

Friedman, L. R. (1982). Unwrapping the riddle of the brain-injured patient by utilizing the beam EEG. *American Journal of Forensic Psychiatry,* **3,** 47–52.

Gauron, E. F.; and Dickinson, J. K. (1966). Diagnostic decision-making in psychiatry: Information usage. *Archives of General Psychiatry,* **14,** 225–232.

Gibbens, T. C. N.; and Williams, J. E. H. (1977). Medical/legal aspects of amnesia. In C. W. M. Whitty and O. L. Vangwill (Eds.), *Amnesia: Clinical, psychological, and medical/legal aspects* (pp. 345–364). London: Butterworth.

Gibbs, E. L.; Gibbs, F. A. (1951). Electroencephalographic evidence of thalamic and hypothalamic epilepsy. *Neurology,* **1,** 136–144.

Gilberstadt, H.; and Duker, J. (1965). *A handbook for clinical and actuarial MMPI interpretation.* Philadelphia: Saunders.

Goebel, R. A. (1983). Detection of faking on the Halstead-Reitan neuropsychological test battery. *Journal of Clinical Psychology,* **39,** 731–742.

Gold, A. V. (1981). Drunkenness and criminal responsibility. In S. J. Hucker, C. D. Webster, and M. H. Ben-Aron (Eds.), *Mental disorder and criminal responsibility* (pp. 63–78). Toronto: Butterworth.

Goldberg, L. R., and Rorer, L. G. (1963). Test-retest item statistics for original and reversed MMPI items. *Oregon Research Institute Monographs, 3,* (Serial No.1).

Golden, C. J. (1979). Diagnosis of multiple sclerosis using double discrimination scales in the Luria-Nebraska neuropsychological battery. *International Journal of Neuroscience, 910,* 51–56.

Golden, C. J. (1980). In reply to Adam's "In search of Luria's battery: A false start." *Journal of Consulting and Clinical Psychology, 48,* 517–521.

Golden, C. J. (1984). The Luria-Nebraska neuropsychological battery in forensic assessment of head injury. *Psychiatric Annals, 14,* 532–538.

Golden, C. J.; Ariel, R. N.; McKay, S. E.; Wilkening, G. N.; Wolf, B. A.; and MacInnes, W. D. (1982). The Luria-Nebraska neuropsychological battery: Theoretical orientation and comment. *Journal of Consulting and Clinical Psychology, 50,* 291–300.

Golden, C. J.; Ariel, R. N.; Moses, J. A.; Wilkening, G. N.; McKay, S. E.; and MacInnes, W. D. (1982). Analytical techniques in the interpretation of the Luria-Nebraska neuropsychological battery. *Journal of Consulting and Clinical Psychology, 50,* 40–48.

Golden, C. J.; Fross, K.; and Graber, B. (1981). Split-half reliability and item consistency of the Luria-Nebraska neuropsychological battery. *Journal of Consulting and Clinical Psychology, 49,* 304–305.

Golden, C. J.; Hammeke, T. A.; and Purisch, A. D. (1978). Diagnostic validity of standardized neuropsychological battery derived from Luria's neuropsychological tests. *Journal of Consulting and Clinical Psychology, 46,* 1258–1265.

Golden, C. J.; Hammeke, T. A.; and Purisch, A. D. (1980). *The Luria-Nebraska battery manual.* Palo Alto, CA: Western Psychological Services.

Golden, C. J.; Moses, J. A.; Fishburne, F. J.; Engum, E.; Lewis, G. P.; Wisniewski, A. M.; Conley, F. K.; Berg, R. A.; and Graber, B. (1981). Cross validation of the Luria-Nebraska neuropsychological battery for the presence, lateralization, and localization of brain damage. *Journal of Consulting and Clinical Psychology, 49,* 491–507.

Golden, C. J.; Moses, J. A.; Zelazowski, R.; Graber, B.; Zatz, L. M.; Horvath, T. B.; Berger, P. A. (1980). Cerebral ventricular size and neuropsychological impairment in young chronic schizophrenics. *Archives of General Psychiatry, 37,* 619–623.

Golding, S. L. (1983, October 6). *The assessment, treatment, and community outcome of defendants found not guilty by reason of insanity.* Paper presented at American Psychology and Law Society Conference, Chicago, IL.

Goldstein, A. S. (1967). *The insanity defense.* New Haven: Yale University Press.

Goldstein, G.; and Shelly, C. (1984). Discriminative validity of various intelligence and neuropsychological tests. *Journal of Consulting and Clinical Psychology, 52,* 383–389.

Goldstein, M. (1974). Brain research and violent behaviour. *Archives of Neurology, 30,* 1–34.

Goldstein, S. G.; Deysach, R. E.; and Kleinknecht, R. A. (1973). Effects of experience and the amount of information on identification of cerebral impairment. *Journal of Consulting and Clinical Psychology, 41, 30–34.*

Goodwin, D. W. (1969). Alcohol and recall: State-dependent effects in men. *Science, 163, 1358–1360.*

Goodwin, D. W.; Alderson, P.; and Rosenthal, R. (1971). Clinical significance of hallucinations in psychiatric disorders. A study of 116 hallucinatory patients. *Archives of General Psychiatry, 24, 76–80.*

Goodwin, D. W.; Crane, J. B.; and Guze, S. B. (1969). Phenomenological aspects of alcoholic "blackout." *British Journal of Psychiatry, 115, 1033–1038.*

Gordon, R. H. (1976). Diagnostic compliance in Rorschach interpretation as a function of group member status. *Journal of Consulting and Clinical Psychology, 44, 826–831.*

Gorman, W. E. (1984). Neurological malingering. *Behavioral Sciences and the Law, 2, 67–74.*

Gough, H. G. (1947). Simulated patterns on the MMPI. *Journal of Abnormal and Social Psychology, 42, 215–225.*

Gough, H. G. (1950). The F-K dissimulation index for the Minnesota Multiphasic Personality Inventory. *Journal of Consulting Psychology, 14, 408–413.*

Gough, H. G. (1957). *California Psychological Inventory manual.* Palo Alto, CA: Consulting Psychologists Press.

Gough, H. G.; Wenk, E. A.; and Rozynko, V. V. (1965). Parole outcome as predicted from the CPI, the MMPI, and a base expectancy table. *Journal of Abnormal Psychology, 70, 432–441.*

Graham, J. R. (1977). *The MMPI: A practical guide.* New York: Oxford University Press.

Green, R. K.; and Schaefer, A. B. (1984). *Forensic psychology: A primer for legal and mental health professionals.* Springfield, IL: Charles C Thomas.

Greenberg, S. W. (1976). The relationship between crime and amphetamine abuse: An empirical review. *Contemporary Drug Problems, 5, 101–130.*

Greene, R. L. (1978). An empirically derived MMPI carelessness scale. *Journal of Clinical Psychology, 34, 407–410.*

Greene, R. L. (1979). Response consistency on the MMPI: The TR index. *Journal of Personality Assessment, 43, 69–71.*

Greene, R. L. (1980). *MMPI, an interpretive manual.* New York: Grune & Stratton.

Greene, R. L. (1984, November). *The MMPI: Its utilization and interpretation in clinical practice* (Workshop presented in Chicago, IL).

Greenspan, E. L. (1978). Insanity and psychiatric evidence. *Crown's Newsletter,* Crown's Attorneys of Ontario, 1–40.

Grinspoon, L.; and Bakalar, J. V. (1978). Drug abuse, crime, and the antisocial personality: Some conceptual issues. In W. H. Reid (Ed.), *The psychopath: A comprehensive study of antisocial disorders and behavior* (pp. 234–243). New York: Bruner-Mazel.

Grisso, T. (1984). *Review of Rogers criminal responsibility assessment scales.* Unpublished draft, Grant MH-37321, National Institute of Mental Health, Washington, D.C.

Grostic, J. M. (1978). The constitutionality of Michigan's guilty but mentally ill verdict. *University of Michigan Journal of Law Reform, 12, 118–199.*

Groth, A. M. (1979). *Men who rape: The psychology of the offender.* New York: Plenum.

Group for the Advancement of Psychiatry. (1983). Criminal responsibility and psychiatric expert testimony. In L. Z. Freedman (Ed.), *By reason of insanity: Essays on psychiatry and the law* (pp. 31–35). Wilmington, DE: Scholarly Resources.

Grove, W. M. (1985). Boot-strapping diagnoses using Bayes's Theorem: It's not worth the trouble. *Journal of Consulting and Clinical Psychology,* **53,** 261–263.

Grow, R.; McVaugh, W.; and Eno, T. D. (1980). Faking and the MMPI. *Journal of Clinical Psychology,* **36,** 910–917.

Gunn, J.; and Bonn, J. (1971). Criminality and violence in epileptic prisoners. *British Journal of Psychiatry,* **118,** 337–343.

Gunn, J.; and Fenton, G. (1969). Epilepsy in prisons: A diagnostic survey. *British Medical Journal,* **4,** 226–328.

Gutheil, T. G.; and Appelbaum, P. S. (1982). *Clinical handbook of psychiatry and the law.* New York: McGraw-Hill.

Gynther, M. D.; Altman, H.; and Sletten, I. W. (1973). Replicated correlates of MMPI two point code types: The Missouri actuarial system. *Journal of Clinical Psychology, Monograph Supplement No. 39.*

Gynther, M. D.; Altman, H.; and Warbin, R. (1973). Interpretation of uninterpretable MMPI profiles. *Journal of Consulting and Clinical Psychology,* **40,** 70–83.

Gynther, M. D.; Altman, H.; Warbin, R. W.; and Sletten, I. W. (1972). A new actuarial system for MMPI interpretation: Rationale and methodology. *Journal of Clinical Psychology,* **28,** 173–179.

Gynther, M. D.; Burkhart, B. R.; and Hovanitz, C. (1979). Do face-valid items have more predictive validity than subtle items? The case of the MMPI Pd scale. *Journal of Consulting and Clinical Psychology,* **47,** 295–300.

Gynther, M. D.; Fowler, R. D.; and Erdberg, P. (1971). False positives galore: The application of standard MMPI criteria to a rural, isolated, Negro sample. *Journal of Clinical Psychology,* **27,** 234–237.

Hain, J. D.; Smith, B. M.; and Stevenson, I. (1966). Effectiveness and processes of interviewing with drugs. *Journal of Psychiatric Research,* **4,** 95–106.

Halleck, S. L. (1967). *Psychiatry and the dilemmas of crime.* New York: Harper & Row.

Halpern, A. L. (1982). Commentary: Reconsideration of the insanity defense and related issues in the aftermath of the Hinckley trial. *Psychiatric Quarterly,* **54,** 260–264.

Hamilton, R. G.; and Robertson, M. H. (1966). Examiner influence on the Holtzman Inkblot Technique. *Journal of Projective Techniques,* **30**(6), 553–558.

Haney, C. (1980). Psychology and legal change: On the limits of factual jurisprudence. *Law and Human Behaviour,* **4,** 147–200.

Hans, V. P.; and Slater, D. (1983). John Hinckley Jr. and the insanity defense: The public's verdict. *Public Opinion Quarterly,* **47,** 202–212.

Harbin, H. T. (1977). Episodic dyscontrol and family dynamics. *American Journal of Psychiatry,* **134,** 1113–1116.

Hare, R. D.; and Cox, D. N. (1978). Psychophysiological research on psychopathy. In W. H. Reid (Ed.), *The psychopath* (pp. 209–222). New York: Brunner-Mazel.

Harrison, A. A.; Hwalek, M.; Raney, D. F.; and Fritz, J. G. (1978). Cues to deception in an interview situation. *Social Psychology,* **41,** 156–161.

Harvey, M. A.; and Sipprelle, C. N. (1976). Demand characteristic effects on the subtle and obvious subscales of the MMPI. *Journal of Personality Assessment,* **40,** 539–544.

Hathaway, S. R. (1946). The multiphasic personality inventory. *Modern Hospital,* **66,** 65–67.

Hathaway, S. R.; and Meehl, P. E. (1951). *An atlas for the clinical use of the MMPI.* Minneapolis: University of Minnesota Press.

Heaton, R. K.; Baade, L. E.; and Johnson, A. L. (1978). Neuropsychological test results associated with psychiatric disorders in adults. *Psychological Bulletin,* **85,** 141–162.

Heaton, R. K.; and Pendleton, M. G. (1981). Use of neuropsychological tests to predict adult patients every day functioning. *Journal of Consulting and Clinical Psychology,* **49,** 807–821.

Heaton, R. K.; Smith, H. H.; Lehman, R. A. W.; and Vogt, A. T. (1978). Prospects of faking believable deficits on neuropsychological testing. *Journal of Consulting and Clinical Psychology,* **46,** 892–900.

Hekimian, L. K.; and Gershon, S. (1968). Characteristics of drug abusers admitted to a psychiatric hospital. *Journal of the American Medical Association,* **205,** 125–130.

Helzer, J. E.; Robins, L. N.; Croughan, J. L.; and Welner, A. (1981). Renard diagnostic interview. *Archives of General Psychiatry,* **38,** 393–398.

Henderson, M. (1983). An empirical classification of non-violent offenders using the MMPI. *Journal of Personality and Individual Differences,* **4,** 671–677.

Hermann, D. J. (1986). Amnesia and the criminal law. *Behavioral Sciences and the Law,* in press.

Herrmann, D. J. (1982). Know thy memory: The use of questionnaires to assess and study memory. *Psychological Bulletin,* **92,** 424–452.

Herrmann, D. J.; and Neisser, U. (1978). An inventory of everyday memory experiences. In M. M. Grunberg, P. E. Morris, and R. N. Sykes (Eds.), *Practical aspects of memory.* New York: Academic Press.

Hersen, M. (1970). Sexual aspects of Rorschach administration. *Journal of Projective Techniques,* **34,** 104–105.

Hilgard, E. R.; and Loftus, E. F. (1979). Effective interrogation of the eye-witness. *International Journal of Clinical and Experimental Hypnosis,* **27,** 342–357.

Hill, D.; and Pond, D. A. (1952). Reflections on 100 capital cases submitted to electroencephalography. *Journal of Mental Science,* **98,** 23–43.

Hill, E. F. (1972). *The Holtzman Inkblot Technique: A handbook for clinical application.* San Francisco: Jossey-Bass.

Hill, R. W. (1981). Drunkenness and criminal responsibility: The psychiatrist's contribution. In S. J. Hucker, C. D. Webster, and M. H. Ben-Aron (Eds.), *Mental disorder and criminal responsibility* (pp. 79–90). Toronto: Butterworth.

Himelstein, P.; and Grunau, G. (1981). Differentiation of aggressive and non-aggressive schizophrenics with the Hand Test: Another failure. *Psychological Reports,* **49,** 556.

Hoivath, F. (1977). The effect of selected variables on interpretation of polygraph records. *Journal of Applied Psychology,* **62,** 127–136.

Holcomb, W. R.; Adams, N. A.; Ponder, H. M.; and Anderson, W. P. (1984). Cognitive and behavioral predictors of MMPI scores in pre-trial psychological evaluations of murderers. *Journal of Clinical Psychology, 40*, 592-597.

Holland, T. R. (1979). Ethnic group differences in MMPI profile pattern and factorial structure among adult offenders. *Journal of Personality Assessment, 43*, 72-77.

Holmes, D. S. (1968). Dimensions of projection. *Psychological Bulletin, 69*, 248-268.

Holmes, D. S. (1974). The conscious control of thematic projection. *Journal of Consulting and Clincal Psychology, 42*, 323-329.

Holtzman, W. H. (1984, September). *Clinical applications in personality assessment and psychodiagnosis.* Paper presented at the 23rd International Congress of Psychology, Acapulco, Mexico.

Holtzman, W. H.; Thorpe, J. S.; Swartz, J. D.; and Herron, E. W. (1961). *Inkblot perception and personality.* Austin: University of Texas Press.

Holtzman, W. H. (1984). *Clinical uses of the HIT with adolescents.* Unpublished manuscript, University of Texas at Austin.

Hook, E. B. (1973). Behavioral implications of the human xyy genotype. *Science, 179*, 139-179.

Hopwood, J. S.; and Snell, H. K. (1933). Amnesia in relation to crime. *Journal of Mental Sciences, 79*, 27-30.

Howard, R. C.; and Clark, C. R. (1983). *When courts and experts disagree: Discordance between insanity recommendations and adjudications.* Unpublished manuscript, Center for Forensic Psychiatry, Ann Arbor.

Howe, E. G. (1984). Psychiatric evaluation of offenders who commit crimes while experiencing dissociative disorders. *Law and Human Behavior, 8*, 253-282.

Huckabee, H. M. (1980). *Lawyers, psychiatrists, and criminal law: Cooperation or chaos?* Springfield, IL: Charles C. Thomas.

Huesmann, L. R.; Lefkowitz, M. M.; and Eron, L. D. (1978). Sum of MMPI scales F, 4, and 9 as a measure of aggression. *Journal of Consulting and Clinical Psychology, 46*, 1071-1078.

Inman, D. J. (1977). Differentiation of intropunitive from extrapunitive female inmates. *Journal of Clinical Psychology, 33*, 95-98.

Insanity Defense Workgroup. (1983). American Psychiatric Association statement on the insanity defense. *American Journal of Psychiatry, 140*, 681-688.

Institute on Mental Disability and the Law. (1984). *The "guilty but mentally ill" verdict: Current state of knowledge.* Williamsburg, VA: National Center for State Courts.

Jacobs, P. A.; Brunton, M.; Melville, M. M.; Brittain, R. P.; and McClemont, W. F. (1965). Aggressive behavior, mental subnormality, and the xyy male. *Nature, 208*, 1351-1352.

Jeffrey, R. W.; and Pasewark, R. A. (1983). Altering opinions about the insanity plea. *Journal of Psychiatry and Law, 6*, 39-40.

Jensen, A. R. (1965). Rorschach. In O. K. Buros (Ed.), *Sixth mental measurements yearbook* (pp. 501-509). Highland Park, NJ: Gryphon Press.

Jesness, C. G. (1966). *The Jesness Inventory manual.* Palo Alto, CA: Consulting Psychologists Press.

Jones, T.; Beidleman, W. B.; and Fowler, R. D. (1981). Differentiating violent and non-violent prison inmates by use of selected MMPI scales. *Journal of Clinical Psychology,* **37,** 673–677.

Jourard, S. M.; and Landsman, M. J. (1960). Cognition, cathexis, and "dyadic effects" in men's self-disclosing behavior. *Merrill-Palmer Quarterly,* **6,** 178–186.

Kahn, M. W. (1967). Correlates of Rorschach reality adherents of murderers who plead insanity. *Journal of Projective Techniques,* **31,** 44–47.

Kahn, M., and Taft, G. (1983). The application of the standard of care doctrine to psychological testing. *Behavioral Sciences and the Law,* **1,** 71–84.

Keasey, C. B.; and Sales, B. D. (1977). Children's conception of intentionality and the criminal law. In B. D. Sales (Ed.), *Psychology in the legal process* (pp. 127–146). Jamaica, NY: Spectrum Publications.

Keilitz, I. (1981). *Mental health examinations in criminal justice settings: Organization, administration, and program evaluation.* Williamsburg, VA: National Center for State Courts.

Keilitz, I. (1984). *The guilty but mentally ill verdict: An empirical study* (Working paper). Williamsburg, VA: Institute on Mental Disability and the Law, National Center for State Courts.

Keilitz, I. (1985). *Researching the insanity defense.* Chapter in preparation (Williamsburg, VA: Institute on Mental Disability and the Law, National Center for State Courts).

Keilitz, I.; and Fulton, J. P. (1983). *The insanity defense and its alternatives: A guide to policy makers.* Williamsburg, VA: National Center for State Courts.

Keller, M. B.; Lavori, P. W.; Andreasen, W. C.; Grove, W. M.; Shapiro, R. W.; Scheftner, W. A.; McDonald-Scott, P. (1981*a*). Reliability of assessing psychiatrically ill patients in a multi-center, test-retest design. *Journal of Psychiatric Research,* **16,** 213–228.

Keller, M. B.; Lavori, P. W.; MacDonald-Scott, P.; Scheftner, W. A.; Anreason, M. C.; Schapiro, R. W.; and Croughan, J. (1981*b*). Reliability of lifetime diagnosis and symptoms in patients with a current psychiatric disorder. *Journal of Psychiatric Research,* **16,** 229–240.

Kelly, J. (1980, July). *Amnesia and forensic psychiatry.* Lecture given at Rush Medical Center, Chicago, IL.

Keltikangas-Jarvinen, L. (1982). Alexithymia in violent offenders. *Journal of Personality Assessment,* **46,** 462–467.

Kiersch, T. (1962). Amnesia, A clinical study of 98 cases. *American Journal of Psychiatry,* **119,** 57–60.

King, D. W.; and Ajmone-Marsan, C. (1977). Clinical features and ictal patterns of epileptic patients with EEG temporal lobe foci. *Annals of Neurology,* **2,** 138–147.

Kleinmuntz, B.; and Szucko, J. J. (1982). On the fallibility of lie detection. *Law and Society Review,* **17,** 85–104.

Klieger, D. M. (1969). An investigation of the influence of response sets on the Holtzman projective technique (Doctoral dissertation, Iowa State University, 1968). *Dissertation Abstracts,* **29,** 4848B.

Kline, M. V. (1979). Defending the mentally ill: The insanity defence and the role of forensic hypnosis. *International Journal of Clinical and Experimental Hypnosis,* **27,** 375–401.

Klopfer, W. G.; and Taubee, E. S. (1976). Objective tests. *Annual Review of Psychology,* **27,** 543-567.

Knapp, M. L.; Hart, R. P.; and Dennis, H. S. (1974). An exploration of deception as a communication construct. *Human Communication Research,* **1,** 15-29.

Knox, S. J. (1968). Epileptic automatism and violence. *Medical Sciences and the Law,* **8,** 96-104.

Kolodny, R. C.; Masters, W. H.; and Hendryx, J. (1971). Plasma testosterone and semen analysis in male homosexuals. *New England Journal of Medicine,* **285,** 1170-1174.

Koson, D.; and Robey, A. (1973). Amnesia and competency to stand trial. *American Journal of Psychiatry,* **130,** 588-592.

Kraiger, K.; Hakel, M. D.; and Cornelius, E. T. (1984). Exploring fantasies of TAT reliability. *Journal of Personality Assessment,* **48,** 365-370.

Kral, V. A. (1959). Amnesia and the amnestic syndrome. *Canadian Psychiatric Association Journal,* **4,** 61-68.

Kral, V. A.; and Durost, H. B. (1953). A comparative study of the amnestic syndrome in various organic conditions. *American Journal of Psychiatry,* **110,** 41-47.

Kraus, J. (1972). Use of Bayes's theorem in clinical decision: Suicidal risk, differential diagnosis, response to treatment. *British Journal of Psychiatry,* **120,** 561-567.

Kreuz, L. E.; and Rose, R. M. (1972). Assessment of aggressive behavior and plasma testosterone in young criminal population. *Psychosomatic Medicine,* **34,** 321-332.

Krieger, M. J.; and Levin, S. M. (1976). Schizophrenic behaviour as a function of role expectation. *Journal of Clinical Psychology,* **32,** 463-467.

Kroger, W. S.; and Douce, R. G. (1979). Hypnosis in criminal investigation. *International Journal of Clinical and Experimental Hypnosis,* **27,** 358-374.

Kurlychek, R. T.; and Jordan, L. (1980). MMPI profiles and code types of responsible and nonresponsible criminal defendants. *Journal of Clinical Psychology,* **36,** 590-593.

Lachar, D.; and Wrobel, T. A. (1979). Validating clinicians' hunches: Construction of a new MMPI critical item set. *Journal of Consulting and Clinical Psychology,* **47,** 277-284.

Lacks, P. B.; Colbert, J.; Harrow, M.; and Levine, J. (1970). Further evidence concerning the diagnostic accuracy of the Halstead organic test battery. *Journal of Clinical Psychology,* **26,** 480-481.

Langevin, R.; Ben-Aron, M. H.; Coulthard, R.; Heasman, G.; Purins, J. E.; Handy, L.; Hucker, S. J.; Russon, A. E.; Day, D.; Roper, V.; and Webster, C. D. (1985). Sexual aggression: Constructing a predictive equation, a controlled pilot study. In R. Langevin (Ed.), *Erotic preference, gender identity and aggression in men: New research studies* (pp. 39-76). Hillsdale, NJ: Lawrence Erlbaum.

Langevin, R.; Ben-Aron, M. H.; Coulthard, R.; Day, D.; Hucker, S. J.; Purins, J. E.; Roper, V.; Russon, A. E.; and Webster, C. D. (1985). The effect of alcohol on penile erection. In R. Langevin (Ed.), *Erotic preference, gender identity and aggression in men: New research studies* (pp. 101-112). Hillsdale, NJ: Lawrence Erlbaum.

Langevin, R.; Hucker, S.; Wortzman, G.; Bain, J.; Handy, L.; Chambers, J.; and Wright, S. (1985). *Neuropsychological impairment in pedophiles.* Unpublished manuscript, University of Toronto.

Langevin, R.; Paitich, D.; Orchard, B.; Handy, L.; and Russon, A. (1982). Diagnosis of killers seen for a psychiatric assessment: A controlled study. *Acta Psychiatrika Scandinavia,* **66,** 216-228.

Laufer, W. S.; Skoog, D. K.; and Day, J. M. (1982). Personality and criminality: A review of the California Psychological Inventory. *Journal of Clinical Psychology,* **38,** 562-573.

Lawrence, S. B. (1978). *Manual for the Lawrence psychological-forensic examination for use within the criminal justice system.* San Bernardino, CA: Author.

Lawson, J. S.; and Inglis, J. (1983). The laterality index of cognitive impairment after hemispheric damage: A measure derived from a principal components analysis of the Wechsler Adult Intelligence Scale. *Journal of Consulting and Clinical Psychology,* **51,** 832-840.

Lentle, B. C. (1983). Diagnostic imaging in transition. *Annals RCPSC,* **16,** 555-559.

Levy, M. R.; and Kahn, M. W. (1970). Interpreter bias on the Rorschach test as a function of patient's socioeconomic status. *Journal of Projective Techniques,* **34,** 106-112.

Lewis, D. O. (1976). Delinquency, psychomotor epileptic symptoms, and paranoid ideation: A triad. *American Journal of Psychiatry,* **133,** 1395-1398.

Lewis, D. O.; Pincus, J. H.; Shanok, S. S.; and Glaser, G. H. (1982). Psychomotor epilepsy and violence in a group of incarcerated adolescent boys. *American Journal of Psychiatry,* **139,** 882-887.

Lewis, D. O.; and Shanok, S. S. (1979). A comparison of medical histories of incarcerated delinquent children and a matched sample of nondelinquent children. *Child Psychiatry and Human Development,* **9,** 210-214.

Lewis, G.; Golden, C. J.; Moses, J.; Osmon, D.; Purisch, A. D.; and Hammeke, T. A. (1979). The localization of cerebral dysfunction with a standardized version of Luria's neuropsychological battery. *Journal of Consulting and Clinical Psychology,* **47,** 1003-1019.

Lezak, M. D. (1978). Neuropsychological assessment. New York: Oxford University Press.

Lidz, C. W.; Meisel, A.; Zerubavel, E.; Carter, M.; Sestak, R. M.; and Roth, L. H. (1984). *Informed consent: A study of decision-making in psychiatry.* New York: Guilford Press.

Lindemann, E. (1932). Psychological changes in normal and abnormal individuals under the influence of sodium amytal. *American Journal of Psychiatry,* **88,** 1083-1091.

Lindzay, G.; and Tejessy, C. (1965). Thematic Apperception Test: Indices of aggression in relationship to measures of overt and covert behavior. In B. I. Murstein (Ed.), *Handbook of projective techniques.* (pp. 575-586). New York: Basic Books.

Lippold, S.; and Claiborn, J. M. (1983). Comparison of the Wechsler Adult Intelligence Scale and the Wechsler Adult Intelligence Scale-Revised. *Journal of Consulting and Clinical Psychology,* **51,** 315.

Lishman, W. A. (1971). Amnesic syndromes and their neuropathology. Special Publication, *British Journal of Psychiatry,* **117,** 25-38(6).

Littlepage, G; and Pineault, T. (1978). Verbal, facial and paralinguistic cues to the detection of truth and lying. *Personality and Social Psychology Bulletin,* **4,** 461-464.

Loevinger, J. (1957). Objective tests as instruments of psychological theory. *Psychological Reports,* **3,** Monograph Supplement IX, 635-694.

Loftus, E. F. (1975). Leading questions and the eye-witness report. *Cognitive Psychology,* **7,** 560-572.

Loftus, E. F. *Eye-witness testimony.* (1979). Cambridge, MA: Harvard University Press.

Loftus, E. F.; and Loftus, T. R. (1980). On the impermanence of stored information in the human brain. *American Psychologist,* **35,** 409-420.

Luisada, P. V. (1978). The phencylidine psychosis: Phenomenology and treatment. In R. C. Petersen and R. C. Stillman (Eds.), *Phencyclidine (PCP) abuse: An appraisal* (pp. 241-255). Rockville, MD: National Institute on Drug Abuse.

Lykken, D. T. (1974). Psychology and the lie detector industry. *American Psychologist,* **29,** 725-739.

Lykken, D. T. (1981). *A tremor in the blood: Uses and abuses of the lie detector.* New York: McGraw-Hill.

Lykken, D. T. (1984). Trial by polygraph. *Behavioral Sciences and the Law,* **2,** 75-92.

Lynch, B. E. (1979). Detection of deception: Its application to forensic psychiatry. *Bulletin of the American Academy of Psychiatry and the Law,* **7,** 239-244.

Lynch, B. E.; and Bradford, J. W. (1980). Amnesia: Its detection by psychophysiological measures. *Bulletin of the American Academy of Psychiatry and Law,* **8,** 288-297.

MacDonald, J. M. (1976). *Psychiatry and the criminal: A guide to psychiatric examinations for the criminal court.* Springfield, IL: Charles C Thomas.

Machover, K. (1949). *Personality projection in the drawing of human figure.* Springfield, IL: Charles C Thomas.

Maier, N. R. S.; and Thurber, J. A. (1968). Accuracy of judgment of deception when an interviewer is watched, heard, and read. *Personnel Psychology,* **21,** 23-30.

Maletzky, V. M. (1973). The episodic dyscontrol syndrome. *Diseases of the Nervous System,* **36,** 178-185.

Maletzky, V. M.; and Klotter, J. (1974). Episodic dyscontrol: A controlled replication. *Diseases of the Nervous System,* **37,** 175-179.

Mark, P. H.; and Ervin, F. R. (1970). *Violence and the brain.* New York: Harper & Row.

Marks, P.; and Seeman, W. (1963). *The actuarial description of abnormal personality: An atlas for use with the MMPI.* Baltimore, MD: Williams & Wilkins.

Markson, E. R.; Greenland, C.; and Turner, R. E. (1965). The life and death of Louis Riel: A study in forensic psychiatry. *Canadian Psychiatric Association Journal,* **10,** 244-264.

Martin, G. A. (1981). Mental disorder and criminal responsibility in Canadian law. In S. J. Hucker, C. D. Webster, and M. H. Ben-Aron (Eds.), *Mental disorder and criminal responsibility* (pp. 15-32). Toronto: Butterworth.

Matarazzo, J. D. (1972). *Wechsler's measurement and appraisal of adult intelligence*. Baltimore, MD: Williams & Wilkins.

Matranga, J. T. (1976). The relationship between behavioral indices of aggression and hostile content on the TAT. *Journal of Personality Assessment, 40,* 130–134.

Mayfield, D. (1976). Alcoholism, alcohol intoxication, and assaultive behaviour. *Diseases of the Nervous System, 37,* 288–291.

McArthur, C. C. (1972). Rorschach. In O. K. Buros (Ed.), *Seventh mental measurements yearbook*. (pp. 340–343). Highland Park, NJ: Gryphon Press.

McBroom, P. (1980). *Behavioral Genetics*. Rockville, MD: National Institute of Mental Health.

McCaldon, R. J. (1964). Automatism. *Canadian Medical Association Journal, 91,* 914–920.

McConaghy, N. (1974). Measurement of change in penile dimensions. *Archives of Sexual Behavior, 4,* 381–388.

McGarry, A. L. (1980). Psycho-legal examinations and reports. In W. J. Curran, A. L. McGarry, and C. S. Petty (Eds.), *Modern legal medicine, psychiatry, and forensic science*. (pp. 739–760). Philadelphia: F. A. Davis.

McGlothlin, W. H.; and Anglin, M. D. (1981). Shutting off methadone. *Archives of General Psychiatry, 38,* 85–89.

McGraw, B. D.; and Keilitz, I. (1984). Guilty but mentally ill: The legislative response to the insanity defense. *State Court Journal, 8,* 4–8.

McKay, S. E.; and Golden, C. J. (1979). Empirical derivation of neuropsychological scales for the lateralization of brain damage using the Luria-Nebraska neuropsychological test battery. *Clinical Neuropsychology, 1,* 19–23.

McKay, S. E.; Golden, C. J.; Moses, J. A.; Fishburne, F.; and Wisniewski, A. (1981). Correlation of the Luria-Nebraska neuropsychological battery with the WAIS. *Journal of Consulting and Clinical Psychology, 49,* 940–946.

McNeil, B. J.; Keeler, E.; and Adelstein, S. J. (1975). Primer on certain elements of medical decision-making. *New England Journal of Medicine, 293,* 211–215.

McRuer, R. (1956). *Report of the Royal Commission on the law of insanity as a defense in criminal cases*. Ottawa: Queen's Printer.

Mednick, S. A.; and Finello, K. M. (1983). Biological factors and crime: Implications for forensic psychiatry. *International Journal of Law and Psychiatry, 6,* 1–15.

Meehl, P. E. (1954). *Clinical versus statistical prediction: A theoretical analysis and review of the evidence*. Minneapolis: University of Minnesota Press.

Megargee, E. I. (1966). Undercontrolled personality types in extreme antisocial aggression. *Psychological Monographs, 80,* (Whole No. 611).

Megargee, E. I. (1977). *The California Psychological Inventory Handbook*. San Francisco: Jossey-Bass.

Megargee, E. I.; Lockwood, V.; Cato, J. L.; and Jones, J. K. (1966, August). The effects of differences in examiner, tone of administration, and sex of subject on scores of the Holtzman Inkblot Technique. *Proceedings of the 74th Annual Convention of the American Psychological Association,* 235–236.

Menuck, M. (1983). Clinical aspects of dangerous behaviour. *Journal of Psychiatry and Law, 11,* 277–304.

Mesritz, G. D. (1976). Guilty but mentally ill: An historical and constitutional analysis. *Journal of Urban Law, 53,* 471–496.

Meyers, T. J. (1965). The psychiatric determination of legal intent. *Journal of Forensic Sciences,* **10**, 347–367.

Miller, T. R.; Bauchner, J. E.; Hocking, J. E.; Fontes, N. E.; Kaminsky, A. P.; and Brendt, D. R. (1981). How well can observers detect deceptive testimony? In B. D. Sales (Ed.), *Perspectives in law and psychology,* Vol. 2, *The trial process.* New York: Plenum.

Millon, T. (1981). *Disorders of personality: DSM III, axis 2.* Toronto: Wiley-Interscience.

Monahan, J. (1978). Report of the task force on the role of psychology in the criminal justice system. *American Psychologist,* **33**, 1099–1113.

Monahan, J. (1980). *Who is the client? The ethics of psychological intervention in the criminal justice system.* Washington, DC: American Psychological Association.

Money, J. (1970a). Behavioral genetics: Principles, methods, and examples from xo, xxy, and xyy syndromes. *Seminars in Psychiatry,* **2**, 11–29.

Money, J. (1970b). Use of an androgen-depleting hormone in the treatment of male sex offenders. *Journal of Sex Research,* **6**, 165–172.

Monroe, R. R. (1970). *Episodic behavior disorders.* Lexington, MA: Lexington Books.

Morse, S. J. (1982). Reforming expert testimony. *Law and Human Behavior,* **6**, 39–43.

Morse, S. J. (1984). Undiminished confusion in diminished capacity. *Journal of Criminal Law and Criminology,* **75**, 1–55.

Moses, J. A.; Golden, C. J.; Wilkening, G. N.; McKay, S. E.; and Ariel, R. (1983). *Interpretation of the Luria-Nebraska neuropsychological battery,* Vol. 2. New York: Grune & Stratton.

Mullen, J. M. (1980). *The forensic psychiatric patient in Texas: Historical perspective and normative research on dangerousness.* Austin: Texas Department of Mental Health and Mental Retardation.

Mullen, J. M.; and Reinehr, R. C. (1982). Predicting dangerousness of maximum security forensic mental patients. *Journal of Psychiatry and Law,* **10**, 223–231.

Mullen, J. M.; Reinehr, R. C.; and Swartz, J. D. (1982). Performance of forensic patients on the Holtzman Inkblot Technique: A normative study. *Perceptual and Motor Skills,* **54**, 275–280.

Mungas, V. (1984). Discriminant validation of an MMPI measure of aggression. *Journal of Consulting and Clinical Psychology,* **52**, 313–314.

Murphy, G. E.; Woodruff, M.; and Herjanic, M. (1974). Validity of clinical course of a primary affective disorder. *Archives of General Psychiatry,* **30**, 757–761.

Murray, H. A. (1943). *Thematic Apperception Test manual.* Cambridge, MA: Harvard University Press.

Murstein, B. I. (Ed.). (1965). *Handbook of projective techniques.* New York: Basic Books.

Mutter, C. B. (1979). Regressive hypnosis and the polygraph: A case study. *American Journal of Clinical Hypnosis,* **22**, 47–50.

Naples, M.; and Hackett, T. P. (1978). The amytal interview: History and current uses. *Psychosomatics,* **19**, 98–105.

Nichols, D. S.; and Greene, R. L. (1983, August). *A new approach to MMPI va-*

lidity. Paper presented at the Eighth International Conference on Personality Assessment, Copenhagen, Denmark.

Orne, M. T. (1961). The potential uses of hypnosis in interrogation. In A. D. Biderman and H. Zimmer (Eds.), *The manipulation of human behavior* (pp. 169–215). New York: Wiley and Sons.

Orne, M. T. (1971). The simulation of hypnosis: Why, how and what it means. *International Journal of Clinical and Experimental Hypnosis, 19,* 277–296.

Orne, M. T. (1972). On the simulating subject as a quasi-control group in hypnosis research: What, why and how. In E. Fromm and R. E. Shor (Eds.), *Hypnosis: Research developments and perspectives* (pp. 399–443). Chicago: Aldine-Atherton.

Orne, M. T. (1979). The use and misuse of hypnosis in court. *International Journal of Clinical and Experimental Hypnosis, 27,* 311–341.

Ossipov, V. B. (1944). Malingering: The simulation of psychosis. *Bulletin of the Menninger Clinic, 8,* 39–42.

Overholser, J. (1962). Criminal responsibility: A psychiatrist's viewpoint. *American Bar Association Journal, 48,* 529–530.

Owen, D. R. (1972). The 47, xyy male: A review. *Psychological Bulletin, 78,* 209–233.

Owens, O. G.; Johnstone, E. C.; Bydder, G. M.; and Kreel, L. (1980). Unsuspected organic disease in chronic schizophrenia demonstrated by computed tomography. *Journal of Neurology, Neurosurgery, and Psychiatry, 43,* 1065–1069.

Packer, I. K. (1981). Use of hypnotic techniques in the evaluation of criminal defendants. *Journal of Psychiatry and Law, 9,* 313–327.

Packer, K. (1983). A meta-analysis of the reliability and validity of the Rorschach. *Journal of Personality Assessment, 47,* 227–231.

Page, S. (1982). Psychologist and physician diagnoses of hospitalized patients with similar MMPI symtomatology. *Canadian Journal of Psychiatry, 27,* 471–473.

Panek, P. E.; and Stoner, S. (1979). Test-retest reliability of the Hand Test with normal subjects. *Journal of Personality Assessment, 43,* 135–137.

Parker, G. (1977). *An introduction to criminal law.* Toronto: Methuen Publications.

Parker, K. (1983). Factor analysis of the WAIS-R at nine age levels between 16 and 74 years. *Journal of Consulting and Clinical Psychology, 51,* 302–308.

Parwatikar, S. D.; Holcomb, W. R.; and Menninger, K. A. (1985). Detection of malingered anmesia in accused murderers. *Bulletin of the American Academy of Psychiatry and the Law, 13,* 97–103.

Patrick, J. (1984). Characteristics of DSM III borderline MMPI profiles. *Journal of Clinical Psychology, 40,* 655–658.

Perlin, M. L. (1980). The legal status of the psychologist in the courtroom. *Mental Disability Law Reporter, 4,* 194–200.

Petersen, R. C.; and Stillman, R. C. (Eds.). (1978). *Phencyclidine (PCP) abuse: An appraisal.* Rockville, MD: National Institute on Drug Abuse.

Petrella, R. C. (1983, October 6–8). *Guilty but mentally ill: A negative view.* Paper presented at the Biannual Conference of the American Psychology-Law Society, Chicago, IL.

Petrella, R. D.; and Poythress, N. G. (1983). The quality of forensic evaluations: An interdisciplinary study. *Journal of Consulting and Clinical Psychology, 51,* 76–85.

Piciucco, L. (1976). *Personality effects of examiner on Rorschach scoring errors* (Doctoral thesis, United States International University, San Diego, California).

Piotrowski, Z. A. (1979). *Perceptanalysis*. Philadelphia: Ex Libris.

Pollack, M.; Levenstein, D. S. W.; and Klein, D. F. (1968). A three year post-hospital follow-up of adolescent and adult schizophrenics. *American Journal of Orthopsychiatry,* **38,** 94–110.

Pollack, S. (1976). The insanity defense as defined by the proposed Federal Criminal Code. *Bulletin of the American Academy of Psychiatry and Law,* **4,** 11–23.

Pollack, S.; Gross, B. H.; and Weinberger, L. E. (1982). Principles of forensic psychiatry for reaching psychiatric-legal opinions. In B. H. Gross and L. E. Weinberger (Eds.), *The mental health professional and the legal system* (pp. 25–44). San Francisco: Jossey-Bass.

Pope, T. (1975). Interpreter bias on the Rorschach test as a function of patients' social class and race. *Dissertation Abstracts International,* **36**(3-B), 1451–1452.

Post, R. M. (1975). Cocaine psychosis: A continuum model. *American Journal of Psychiatry,* **132,** 225–231.

Potkay, C. R. (1972). Clinical judgement under varied informational conditions. *Journal of Consulting and Clinical Psychology,* **39,** 513.

Prandoni, J. R.; and Swartz, C. P. (1978). Rorschach protocols for three diagnostic categories of adult offenders: Normative data. *Journal of Personality Assessment,* **42,** 115.

Pratt, R. T. C. (1977). Psychogenic loss of memory. In C. W. M. Whitty and O. L. Vangwill (Eds.), *Amnesia: Clinical, psychological, and medical/legal aspects* (pp. 224–232). London: Butterworth.

Price, W. H.; Strong, J. A.; Whatmore, P. B.; and McClemont, W. (1966). Criminal patients with xyy sex chromosome complement. *Lancet,* **1,** 565–566.

Prifitera, A.; and Ryan, J. J. (1981). Validity of the Luria-Nebraska intellectual process scale as a measure of adult intelligence. *Journal of Consulting and Clinical Psychology,* **49,** 755–766.

Purcell, K. (1956). The Thematic Apperception Test and antisocial behavior. *Journal of Consulting Psychology,* **20,** 449–456.

Purisch, A. D.; Golden, C. J.; and Hammeke, T. A. (1978). Discrimination of schizophrenic and brain-injured patients by a standardized version of Luria's neuropsychological tests. *Journal of Consulting and Clinical Psychology,* **46,** 1266–1273.

Putnam, W. H. (1979). Hypnosis and distortions in eye-witness memory. *International Journal of Clinical and Experimental Hypnosis,* **27,** 437–448.

Pykett, I. L. (1982). NMR imaging in medicine. *Scientific American,* **246,** 78–91.

Quen, J. M. (1978). Isaac Ray and Charles Doe: Responsibility and justice. In W. E. Barton and C. J. Sanborn (Eds.), *Law and the mental health professions* (pp. 235–250). New York: International Universities Press.

Quen, J. M. (1981). Anglo American concepts of criminal responsibility. In S. J. Hucker, C. D. Webster, and M. H. Ben-Aron (Eds.), *Mental disorder and criminal responsibility* (pp. 1–10). Toronto: Butterworth.

Quinsey, V. L.; Arnold, L. S.; Pruesse, M. G. (1980). MMPI profiles of men referred for a pre-trial psychiatric assessment as a function of offense type. *Journal of Clinical Psychology,* **36,** 410–417.

Quinsey, V. L.; Chaplin, T. C.; and Varney, G. W. (1981). A comparison of rapists' and non-sex offenders' sexual preferences for mutually consenting sex, rape, and sadistic acts. *Behavioral Assessment,* **3,** 127–135.

Quinsey, V. L.; MacGuire, A.; and Varney, G. W. (1983). Assertion and overcontrolled hostility among mentally disordered murderers. *Journal of Consulting and Clinical Psychology,* **51,** 550–556.

Rachlin, S.; Halpern, A. L.; and Portnow, S. L. (1984). The volitional rule, personality disorders and the insanity defense. *Psychiatric Annals,* **14,** 139–147.

Rada, C. M. (1977). MMPI profile types of exposers, rapists and assaulters in a court services population. *Journal of Consulting and Clinical Psychology,* **45,** 61–69.

Rada, R. T. (1975). Alcoholism and forcible rape. *American Journal of Psychiatry,* **132,** 444–446.

Rada, R. T. (1978). *Clinical aspects of the rapist.* New York: Grune & Stratton.

Rada, R. T. (1980). Plasma androgens and the sex offender. *Bulletin of the American Academy of Psychiatry and Law,* **8,** 456–464.

Rada, R. T.; Kellner, R.; and Winslow, W. W. (1976). Plasma testosterone and aggressive behavior. *Psychosomatics,* **17,** 138–142.

Rada, R. T.; Kellner, R.; Laws, D. R.; and Winslow, W. W. (1978). Drinking, alcoholism and the mentally disordered sex offender. *Bulletin of American Academy of Psychiatry and Law,* **6,** 296–300.

Rada, R. T.; Laws, D. R.; and Kellner, R. (1976). Plasma testosterone levels in the rapist. *Psychosomatic Medicine,* **38,** 257–268.

Rada, R. T.; Laws, D. R.; Kellner, R.; Stivastava, L.; and Peake, G. (1983). Plasma androgens in violent and non-violent sex offenders. *Bulletin of the American Academy of Psychiatry and the Law,* **11,** 149–158.

Radar, C. M. (1977). MMPI profile types of exposers, rapists, and assaulters in a court services population. *Journal of Clinical and Consulting Psychology,* **45,** 61–69.

Rakoff, V. M.; Stancer, H. C.; and Kedward, H. B. (1977). *Psychiatric diagnosis.* New York: Brunner-Mazel.

Rappeport, J. R. (1985). Reasonable medical certainty. *Bulletin of the American Academy of Psychiatry and the Law,* **13,** 5–16.

Ratner, R. A.; and Shapiro, D. (1978). The episodic dyscontrol syndrome and criminal responsibility. *Bulletin of the American Academy of Psychiatry and the Law,* **7,** 422–431.

Rawlin, J. W. (1968). Street level abusage of amphetamines. In J. R. Russo (Ed.), *Amphetamine abuse* (pp. 51–65). Springfield, IL: Charles C Thomas.

Redlich, F. C.; Ravitz, L. J.; and Dession, G. H. (1951). Narcoanalysis and truth. *American Journal of Psychiatry,* **106,** 586–593.

Reed, A.; and Kane, A. W. (1973). *Phencyclidine.* Rockville, MD: National Clearing House for Drug Abuse Information.

Regier, D. A.; Myers, J. K.; Kramer, M.; Robins, L. N.; Blazer, D. G.; Hough, R. L.; Eaton, W. W.; and Locke, B. Z. (1984). The NIMH epidemiologic catchment area program. *Archives of General Psychiatry,* **41,** 934–941.

Reich, T.; Robins, L. N.; Woodruff, R. A.; Taibleson, M.; Rich, C.; and Cunningham, L. (1975). Computer-assisted derivation of screening interview for alcoholism. *Archives of General Psychiatry,* **32,** 847–852.

Reiser, M. (1974). Hypnosis as an aid in homicide investigation. *American Journal of Clinical Hypnosis*, **17**, 84–87.

Reiser, M.; and Nielson, M. (1980). Investigative hypnosis: A developing specialty. *American Journal of Clinical Hypnosis*, **23**, 75–84.

Reitan, R. M. (1955). Certain differential effects of the left and right cerebral lesions in human adults. *Journal of Comparative and Physiological Psychology*, **48**, 474–477.

Reitan, R. M.; and Davison, L. A. (1974). *Clinical neuropsychology: Current status and applications*. New York: Winston-Wiley.

Relinger, H.; and Stern, T. (1983). Guidelines for forensic hypnosis. *Journal of Psychiatry and Law*, **11**, 69–74.

Resnick, P. J. (1984). The detection of malingered mental illness. *Behavioral Sciences and the Law*, **2**, 21–38.

Richman, J. (1985). Sociological perspectives on illegal drug abuse: Definitional, reactional, and etiologic insights. *Behavioral Sciences and the Law*, in press.

Rioch, M. J.; and Lubin, A. (1959). Prognosis of social adjustment for mental hospital patients under psychotherapy. *Journal of Consulting Psychology*, **23**, 313–318.

Roback, H. B. (1968). Human figure drawings: Their utility in the clinical psychologist's armamentarium for personality assessment. *Psychological Bulletin*, **70**, 1–19.

Roberts, A. C. (1982). The abuse of hypnosis in the legal system. *American Journal of Forensic Psychiatry*, **3**, 67–78.

Roberts, B. (1978). A look at psychiatric decision-making. *American Journal of Psychiatry*, **135**, 1384–1387.

Roberts, J. K. A.; and Lishman, W. A. (1984). Use of the CAT headscanner in clinical psychiatry. *British Journal of Psychiatry*, **145**, 152–158.

Robey, A. (1978). Guilty but mentally ill. *Bulletin of the American Academy of Psychiatry*, **6**, 374–381.

Robins, L. N.; Helzer, J. E.; Croughan, J.; and Ratcliff, K. S. (1981). National Institute of Mental Health diagnostic interview schedule. *Archives of General Psychiatry*, **38**, 381–399.

Robitscher, J. B. (1966). *Pursuit of agreement: Psychiatry and the law*. Philadelphia: J. B. Lippincott.

Rockwell, D. A.; and Oswald, P. (1968). Amphetamine use and abuse in psychiatric patients. *Archives of General Psychiatry*, **18**, 612–616.

Rodin, E. A. (1973). Psychomotor epilepsy and aggressive behaviour. *Archives of General Psychiatry*, **28**, 210–213.

Roesch, R.; and Golding, S. L. (1980). *Competency to stand trial*. Urbana, IL: University of Illinois Press.

Rogers, J. L.; and Bloom, J. D. (1982). Characteristics of persons committed to Oregon's Psychiatric Security Review Board. *Bulletin of American Academy of Psychiatry and the Law*, **5**, 391–402.

Rogers, R. (1983). Malingering or random? A research note on obvious vs. subtle subscales on the MMPI. *Journal of Clinical Psychology*, **39**, 257–258.

Rogers, R. (1984a). *Rogers criminal responsibility assessment scales (RCRAS) and test manual*. Odessa, FL: Psychological Assessment Resources, Inc.

Rogers, R. (1984*b*). Towards an empirical model of malingering and deception. *Behavioral Sciences and the Law,* **2,** 93-112.

Rogers, R.; and Cavanaugh, J. L. (1980). Differences in select psychological variables between criminally responsible and insane subsamples. *American Journal of Forensic Psychiatry,* **1,** 29-37.

Rogers, R.; and Cavanaugh, J. L. (1981*a*). Application of the SADS diagnostic interview to forensic psychiatry. *Journal of Psychiatry and Law,* **9,** 329-344.

Rogers, R.; and Cavanaugh, J. L. (1981*b*). Rogers criminal responsibility assessment scales. *Illinois Medical Journal,* **160,** 164-169.

Rogers, R.; and Cavanaugh, J. L. (1981*c*). A treatment program for potentially violent offender patients. *International Journal of Offender Therapy and Comparative Criminology,* **25,** 53-59.

Rogers, R.; and Cavanaugh, J. L. (1983*a*). "Nothing but the truth" . . . A reexamination of malingering. *Journal of Psychiatry and Law,* **11,** 443-460.

Rogers, R.; and Cavanaugh, J. L. (1983*b*). Usefulness of the Rorschach: A survey of forensic psychiatrists. *Journal of Psychiatry and Law,* **11,** 55-67.

Rogers, R.; Cavanaugh, J. L.; and Dolmetsch, R. (1981). Schedule of affective disorders and schizophrenia, a diagnostic interview in evaluations of insanity: An exploratory study. *Psychological Reports,* **49,** 135-138.

Rogers, R.; Cavanaugh, J. L.; Seman, W.; and Harris, M. (1984). Legal outcome and clinical findings: A study of insanity. *Bulletin of the American Academy of the Psychiatry and the Law,* **12,** 75-83.

Rogers, R.; and Clark, C. (1985, October). *Diogenes revisited: Another search for the ultimate NGRI standard.* Paper presented at the American Academy of Psychiatry and Law Conference, Albuquerque.

Rogers, R.; and Cunnien, A. J. (1986). Multiple SADS evaluation in the assessment of criminal defendants. *International Journal of Offender Therapy and Comparative Criminology,* in press.

Rogers, R.; Dolmetsch, R.; and Cavanaugh, J. L. (1981). An empirical approach to insanity evaluations. *Journal of Clinical Psychology,* **37,** 683-687.

Rogers, R.; Dolmetsch, R.; and Cavanaugh, J. L. (1983). Identification of random responders on MMPI protocols. *Journal of Personality Assessment,* **47,** 364-368.

Rogers, R.; Harris, M.; and Wasyliw, O. E. (1983). Observed and self-reported psychopathology in NGRI acquittees in court-mandated outpatient treatment. *International Journal of Offender Therapy and Comparative Criminology,* **27,** 143-149.

Rogers, R.; Resnick, P.; and Seman, W. (1984, August). *Clinical approaches to malingering and deception.* Symposium presented at the American Psychological Association Annual Convention, Toronto.

Rogers, R.; and Seman, W. (1983). Murder and criminal responsibility: An examination of MMPI profiles. *Behavioral Sciences and the Law,* **1,** 89-95.

Rogers, R.; Seman, W.; and Clark, C. C. (1985). Assessment of criminal responsibility: Intital validation of the RCRAS with the M'Naghten and GBMI standards. *International Journal of Law and Psychiatry* (in press).

Rogers, R.; Seman, W.; and Stampley, J. (1984). Individuals evaluated for insanity: A comparative study of social and demographic variables. *International Journal of Offender Therapy and Comparative Criminology,* **28,** 3-10.

Rogers, R.; Seman, W.; and Wasyliw, O. E. (1983). The RCRAS and legal insanity: A cross validation study. *Journal of Clinical Psychology,* **39,** 554–559.

Rogers, R.; Thatcher, A. A.; and Cavanaugh, J. L. (1984). Use of the SADS diagnostic interview in evaluating legal insanity. *Journal of Clinical Psychology,* **40,** 1538–1541.

Rogers, R.; Thatcher, A. A.; and Harris, M. (1983). Identification of random responders on the MMPI: An actuarial approach. *Psychological Reports,* **53,** 1171–1174.

Rogers, R.; Wasyliw, O. E.; and Cavanaugh, J. L. (1984). Evaluating insanity: A study of construct validity. *Law and Human Behavior,* **8,** 293–303.

Rogers, R.; Wasyliw, O. E.; and Dolmetsch, R. (1982). Accuracy of MMPI decision rules in DSM III diagnoses. *Psychological Reports,* **51,** 1283–1286.

Rogers, R.; and Zinbarg, R. (1985). Sociopathy and substance abuse in NGRI evaluatees. Unpublished manuscript, University of Toronto.

Ron, M. A. (1983). The alcoholic brain: CT scan and psychological findings. *Psychological Medicine Monograph,* Supplement 3. Whole issue.

Rosen, G. (1975). On the persistence of illusory correlations with the Rorschach. *Journal of Abnormal Psychology,* **84,** 571–573.

Rosen, R. C.; and Keefe, F. J. (1978). The measure of human penile tumescence. *Psychophysiology,* **15,** 366–376.

Rosenberg, C. E. (1968). *The trial of assassin Guiteau: Psychiatry and law in guilded age.* Chicago: University of Chicago Press.

Rosenhan, D. L. (1983). Psychological abnormality and law. In C. J. Scheirer and B. L. Hammonds (Eds.), *Psychology and the Law* (pp. 89–118). Washington, D.C.: American Psychological Association.

Roth, M. (1981). Modern neurology and psychiatry and the problem of criminal responsibility. In S. J. Hucker, C. D. Webster, and M. H. Ben-Aron (Eds.), *Mental disorder and criminal responsibility* (pp. 91–110). Toronto: Butterworth.

Rubinsky, E. W. & Brandt, J. (1986). Amnesia as a criminal defense. *Behavioral Sciences and the Law,* in press.

Russell, E. W.; Nueringer, C.; and Goldstein, G. (1970). *Assessment of brain damage: A neuropsychological key approach.* New York: Wiley-Interscience.

Russell, W. R.; and Nathan, P. W. (1946). Traumatic amnesia. *Brain,* **69,** 280–300.

Ruzicka, W. J. (1979). *Psychodiagnostic assessment procedures in the criminal justice system.* Palo Alto, CA: Psychological Health Services.

Ryan, J. J.; Prifitera, A.; and Powers, L. (1983). Scoring reliability on the WAIS-R. *Journal of Consulting and Clinical Psychology,* **51,** 149–150.

Sauer, R. H., and Mullens, P. M. (1976). The insanity defense: M'Naghten vs. ALI. *Bulletin of the American Academy of Psychiatry and the Law,* **4,** 73–75.

Schacter, D. L. (1986a). Amnesia and crime: How much do we really know? *American Psychologist,* in press.

Schacter, D. L. (1986b). Feeling-of-knowing ratings distinguish between genuine and simulated forgetting. *Journal of Experimental Psychology,* in press.

Schacter, D. L. (1986c). On the relation between genuine and simulated amnesia. *Behavioral Sciences and the Law,* in press.

Schiffer, M. E. (1978). *Mental disorder and the criminal trial process.* Toronto: Butterworth.

Schuckit, M. A. (1979). *Drug and alcohol abuse: A clinical guide to diagnosis and treatment.* New York: Plenum.

Schuckit, M. A.; and Morrissey, E. R. (1978). Propoxyphene and phencyclidine (PCP) use in adolescence. *Journal of Clinical Psychiatry,* 7-13.

Schwade, E. D.; and Geiger, S. G. (1956). Abnormal electroencephalographic findings in severe behavior disorders. *Diseases of the Nervous System,* 17, 307-317.

Schwade, E. D.; and Geiger, S. G. (1960). Severe behavior disorders with abnormal electroencephalograms. *Diseases of the Nervous System,* 21, 616-620.

Schwartz, F.; and Lazar, Z. (1979). The scientific status of the Rorschach. *Journal of Personality Assessment,* 43, 3-11.

Scott, R. L. (1982). Analysis of the need systems of 20 male rapists. *Psychological Reports,* 51, 1119-1125.

Sears, J. D.; Hirt, M. L; and Hall, R. W. (1984). A cross validation of the Luria-Nebraska neuropsychological battery. *Journal of Consulting and Clinical Psychology,* 52, 309-310.

Sehulster, J. R. (1981a). Phenomenological correlates of the self-theory of memory. *American Journal of Psychology,* 94, 527-537.

Sehulster, J. R. (1981b). Structure and pragmatics of the self-theory of memory. *Memory and Cognition,* 9, 263-276.

Shanok, S. S.; and Lewis, D. O. (1981). Medical history of abused delinquents. *Child Psychiatry and Human Development,* 11, 222-231.

Shapiro, D. L. (1984). *Psychological evaluation and expert testimony.* New York: Van Nostrand Reinhold.

Sharpe, G.; and Richter, J. (1984). *Mental disorder project, Criminal law review, Draft report.* Toronto: Department of Justice.

Sheppard, G.; Gruzelier, J.; Manchanda, R.; Hirsch, S. R.; Wise, R.; Fracowiak, R.; and Jones, T. (1983). O positron emission tomographic scanning in predominantly never-treated acute schizophrenic patients. *Lancet,* 2, 1448-1452.

Siegel, R. K. (1978a). Phencyclidine, criminal behavior, and the defense of diminished capacity. In R. C. Petersen and R. C. Stillman (Eds.), *Phencyclidine (PCP) abuse: An appraisal* (pp. 272-288). Rockville, MD: National Institute on Drug Abuse.

Siegel, R. K. (1978b). Phencyclidine and ketamine intoxication: A study of four populations of recreational users. In R. C. Petersen and R. C. Stillman (Eds.), *Phencyclidine (PCP) abuse: An appraisal* (pp. 119-147). Rockville, MD: National Institute on Drug Abuse.

Sierles, F. S. (1984). Correlates of malingering. *Behavioral Sciences and the Law,* 2, 113-118.

Silber, D. E.; and Courtless, T. F. (1968). Measures of fantasy aggression among mentally retarded offenders. *American Journal of Mental Deficiency,* 72, 17-27.

Silver, S. B. (1982, July 14). Treatment in aftercare for insanity acquittees in Maryland. Testimony given before the United States Senate.

Silver, S. B. (1983). Treatment and aftercare of insanity acquittees in Maryland. Testimony before the Subcommittee on Criminal Law of the Committee on the Judiciary, United States Senate (Serial #J-97-122). Washington, DC: U.S. Government Printing Office. pp. 374-383.

Silver, S. B.; and Spodak, M. K. (1983). Dissection of the prongs of ALI: A retrospective assessment of criminal responsibility by the psychiatric staff of the Clifton T. Perkins Hospital Center. *Bulletin of American Academy of Psychiatry and Law,* **11,** 383-387.

Simkins, L. D. (1960). Examiner reinforcement and situational variables in a projective testing situation. *Journal of Consulting Psychology,* **24,** 541-547.

Simon, R. A. (1967). *The jury and the defense of insanity.* Boston: Little, Brown.

Simon, R. J. (1983). The defense of insanity. *Journal of Psychiatry and the Law,* **11,** 183-202.

Sines, L. K.; Silver, R. J.; and Lucero, R. J. (1961). The effect of therapeutic intervention by untrained therapists. *Journal of Clinical Psychology,* **17,** 394-396.

Slobogin, C.; Melton, G. B.; and Showalter, C. R. (1984). The feasibility of a brief evaluation of mental state at the time of the offense. *Law and Human Behavior,* **8,** 305-320.

Smith, B. M.; Hain, J. D.; and Stephenson, I. (1970). Controlled interviews using drugs. *Archives of General Psychiatry,* **22,** 2-10.

Smith, G. A.; and Hall, J. H. (1982). Evaluating Michigan's guilty but mentally ill verdict: An empirical study. *Michigan Journal of Law Reform,* **16,** 80-85.

Smith, R. S. (1983). A comparison study of the Wechsler Adult Intelligence Scale and the Wechsler Adult Intelligence Scale-Revised in a college population. *Journal of Consulting and Clinical Psychology,* **51,** 414-419.

Snyder, S.; Pitts, W. M.; Goodpastor, W. A.; Sajadi, C.; and Gustin, Q. (1982). MMPI profile of DSM III borderline personality disorder. *American Journal of Psychiatry,* **139,** 1046-1048.

Speckart, G.; and Anglin, M. D. (1985). Narcotics and crime: An analysis of existing evidence for a causal relationship. *Behavioral Sciences and the Law,* **3,** in press.

Spiegel, D.; and Spiegel, H. (1984). Uses of hypnosis in evaluating malingering and deception. *Behavioral Sciences and the Law,* **2,** 51-65.

Spiers, P. A. (1981). Have they come to praise Luria or to bury him? The Luria-Nebraska battery controversy. *Journal of Consulting and Clinical Psychology,* **49,** 331-341.

Spitzer, R. L.; and Endicott, J. (1974). *Mental status evaluation record.* New York: Biometrics Research.

Spitzer, R. L.; and Endicott, J. (1978). *Schedule of affective disorders and schizophrenia.* New York: Biometrics Research.

Spitzer, R. L.; Endicott, J.; and Robbins, E. (1978). Research diagnostic criteria for use in psychiatric research. *Archives of General Psychiatry,* **35,** 773-782.

Spitzer, R. L.; and Fleiss, J. L. (1974). A re-analysis of psychiatric diagnosis. *British Journal of Psychiatry,* **125,** 341-347.

Spotts, J. V.; and Spotts, C. A. (1980). *Use and abuse of amphetamine and its substitutes.* Rockville, MD: National Institute on Drug Abuse.

Squire, L. S. (1977). E.C.T. and memory loss. *American Journal of Psychiatry,* **134,** 997-1001.

Stafford-Clark, D.; and Taylor, F. H. (1949). Clinical and electroencephalographic studies of prisoners charged with murder. *Journal of Neurology, Neurosurgery, and Psychiatry,* **12,** 325-330.

Standing Committee on Association Standards of Criminal Justice. (1983). *Criminal justice and mental health standards.* Chicago: American Bar Association.

Stanley, B.; and Howe, J. G. (1983). Identification of multiple sclerosis using double discrimination scales derived from the Luria-Nebraska neuropsychological battery: An attempt at cross validation. *Journal of Consulting and Clinical Psychology,* **51,** 420-423.

Steadman, H. J.; and Cocozza, J. J. (1978). Psychiatry, dangerousness, and the repetitively violent offender. *Journal of Criminal Law and Criminology,* **69,** 226-231.

Stearns, A. W. (1945). Isaac Ray, psychiatrist and pioneer in forensic psychiatry. *American Journal of Psychiatry,* **101,** 573-583.

Stelzner, L. G.; and Piatt, R. (1983). The guilty but mentally ill verdict and plea in New Mexico. New Mexico Law Review, **13,** 99-116.

Stevenson, I.; Buckman, J.; Smith, B. M.; and Hain, J. D. (1974). The use of drugs in psychiatric interviews: Some interpretations based on controlled experiments. *American Journal of Psychiatry,* **131,** 707-710.

Stone, A. A. (1975). *Mental health and law: A system in transition.* Rockville, MD: National Institute of Mental Health.

Stone, L. A. (1965). Test-retest stability of MMPI scales, *Psychological Reports,* **16,** 619-620.

Suarez, J. M.; and Pittluck, A. T. (1975). Global amnesia: Organic and functional considerations. *Bulletin of the American Academy of Psychiatry and Law,* **3,** 17-24.

Subcommittee on Criminal Law of the United States Senate Judiciary Committee (1982). *Hearings on limiting the insanity defense.* Washington, DC: U. S. Government Printing Office.

Sue, S.; and Sue, D. W. (1974). MMPI comparisons between Asian American and non-Asian students utilizing a student health psychiatric clinic. *Journal of Counseling Psychology,* **21,** 423-427.

Sunderland, A. (1980). *Everyday memory questionnaire.* Unpublished manuscript, Applied Psychological Unit, Cambridge, England.

Swartz, J. D. (1978). Thematic Apperception Test. In O. K. Buros (Ed.), *Mental measurements yearbook* (8th ed.). (pp. 1127-1130). Highland Park, NJ: Gryphon Press.

Swartz, J. D.; Reinehr, R. C.; and Holtzman, W. H. (1983). *Holtzman Inkblot Technique, 1956-1982: An annotated bibliography.* Austin: University of Texas.

Swensen, C. H. (1957). Empirical evaluations of human figure drawings. *Psychological Bulletin,* **54,** 431-466.

Swensen, C. H. (1968). Empirical evaluations of human figure drawings: 1957-1966. *Psychological Bulletin,* **70,** 20-44.

Szucko, J. J.; and Kleinmuntz, B. (1985). Psychological methods of truth detection. In C.P. Ewing (Ed.), *Psychology, psychiatry, and the law: A clinical and forensic handbook* (pp. 441-466). Sarasota, FL: Professional Resource Exchange.

Talkington, L.; and Reed, K. (1969). An evaluation of Rorschach indicators of psychosis among mentally retarded. *Journal of Protective Techniques,* **33,** 474-475.

Talland, G. A. (1965). *Deranged memory.* New York: Academic Press.

Tanay, E. (1978). Psychodynamic differentiation of homicide. *Bulletin of the American Academy of Psychiatry and Law*, 6, 364-369.

Taylor, D. A.; Altman, I.; Wheeler, L.; and Kushner, E. N. (1969). Personality factors related to response to social isolation and confinement. *Journal of Consulting and Clinical Psychology*, 33(4), 411-419.

Taylor, S. P. (1967). Aggressive behavior and physiological arousal as a function of provocation and the tendency to inhibit aggression. *Journal of Personality*, 35, 297-310.

Taylor, S. P.; and Leonard, K. E. (1983). Alcohol and human physical aggression. In R. G. Geen and E. I. Donnerstein (Eds.), *Aggression: Theoretical and empirical reviews* (Vol. 2) (pp. 77-101). New York: Academic Press.

Theilgaard, A. (1983). Aggression and the xyy personality. *International Journal of Law and Psychiatry*, 6, 413-421.

Tinklenburg, J. R. (1973). Alcohol and violence. In T. Bourne and R. Fox (Eds.), *Alcoholism: Progress in research and treatment*. New York: Academic Press.

Tomkins, S. S. S. (1947). *The Thematic Apperception Test: The theory and technique of interpretation*. New York: Grune & Stratton.

Trachtman, J. P. (1970). Socio-economic class bias in Rorschach diagnoses: Contributing psychosocial attributes of the clinician. *Journal of Projective Techniques*, 34, 229-240.

Tsai, L.; and Tsuang, M. T. (1981). How can we avoid unnecessary CT scanning for psychiatric patients? *Journal of Clinical Psychiatry*, 42, 452-454.

Tucker, G. W.; Detre, T.; Harrow, M.; and Glaser, G. H. (1965). Behavior and symptoms of psychiatric patients and the electroencephalogram. *Archives of General Psychiatry*, 12, 278-286.

Uniform Law Commissioners. (1984, August 3). Model Insanity Defence and Post-Trial Disposition Act. Model legislation approved at the National Conference of Commissioners on Uniform State Laws, Keystone, Colorado.

Vega, A.; and Parsons, O. A. (1967). Cross validation of the Halstead-Reitan test for brain damage. *Journal of Consulting Psychology*, 31, 619-625.

Verdun-Jones, S. N. (1979). The evolution of the defences of insanity and automatism in Canada from 1843 to 1979: A saga of judicial reluctance to sever the umbilical cord to the mother country? *University of British Columbia Law Review*, 14, 1-76.

Vincent, K. R. (1983). MMPI code types and DSM III diagnosis. *Journal of Clinical Psychology*, 39, 829-842.

Von Rosenstiel, L. (1973). Increase in hostility responses in the HIT after frustration. *Journal of Personality Assessment*, 37(1), 22-24.

Voss, H. L.; and Hepburn, J. R. (1968). Patterns in criminal homicide in Chicago. *Journal of Criminal Law, Criminology, and Police Science*, 59, 499-508.

Wade, T. C.; and Baker, T. E. (1977). Opinions in use of psychological tests: A survey of clinical psychologists. *American Psychologist*, 32, 874-882.

Wagner, E. E.; and Medvedeff, E. (1963). Differentiation of aggressive behavior of institutionalized schizophrenics with the Hand Test. *Journal of Projective Techniques and Personality Assessment*, 27, 111-113.

Walker, E. (1961). Murder or epilepsy. *Journal of Nervous and Mental Diseases*, 133, 430-437.

Walker, P. A. (1978, October). *The role of anti-androgens in the treatment of sex offenders.* Paper presented at the American Academy of Psychiatry and Law Conference, Baltimore, MD.

Ward, C. H.; Beck, A. T.; Mendelson, M. (1962). The psychiatric nomenclature. *Archives of General Psychiatry,* **7,** 198–205.

Wasyliw, O. E.; Cavanaugh, J. L.; and Rogers, R. (1985). Beyond the scientific limits of expert testimony. *Bulletin of the American Academy of Psychiatry and the Law,* **13,** 147–158.

Watkins, C. M. (1981). Guilty but mentally ill: A reasonable compromise for Pennsylvania. *Dickinson Law Review,* **85,** 289–319.

Webster, C. D.; Menzies, R. J.; and Jackson, M. A. (1982). *Clinical assessment before trial: Legal issues and mental disorder.* Toronto: Butterworth.

Webster, J. S.; and Dostrow, V. (1982). Efficacy of a decision-tree approach to the Luria-Nebraska neuropsychological battery. *Journal of Consulting and Clinical Psychology,* **50,** 313–315.

Wechsler, D. (1955). *The Wechsler Adult Intelligence Scale.* New York: Psychological Corporation.

Wechsler, D. (1981). *The Wechsler Adult Intelligence Scale-Revised.* New York: Psychological Corporation.

Wedding, D. (1983*a*). Clinical and statistical prediction in neuropsychology. *Clinical Neuropsychology,* **5,** 49–54.

Wedding, D. (1983*b*). Comparison of statistical and actuarial models for predicting lateralization of brain damage. *Clinical Neuropsychology,* **5,** 15–20.

Weinberger, D. R. (1984). Brain disease and psychiatric illness: When should a psychiatrist order a CAT scan? *American Journal of Psychiatry,* **141,** 1521–1527.

Weinberger, D. R.; Wagner, R. L.; and Wyatt, R. J. (1983). Neuropathological studies of schizophrenia: A selective review. *Schizophrenia Bulletin,* **9,** 493–512.

Weiner, B. A. (1980). Not guilty by reason of insanity: A sane approach. *Chicago Kent Law Review,* **56,** 1057–1085.

Weiner, B. A. (1985). Insanity evaluation. In S. J. Brakel; J. Parry, and B. A. Weiner (Eds.), *Mentally disabled and the law.* Chicago: American Bar Association, in press.

Weiner, D. N.; and Haromon, L. R. (1946). *Subtle and obvious keys for the MMPI: Their development.* (Advisement Bulletin No. 16). Regional Veterans Administration Office, Minneapolis.

Weiner, J. M. (1966). An EEG study of delinquent and non-delinquent adolescents. *Archives of General Psychiatry,* **15,** 144–148.

Weiner, R. D. (1983). Amnesia. In J. O. Cavenar and K. H. Brodie (Eds.), *Signs and symptoms in psychiatry* (pp. 575–596). Philadelphia: J. B. Lippincott.

Weinstein, M. C.; and Fineberg, H. B. (1980). *Clinical decision analysis.* Philadelphia: W. B. Saunders Company.

Weisstub, D. N. (1980). *Law and psychiatry in the Canadian context.* New York: Pergamon Press.

Whitaker, L. C. (1976). Psychological test evaluation. In J. M. MacDonald, *Psychiatry and the criminal: A guide to psychiatric examinations for the criminal court* (pp. 151–178). Springfield, IL: Charles C Thomas.

Whitlock, F. A. (1963). *Criminal responsibility and mental illness.* London: Butterworth.

Wing, J. K.; Cooper, J. E.; and Sartorius, M. (1974). *Measurement and classification of psychiatry symptoms.* New York: Cambridge University Press.

Winter, D. G.; and Stewart, A. J. (1977). Power motive reliability as a function of retest instructions. *Journal of Consulting and Clinical Psychology, 45,* 436–440.

Witkin, H. A.; Mendick, S. A.; Schulisinger, F.; Bakkestrom, E.; Christiansen, K. O.; Goodenough, D. R.; Hirschhorn, K.; Lundsteen, C.; Owen, D. R.; Philip, J.; Rubin, D. B.; and Stocking, M. (1976). Criminality in xyy and xxy men. *Science, 193,* 547–555.

Wolfgang, M. E. (1958). *Patterns in criminal homicide.* Philadelphia: University of Pennsylvania Press.

Woods, S. M. (1961). Adolescent violence and homicide. *Archives of General Psychiatry, 5,* 528–534.

Wydra, A.; Marshall, W. L.; Earls, C. M.; and Barbaree, H. E. (1983). Identification of cues and control of sexual arousal by rapists. *Behavior Research and Therapy, 21,* 469–476.

Yesavage, J. A.; and Freman, A. M. (1978). Acute phencyclidine (PCP) intoxication: Psychopathology and prognosis. *Journal of Clinical Psychiatry, 39,* 664–666.

Zeegers, M. (1981). Diminished responsibility: A logical, workable, and essential concept. *International Journal of Law and Psychiatry, 4,* 433–444.

Zelig, M., and Beidleman, W. B. (1981). The investigative use of hypnosis: A word of caution. *International Journal of Clinical and Experimental Hypnosis, 29,* 401–412.

Ziskin, J. (1981). *Coping with psychiatric and psychological testimony.* Beverly Hills: Law and Psychology Press.

Ziskin, J. (1984). Malingering of psychological disorders. *Behavioral Sciences and the Law, 2,* 39–50.

Zonana, H. V. (1979). Hypnosis, sodium amytal, and confessions. *Bulletin of the American Academy of Psychiatry and the Law, 7,* 18–28.

Zubin, J.; Eron, L. D.; and Schumer, F. (1965). *An experimental approach to projective techniques.* New York: Wiley & Sons.

Zuckerman, M. (1971). Physiological measures of sexual arousal in the human. *Psychological Bulletin, 75,* 297–329.

Zuckerman, M., Larrance, D. T.; Hall, J. A.; DeFrank, R. S.; and Rosenthal, R. (1979). Posed and spontaneous communication of emotion via facial and vocal cues. *Journal of Personality, 47,* 712–733.

Zuckerman, M.; Lipets, M. S.; Koivunaki, J. H.; and Rosenthal, R. (1975). Encoding and decoding on verbal cues of emotion. *Journal of Personality and Social Psychology, 32,* 1068–1076.

Zusman, J.; and Simon, J. (1983). Differences in repeated psychiatric examinations of litigants to a lawsuit. *American Journal of Psychiatry, 140,* 1300–1304.

Zwick, R. (1983). Assessing the psychometric properties of psychodiagnostic systems: How do the research diagnostic criteria measure up? *Journal of Consulting and Clinical Psychology, 51,* 117–131.

Author Index

Subject Index

About the Author

RICHARD ROGERS is senior psychologist and coordinator of research at the Metropolitan Toronto Forensic Service (METFORS), Clarke Institute of Psychiatry. He is also assistant professor of psychiatry and special lecturer in psychology at the University of Toronto. Prior to his current positions, Dr. Rogers was unit program director at Chester Mental Health Center, an inpatient forensic hospital, and subsequently senior clinical psychologist at the Isaac Ray Center in Chicago, a university-based forensic clinic. Dr. Rogers is best known for his research on insanity evaluations that resulted in the R-CRAS, an empirically based measure for the assessment of criminal responsibility. He was honored in 1985 as the first recipient of the Distinguished Contributions to Forensic Psychology Award by the American Academy of Forensic Psychologists. Dr. Rogers is a diplomate of the American Board of Forensic Psychology and is widely published in forensic psychology and psychiatry. Since 1981, he has been the founding coeditor of the interdisciplinary journal, *Behavioral Sciences and the Law.*